THERE WAS A LAD

By the same Author

Biography
RUDYARD KIPLING

Fiction
DISMISS!
DICTATORS LIMITED
SUSANNA
OSTRICH EYES
LOCUST FOOD
TORTEVAL
THE HARE OF CLOUD
THAT STATE OF LIFE
HUMBUG HALL
STANDS MY HOUSE

Collected Verse
THE SECOND LUSTRE
BOTH SIDES OF SUEZ
THE GOLD AND THE GREY

Also
THE CIVILIAN'S SOUTH INDIA
THE SAHIBS

ROBERT BURNS

THERE WAS A LAD

AN ESSAY ON ROBERT BURNS

BY

HILTON BROWN

'The biography of a celebrated man usually
reminds me of the outside of a coastguards-
man's cottage—all tar and whitewash.'
AUGUSTINE BIRRELL

HAMISH HAMILTON
LONDON

First published by Hamish Hamilton, Ltd.
1 949

MADE AND PRINTED IN GREAT BRITAIN
AT THE STANHOPE PRESS LTD.,
ROCHESTER, KENT

CONTENTS

LIST OF ILLUSTRATIONS

The portrait of Maria Riddell by Sir Thomas Lawrence, P.R.A., is repro-
duced by the courtesy of the owner of the original, Ralph Bankes, Esq.
The originals of the other illustrations are in the Scottish National Portrait
Gallery and are reproduced here by courtesy of the Trustees of the National
Galleries of Scotland.

AUTHOR'S FOREWORD

'THIS is so exhausted a subject that any new idea on the business is not to be expected; 'tis well if we can place an old idea in a new light.' So Robert Burns, writing to Mrs. Dunlop; so Franklyn B. Snyder, quoting it to the students at Toronto; so I, doubly indebted, repeating it again here because—as so often with Burns—the thought could not be better expressed. I have no new manuscript or virgin material to offer—though that is a discrepancy which has not in the past deterred a number of persons from putting forward their views on what must be one of the most interesting lives in history. On the other hand, I can claim to carry one important chapter of the Burns story further than does any other book I know, and I have examined developments and discoveries made since the last authoritative biographies were published. Here and there a 'new light' may flicker. I am writing mainly for those whose knowledge of Burns is slight; the initiate must excuse what will be to them many twice-told tales.

I have read almost all that Burns ever wrote—or such of it as has survived, and a great deal of what has been written about him; and, like many others who have done the same, I find myself, on many points, left guessing. Indeed, one of the most exciting features of this highly unusual life is its abiding mysteries, its unanswered riddles. Why did Burns marry Jean Armour just when he did? What really happened between Burns and Highland Mary? What *did* take place at Friar's Carse—if it *was* Friar's Carse—on that disastrous evening of misconduct? I do not know the answers, but I have tried to set down the latest evidence. On firmer ground, I have attempted some analysis of Burns's writings; as one who has struggled for thirty years with the devilments of metre and rhyme, I think I may claim to sympathise with his difficulties and

9

his triumphs in the sphere of verse; and I should like to add myself to the muster—not such a long one—of those who have recognised the excellence of his prose.

I am afraid this book will annoy some of my country-men; any intelligent work on Burns would. I am sorry for that, but I shall regret it the less if my essay leads one—or a score—of them to do something to remove the reproach—that, for all the talk, all the enthusiasm, all the idolatry of Burns in Scotland, the most complete and reliable modern life of him has been written by an American; and the next best by a Professor in Germany.[1]

[1] Franklyn Bliss Snyder (1932) and Hans Hecht (1919: *Trans.* 1936). I do not forget the late Mrs. Carswell's vivid, intimate, imaginative, but sadly undocumented work.

THERE WAS A LAD

PART ONE

THE BURNS STORY

I CLAIM credit at the outset for heading this section the Burns Story and not the Burns Legend or the Burns Myth; the temptation to employ one of these latter words is not inconsiderable. The popular picture of Burns, which persisted for a century after his death, ran somewhat as follows. Burns was an Ayrshire ploughman, unlettered but inspired, who suddenly and by the divine afflatus burst into nightingale song. He was promiscuous with women and peopled south Scotland with bastards; according to one self-constituted authority, he had seventy. But all this disgraceful promiscuity was purged and sanctified and absolved by his wholly uncarnal love for an ethereal creature called Highland Mary. He drank himself to death at an early age, thereby cutting short a career of marvellous promise; he thus came suitably to that Bad End so beloved of Victorian morals. And so on.

This was, of course, a thoroughly attractive picture. It pleased the men, who could condone their conviviality (in an age when drink was procurable and cheap) by the reflection that they were but emulating the national hero. It pleased the women, who—whatever they may profess to the contrary—have always at heart a sneaking admiration for a stallion, and who could forgive his crudities with their sex because of his spiritual salvation through a member of it. Yes, it was a satisfying picture and highly coloured; but unfortunately it was almost completely at variance with the facts. To take only a few aspects, Burns was not 'unlettered'; he did not drink himself to death; his women were few and his bastards fewer; he long outlived his early promise; and his spiritual love for

Highland Mary was moonshine. There may be a tendency today to go to the other extreme and disbelieve *all* the cherished traditions—to deny that he sent the Rosamond's 'carronades' to the French Republic, or composed *Tam o' Shanter* and *To Mary in Heaven* under the circumstances commonly alleged, or got his death lying alcoholically insensible in the snow of Dumfries. This, or some of it, may be going too far; but the facts remain that in the harsh light of modern research too many of these stories collapse, and that the main lines of the Victorian picture will stand no better.

One of the falsest statements in the unveracious catalogue was that Burns was a 'ploughman'; he was nothing of the kind—though he may have called himself one when it suited him. He would indeed have been better off—financially at least—if he *had* been, instead of being a partner in his father's ruinous succession of farms. There was a limit, even in 1780, to the labour that could be exacted from hirelings; there was no limit to that expected from a son of the house. And his share of the farming profits—if any—being but seven pounds a year, he could hardly have drawn less as a feed servant. But, of course, he was not a farm-servant, and he never really thought of himself as one; he was a tenant farmer, small if you like, but still a tenant farmer. In this he but followed his long and farming ancestry descending from that Walter Burness of Bogjorgan and Brawlinmuir in the county of Kincardine who was gathered to his fathers as long ago as 1670. On the side of his mother, the chestnut-haired, fair-skinned Agnes Broun, to whom he owed the light-hearted and adventurous side of his being, the same tradition went back into the generations. It is true that all the Burness family were, as farmers, either incompetent or unlucky; but that did not cure them of their inherited passion for farming. It did, however, in 1748, drive William Burness, son of Robert Burness and father of the poet, to the alternative of leaving his father's roof at Clochnahill or starving under it; he chose the former—wisely, as the farm soon afterwards failed, and old Robert was left to the compassion of his son-in-law, who had the sense to be an artisan. Son William, migrating southward by stages and earning his living as a gardener, found himself at last at Alloway in Ayrshire, where, in 1756, he feud a seven-acre plot from Doctor Campbell, and grew on it market vegetables and built on it the celebrated cottage where the poet passed the first seven years (perhaps the best seven years) of his life.

But William Burness had no intention of remaining a market gardener or any other kind of gardener; he knew he was a farmer and when at last an opportunity presented itself of turning this faith into works, he seized it eagerly. Then began the unhappy sequence of family failures—Mount Oliphant with its 'churlish and ungrateful' soil; Lochlie,[1] swampy and sour; Mossgiel with its panoramic view which so delighted Wordsworth—and its panoramic rent of a pound an acre. Allowance must be made for the optimistic but consistently unsuccessful Burness; the agricultural system of the day was as crazy as the agricultural implements—witness the 'run rig' and the enormous four-horse ploughs; the tenant farmer was too often faced with the alternative—owe for the rent or starve. Yet with all this it must be admitted that Burness was either very unworldly or very stupid; he was done time after time. He advanced upon his enterprises with hopelessly inadequate capital, and his eagerness to achieve his aim closed his eyes to quite manifest and palpable snags. At Lochlie, for instance, he committed himself to a crushing rent on a mere gentleman's agreement—not a word in writing—with an Ayr merchant, David Maclure, whose own finances were in the most precarious state, and who had therefore no hesitation in preferring false and inequitable claims against his tenant;[2] hence litigation in the Court of Session, dequestration, and—for William Burness—a miserably unhappy death. Burns could refer loyally to his father as one who had 'figured pretty well as *un homme des affaires*';

looking back on his father's procession of bad bargains, he could hardly have believed it.

Burness's failure to achieve the dream of his life is the more pitiable because he was a man of the highest— indeed of an extraordinarily high—character, a fact undisputed since the days of Carlyle. He had the typically Scots appetite for education, the typically Scots ambition to better his children by the acquisition of book learning, the typically Scots austere ungraciousness of manner. He was of course intensely religious—otherwise he could hardly have been contemporary with his epoch; but he was no bigot, he was no hidebound Calvinist. He believed—or at least he hoped—that a repentant sinner had some chance of a Heaven which was not reserved for the Calvinist 'elect'. He had a tolerance in advance of his time; on reflection he could withdraw his embargo on the dancing-class his family wished to attend; and in his *Manual of Religious Belief*, 'Transcribed with Grammatical Corrections by John Murdoch, Teacher', he allowed the child to interrogate the parent. These—especially the last—were, for his age and class, revolutionary. According to Doctor John Mackenzie, who saw him often, he produced upon the stranger an impression either of frigid reserve or of mental vacuity; but he warmed up very soon when he met a companion to his taste and subsequently conversed with astonishing breadth and judgment. He would, in fact, have been a more successful farmer had he been more of the fool he looked at first sight; but, like his son, he fell between the two stools of humdrum husbandry and the allure of intellectual attainments. He was, of course, no more the simple peasant, no more the 'ploughman' than his son was; if he spelt 'wrote' 'wrott' and 'daughter' 'douther', he read whatever he could lay hands on and digested whatever he read. As a litigant he was obstinate and hard-headed, fighting the objectionable Maclure to the last ditch with the same undaunted courage with which he battled with the unrewarding divots of Mount Oliphant and Lochlie. He was upright, broad-minded, earnestly bent on self-improvement—a *good* man if ever there was one. The tragedy is that, by his mania for farms which required the labour of a Hercules to make them even balance, he killed his eldest son.

He was fortunate in his wife; Agnes Broun doted on him and sat spellbound whenever he opened his mouth. Whether his children, and especially his eldest, regarded him with the same unquestioning love is open to doubt. The principal effect of his death upon son Robert was apparently a feeling of relief from grinding discipline and slavery, a wide sense of emancipation. The young man took the first holiday of his life; he burst into redoubled song; he seized Elizabeth Paton and begat on her the first of his brood; new and dazzling ambitions appeared on his horizon. For an excitable youth, he bore his loss with remarkable fortitude; on 21st June 1783 he wrote laconically to his uncle in Montrose: 'My father . . . is in a dying condition', and with that abandoned the subject for a copy-book dissertation on the state of farming in Ayrshire. His announcement of the subsequent death is a similar exhibition piece; and he fell back on Goldsmith for his father's epitaph. No son could have failed to respect such a parent, and Burns was to pay many tributes to him in after life; but love seems another story. One can say at least that though the parent's death closed a chapter, other and far more exciting chapters were simultaneously and consolingly revealed.

The main outlines of the Burns Story are, or should be, well known to any reader of this book; they have been set out in many good and authoritative and very many bad and unreliable works. I do not therefore propose here to enter into any detail; merely to present the time-space background without which it is impossible to assess this extraordinary character; one must know roughly what he did and what happened to him. The essentials can be stated in a paragraph. He endured a boyhood and adolescence of grinding poverty and toil on those murderous

small Scottish farms with which, in series, his father so
indomitably or perhaps pig-headedly persisted. He received practically no systematic education, but by an
exceptional glegness in the uptak' made the very most of
what he did encounter; which amounted to two years'
intermittent work under young John Murdoch; a week at
Dalrymple on handwriting and grammar; French in
three weeks—again with Murdoch; and a summer
quarter at Kirkoswald imbibing such elementary mathe-
matics as is implied in a course of land-surveying. This
was literally all his benefit from outside sources; the rest
he taught himself. He drew his conception of international
affairs from the Geographical Grammar; his ancient
history from Stackhouse's *History of the Bible*; goodness
knows what from *Pamela* and *Peregrine Pickle*—the latter
incomplete; and a good foundation for most of his poetical
errors from Pope, Young, Shenstone, Thomson and
Macpherson's Ossian; there was also *The Man of Feeling*,
'a book I prize next to the Bible'. The result of this mixture
was a limited and fairly indigestible compendium; still,
there were few 'unlettered ploughmen' of that day (or
any other) who had read much more. He developed in
the meantime a need to express himself in verse, whose
excellence of technique, aided by the parochial character
of its themes, attracted local notice. This, spreading, took
him for a brief period to Edinburgh and the great literary
world; nothing came of this except that Edinburgh and
the great literary world chilled and killed his Muse and
left him disgruntled for life. For some months he wandered
rather aimlessly and fruitlessly about Scotland, reverting
in the end to his origins. He made one more attempt at
farming, which—though under better auspices than
before—failed equally. This, combined with the need to
buttress his farmer brother and help to maintain his
mother and his unmarried or tardily marrying sisters,
drove him to accept a bread-and-butter post in the
Excise which he continued to hold steadily and not without credit and advancement till his early death. He was
handicapped throughout his career by the stealthy progress

BURNS AT THE LODGE OF CANONGATE KILWINNING, 1787

In this composite—which was executed nearly sixty years after the event—the R.W.M. addressing Burns from the rostrum is Alexander Fergusson of Craigdarroch. Behind Burns, in full regalia, stands Willie Dunbar; and a few paces behind him, with his hands clasped, Sir James Hunter-Blair, with Boswell on his right. Lord Monboddo's aquiline beak stands out in the bottom left-hand corner; Henry Erskine sits there also with arms folded. A little behind Hunter-Blair, the distinguished paunch of that 'fine fat fodgel wight' Grose is a salient feature. Dugald Stewart sits cross-legged in the centre of the picture between Dunbar and Hunter-Blair.

of an undiagnosed and incurable disease. He further complicated a sufficiently difficult life by attachments to a series of women, some of which he took very seriously. One of these women, Jean Armour, he suddenly and belatedly, and for inscrutable reasons, married. He died at the early age of thirty-seven, leaving five legitimate children, two illegitimate but absorbed into his family, and two (known) illegitimate and discarded or unsurviving. All of these, the sheep alike with the goats, did reasonably if not outstandingly well; most were prolific, but by the year 1924 Burns's surviving descendants numbered only six. None of these bore the name of Burns.

The above bare summary no doubt covers the salient facts, but there are episodes in the story which demand much more detailed consideration. Let us begin with that boyhood and adolescence of toil that eventually killed him; those incredibly lean years at Mount Oliphant, 'vile with stones', which Provost Ferguson of Doonholm leased to William Burness with such remarkably disinterested philanthropy; at Lochlie, where flax was to be grown which young Robert could learn to heckle, and where nothing was, in fact, grown except a crop of ill will, debts and disappointment, where the stout heart of Burns's father was finally broken and whence his sons only escaped by a piece of rather sharp practice; at the sodden and clay-bound Mossgiel, where another kind protector exacted another unprotective rent. It is a sorry picture—especially in the earlier stages; a lad in his teens doing the whole work of an adult labourer, living on slops with never a bite of butcher meat, struggling meanwhile to assimilate the 'best' authors, 'especially the sentimental kind', suffering from headaches and palpitations and fainting fits which he tried to cure alternately by writing prayers in verse and by plunging his body into an ice-cold bath. That is indeed a picture on which one does not care to dwell.

Fortunately, however, it had also its brighter side; it was not all 'the unceasing moil of a galley-slave'. There was the Tarbolton Bachelors Club, which debated Rousseau and demanded of its members a professed love affair with 'one or more of the female sex'; there was that later and more progressive body the Rebel Four, which demanded of its members at least one certified and productive fornication;[3] there were the Masonic Lodges which were to play a large and on the whole a useful part in Burns's life. There was Captain Richard Brown, the sea-faring man, at Irvine, 'open-handed and brave, unlucky and lecherous'.[4] The evil influence of Brown on Burns has been a subject of controversy in which the bold sea Captain took a leading part; it would seem that his principal effect was to make the young Robert believe that he *could* do the things he desired to do, whether these were the conquest of women or the publication of literary products. The Captain's young friend would appear, at first at any rate, to have been more receptive to the former of these suggestions than to the latter. Be that as it may, there is no doubt that Captain Richard Brown introduced an element of gaiety into life which was conspicuously absent in the entourage of William Burness.

Meanwhile the verse-writing budded, bloomed and at Mossgiel burst into full flower. And with the verses came the germ of what its author was later to call 'philosophy'; the twenty-four-year-old Burns opened a Commonplace Book. (It was the predecessor of others, but the only one that lasted for any considerable length of time; its first entry is April 1783 and its last October 1785.) It is an illuminating if slightly pathetic document; it is impossible not to be drawn to the very young and ingenuous mind that penned it—now in copperplate, now in an untidy scrawl with the characteristic long-tailed 'd's'. It is headed very self-consciously 'Observations, Hints, Songs, Scraps of Poetry, etc., by Robt. Burness: a man who had little art in making money, and still less in keeping it; but was, however, a man of some sense, a great deal of honesty and unbounded goodwill to every creature, rational or irrational'. The contents are to exhibit how a 'ploughman' (I have said that he could use the word when it suited him without meaning it in the least) 'thinks and feels under the pressure of Love, Ambition, Anxiety and Grief'. The book opens with admired—and very apt—quotations from Shenstone, and many of its ideals are as bogus as Shenstone's sentimentality; but many are otherwise—for instance, the well-known passage regretting that no poet has so far celebrated 'my dear native country, the ancient Baileries of Carrick, Kyle and Cunningham'. This defect the writer would gladly remedy, but is 'far unequal to the task'. 'Obscure I am and obscure I must be, though no young Poet nor young Soldier's heart ever beat more fondly for fame than mine.' (This is in August of 1785; the Kilmarnock edition was to appear eleven months later!) The book terminates abruptly in religious mood with the words 'let my Pupil, as he tenders his own peace, keep up a regular, warm intercourse with the Deity'. I cannot cite its contents here in detail; but it makes rewarding reading. It is interlarded with much later comments by 'J.S.'—John Syme—and with contemporary (and imbecile) remarks by the unidentified 'W.R.'; the amateur of unconscious humour will find both these highly diverting. In August of 1785, among the last entries, Jean Armour appears for the first time—in cypher.

Ere half the Commonplace Book was filled young Robert Burns had become a local celebrity; he had won himself the reputation of a rather dangerous and tiresome but undoubtedly amusing young man who would pay for watching. He was taken up by such social lights as Aiken (who was to 'read him into fame'), Gavin Hamilton of Mauchline, Ballantyne of Ayr. He could score off such as snooping Willie Fisher, the type hypocrite, or pretentious John Wilson of Tarbolton with his medical nostrums, the type charlatan; *Death and Doctor Hornbook* is perhaps the best exposition ever written on the text *ne sutor*, just as Holy Willie is the world's finest denunciation of the Pharisee. He was conspicuous enough indeed to attract enemies who were fortunately—like the egregious Sanders Tait[5]—easy meat for slaughter. For the rest, the farmers and cottars and merchants and magnates of Ayrshire sat back watching speculatively this promising colt who kicked so handsomely in the breaking-harness; give him his head, they thought, and how far and how fast may he go?

Early in 1786, however, a brake was put upon this light-hearted career by the intolerable mess into which he had got himself, first with one woman, then with two at once. That Jean Armour whose name had been so secretly hidden in the Commonplace Book was now in a condition which could be kept secret no longer. Her father was a respectable master mason in Mauchline, a grim man—though his wife was reputed to be lighter-hearted. Grim or light-hearted, they both violently disapproved of Robert Burns, not so much because he was a notorious or at any rate a self-proclaimed rake, but because he was a poverty-stricken farmer with the wrong religious and political views. James Armour had no use for the Radical, whether he appeared as a New Light or as a Whig; there was thus no single redeeming feature to soften the blow which their daughter's confessed condition struck them. Jean was hastily removed to relatives in Paisley; her lover, regarding this as desertion, turned the more eagerly to another sweetheart of the moment, the celebrated 'Highland Mary' Campbell, with whom it is to be feared he had already gone a very considerable way indeed. The Armours, anxious for the future maintenance of the coming child and hearing that the Lothario was proposing to flee the country, took out a warrant against him *in meditatione fugae*; and though Burns eluded this by transferring all his property to his brother Gilbert—not so bad for a simple 'unlettered ploughman'—the situation grew so tense that he began seriously to contemplate putting his idea of flight into effect. He had long toyed with the notion of going out to Jamaica—an island he was to hear of again in curious circumstances—where fabulous wealth was said to await the enterprising; and he now announced that his passage was actually booked. It seems doubtful, however, if he was entirely serious about this or ever really saw himself dragooning slaves on the sugar plantations of Port Antonio; as Mrs. Carswell says, it was 'less a decision than a dramatisation', and nothing that he said or wrote on the subject has the ring of conviction.

It is certain, however, that in Ayrshire he was in a fix. The full details—which were involved in the extreme— may be reserved for consideration later; it will suffice to say meantime that he had compromised himself matrimonially with both Jean Armour and Highland Mary, and with one of them at least—and perhaps with both— he had compromised himself to the further extent of a forthcoming child. At the same time a dazzling possibility of a quite different sort was opening before him; the carefully vetted edition of his Poems just printed at Kilmarnock had been a *succès fou*, well-wishers had brought it to the notice of Edinburgh and now it was suggested to him that he should visit the capital with a view to a second and larger edition to be issued at the fountainhead of wisdom and culture itself. What was he to do? Risk the entanglements and hang on for the chance of Edinburgh, or take himself at his own word and sail for Kingston? He did, in fact, what he was to do again several times—he shilly-shallied; he played cannily for time, dodging about the country and doing nothing beyond writing hysterical letters on the subject of his—understandable—mental stress. He was rewarded for his off-putting; Mary Campbell, 'Highland Mary', obligingly died, the Armours to their chagrin were unable to execute their warrant in default of anything to distrain, the great Blacklock, D.D., in Edinburgh—himself a poet who had risen from the humble origins of a bricklayer's cottage—wrote an encouraging letter. The storm was weathered; the skies magically cleared. Burns, drawing no doubt a breath of profound relief, decided to forget about Port Antonio, and while the *Roselle* headed out into the Atlantic her prospective passenger was riding eastwards across the Lanarkshire moors instead. He was at this time twenty-seven years of age.

There is no use denying that the Edinburgh visit was a flop. It was like one of those plays where the first act goes swingingly and with promise, the second begins to drag, and the third is played out to a melancholy accompaniment of departing spectators. Why did this happen? Why did the bright dawn turn into such a dreary evening? The reasons remain obscure, but the conclusion seems inescapable that they must be sought in the character and conduct of Burns himself.

The Edinburgh society in the winter of 1786-7 was not altogether easy to deal with. The period was one of transition between the Augustan age of the mid-century and the coming explosion of Scott and Jeffrey. Yet it was by no means a period of calm; Edinburgh was peopled—much as was London in the nineteen-twenties—by a bustling set of minor luminaries dragging with them a tail of luminaries lesser still, hurrying and scurrying from this to that with the self-importance of a hill of ants. They played golf, they went horse-racing and cock-fighting, they danced a great deal, they patronised the theatres, they spent ambrosial nights in taverns dancing reels and drinking claret, while the ladies—the very best ladies—consumed quantities of stout and oysters. With all this they took themselves very seriously indeed, never forgetting that they upheld on their shoulders the Modern Athens. Harry Erskine, the dean of the Faculty of Advocates, the Rev. Dr. Blair, Blacklock and Man-of-Feeling Mackenzie dominated the literary scene as that other legal luminary, the great Dundas, lowered over the political. Morals were theoretically high, but in fact easy; heavy drinking was not only condoned, it was obligatory; and one could not walk far along the streets at evening without being accosted by a lady of the town. Burns found himself plunged suddenly into a bewildering array of cliques and cabals; the tempo of life in Mauchline was speeded up by at least five hindred per cent; day and night were one long search for novelty and a new 'rage' was discovered almost hourly. The life of any 'rage' in such a society was therefore precarious, and it was a quicksand in which it was none too easy for a 'Ploughman Poet' to keep his feet. It was necessary to walk warily, and for a time Burns did walk warily; but perhaps he was not wary enough.

Burns spent his first week in Edinburgh lying sick in the horrid little rooms he shared with the long-suffering Richmond; they were 'down a long dark nesty closs'[6] and had some riotous harlots on the floor above. He had an attack of his 'hypochondriacs', as the poor fellow called them—aggravated, as he himself admitted, by a hangover consequent on the 'savage hospitality' of his hosts *en route* from Ayrshire. It was a deplorable lodging enough; yet in a short time he was able to paste above the mantelpiece a piece of white paper with his dinner and supper engagements for some weeks to come; formidable indeed was the list of hosts it displayed—Earl Glencairn, Sir John Whiteford, Dr. Blair, Mr. Henry Erskine and so on. For Burns's friends—and more especially his Masonic friends —had certainly got him away to a flying start. Within a month of his arrival he was able to write home a complacent letter to Dr. John Mackenzie, whose introductions to Sir John Whitefoord and Professor Dugald Stewart of Edinburgh University had laid the first stepping-stones: he had been taken up by everybody; Stewart had 'even got me into the periodical paper *The Lounger*'—copy enclosed. This sounds magnificent, but requires examination. If not a clique, his sponsors were certainly a chain; Whitefoord and Dalrymple of Orangefield passed him on to Glencairn, who introduced him to his relative the Earl of Buchan; Henry Erskine was Buchan's brother; Creech, who published the poems, was an ex-tutor of Glencairn. So far so good, but how far beyond these did he ever

23

advance? True, he 'captivated' that whirlwind creature
the Duchess of Gordon, but not much more came out of
that than a visit (later on) to Gordon Castle; the Great
Panjandrum Blair, as mighty in letters as in the Church,
after some preliminary interest seems to have gently
dropped him. The Dundas faction would not look at him
at all. Yet for a time he was the rage and the lion; the
'Ploughman Poet'—as he allowed himself to be called in
public—was essential to any party pretending to smart-
ness. The Edinburgh Edition of his poems, heartily over-
subscribed, was presently a resounding success. That
Burns, that Edinburgh winter, had his foot upon the
ladder is as evident as anything can be: why didn't he
climb it?

Allowing for the fickleness of the society in which he
moved, the root cause can only be found in Burns himself.
He seemed curiously unable to visualise the opportunities
that were lying at his feet; or if he did see them, he
sheered off from them in alarm. Perhaps they were too big
and too sudden for him altogether. But from the first he
was resolutely realistic as to his prospects; in December
1786 he wrote to the Rev. Mr. Greenfield 'bear me witness, when my bubble of fame was at the highest, I stood,
unintoxicated, with the inebriating cup in my hand,
looking forward with rueful resolve, to the hastening time
when the stroke of envious calumny . . . should dash it
to the ground'. The metaphor pleased him, for he repeated it to Lawrie—'I have no great temptation to be
intoxicated with the cup of Prosperity' . . . 'to this
[i.e. novelty] I owe my present *éclat*'. Much of this was, no
doubt, pose—so far at least there had been no 'envious
calumny' at all, nor shadow of it; but it was an unfortunate
line to take up because—as with all his poses—Burns
could talk himself into believing it. Perhaps he did; perhaps he was only—again as usual—lazy-minded, and the
prospect of a golden staircase rising to indefinite heights
affected him only with disinclination for the labour of
ascending it.

Yet he must have seen how very bright his prospects

were. He had completely avoided the two pitfalls one might have feared for him—clodhopping and bounce; indeed, his demeanour everywhere gave the greatest satisfaction and was sincerely admired. 'The man will be spoiled if he can spoil,' wrote that sprightly lion-collector Lady Cockburn, 'but he keeps his simple manners and is quite sober.' Dugald Stewart told Burns's biographer Currie that his manners were simple, manly and independent; he had no forwardness or vanity; he shared in but did not arrogate conversation. (His conversation surprised and delighted everybody.)[7] Scott, calling up a boyhood recollection, rated him 'rustic, not clownish', 'firm not forward', and Josiah Walker, the literary-minded factor at Athol, on their first meeting found no 'grace', but 'no clownish constraint either'. He dressed quietly and simply, 'like a farmer in his best to dine with the Laird'; he avoided serious eccentricities; he was first-class company almost anywhere. He was even clever with the women—another deadly trap; he had apparently outgrown that 'coarseness' and 'boisterousness of approach' which offended Miss Janet Logan of Cumnock in the Mossgiel days, for Scott could write that 'his address to females was extremely deferential and always with a view either to the pathetic or the humorous which engaged their attention particularly': this Scott had heard from no less exalted a source than Her Grace of Gordon. (No doubt the celebrated eye which 'glowed, I say literally *glowed*,' had something to do with it, too.) In other words, Burns in his first Edinburgh winter, was much more than a 'rage' with the hare-brained; he had passed muster—and with flying colours—with the best and most cultured men of the time, who were ready to forget the Ploughman Poet and receive this brilliant newcomer on equal terms. What, then, went wrong?

It is difficult to say. True, he characteristically complicated his life by a fresh and desperate entanglement; this time with a married woman—Mrs. Agnes McLehose ('Clarinda'), a grass widow of the plump, fluffy, hot-and-cold-blowing type so dangerous to the susceptible. But this, though no great help, was not necessarily ruinous; and in any case it did not occur till his second Edinburgh winter, by which time the position had already slipped. Simultaneously, too, he succeeded in putting a servant-girl in the family way, but such errors of judgment were regarded as venal enough. It is usual to lay the blame for his decline in prestige on his increasing association with the Crochallan Fencibles (or worse), and certainly that circle of boon companions was not distinguished for the loftiness of its ideals, the purity of its conversation or its exclusiveness; but this again could hardly have been fatal in a society where everyone who was anyone belonged to one tavern club or another. Perhaps, however, Burns's inexcusable fault lay in his failure to distinguish between Edinburgh theory (which was highly moral) and Edinburgh practice (which was loose); he failed to understand that Saturday night and Sunday morning—or Monday morning for that matter—were strictly separate compartments. He would not keep up appearances, he would not sustain the convention that the Crochallans and their like were outside normal existence, he carried his taverns and his tavern friends into his daily life. He deserted the elevated menage of Dr. Blair for the more congenial but much less suitable company of Smellie, Nicol and Cleg-horn; and—here was the cardinal sin—he did this openly. He preferred the Crochallans and had not the wit to disguise it. He became 'impossible' and he was dropped; as Dugald Stewart wrote regretfully to Currie, 'afterwards [i.e. after the first winter] we met but seldom'. Why not—unless that Burns, failing to see and profit by his chance or not perhaps very greatly liking the look of it, had voluntarily descended?

There is another aspect. All through his life Burns was extraordinarily obtuse in one respect—he believed that he could say what he liked, however bitter, however wounding, and still get away with it; when the worm turned or the kicked dog snapped at his calves he was at once amazed and furious. There was something of this in his Edinburgh behaviour. He was injudicious enough to express vehement opinions—often the reverse of laudatory—upon the great and good of Edinburgh; it can hardly be supposed—especially as he did it quite publicly —that these were not carried to the ears of their subjects. Satire, wrote Maria Riddell long afterwards, was at once his forte and his foible—'for every ten jokes he got a hundred enemies'. The danger signals are to be noticed quite early; Dugald Stewart, his friend, sponsor and admirer, could shake his head over Burns's biting sarcasms and could write 'if there had been a little more of gentleness and accommodation in his temper, he would, I think, have been still more interesting; but he had been accustomed to give the law in the circle of his ordinary acquaintance, and his dread of anything approaching to meanness or servility rendered his manner somewhat dry and hard'. A good deal can be read between those few but illuminative lines; a man who could burst out to a fellow guest at table—and a minister of the church at that— 'Sir, I perceive that a man may be an excellent judge of poetry by square and rule, and after all be a damned blockhead!' was obviously capable of giving quite considerable offence. Josiah Walker, who was inclined to like Burns but saw through him a good deal, said he was 'powerful' in conversation but 'somewhat authoritative'; he lacked experience of those 'modes of smoothing dissent' characteristic of 'polished manners'. He was always ready to repel insult 'with decision at least if not with roughness.' In fact, a prickly character altogether. If such a man, at first disarmingly modest, became increasingly prone to be insulted—as the 'stateliness of the Patricians in Edinburgh' became more marked—if he became increasingly aggressive and took to calling his opponents in argument blockheads or worse, then one can see shoulders being shrugged and doors beginning to close. Probably a combination of all these—the low company for which he almost vauntingly deserted the 'Patricians', a growing as time went on a little above himself, an 'independence' which became mere boorishness—brought him down; at any rate, down he came. The graph of Burns in Edinburgh is a falling slant; from that first brilliant blaze the fire goes steadily out. Forward he could not go.

Instead he went backward—as he had said he would do —to Mauchline. His repute had preceded him; the Armours, whose opposition had been so implacable, were now extending hands in sycophantic welcome; and finally he sealed himself into his past by marrying their daughter Jean, that old flame of whom he had just been writing to his Edinburgh friends with a degree of scurrility which must be read to be believed. The chance—such as it ever had been—was lost; he became a person not of no importance, but of less importance than had seemed at one time probable.

The old problem of a livelihood now presented itself— and naturally with renewed urgency. The Edinburgh edition had sold out, and badly as Burns's affairs had been handled by himself and his friends, he had reaped what was for these days a substantial profit. A second volume would no doubt have done equally well; but alas! no second volume was forthcoming. Edinburgh seemed to have withered him; he had produced next to nothing of any value during his two winters there and he was writing little or nothing now. He had no follow-up to his success; it was obvious therefore that an income must be sought elsewhere. He had long, perhaps ever since Lochlie, alternately aimed at and fobbed off a post in the Excise— in 1786 he had bemoaned the fact that want of patronage should drive him to exile in Jamaica 'in a very humble situation', when all he asked for was such an appointment; and he now achieved his desire to the extent of being nominated to the approved list of candidates. This was the sole tangible fruit of the Edinburgh excursion—apart, of course, from the success of his book. It seems incredible that with a little ingenuity or perseverance he (or his friends on his behalf) could not have found some con- genial and remunerative work in the capital—which at one time had dangled no less an allurement than a Chair of Agriculture; but the fact remains that no such occupation was forthcoming. Perhaps he never very earnestly sought it.

Common sense now suggested that he should apply for an immediate posting in the Excise Department; but he was still haunted by the evil genius of his family—the longing to be a successful farmer. Here again the Edinburgh visit seemed to throw out a promise that might not be wholly delusive. In Edinburgh he had made some contact with Patrick Miller, brother of Thomas Miller of Barskimming (on the Ayr), the Lord Justice Clerk, and Miller, who was a man of kind intention, had taken an interest in the Ayrshire poet—a warmer interest perhaps than the Ayrshire poet took in him. Miller was not only a Man of Feeling; he was a Man of Ideas, some of which—for example, steam navigation—were good. His latest idea was agricultural research, and he was on the outlook for a *vile corpus* for development. Why not at the same time do a good turn to poor Burns? Miller had recently bought a derelict and neglected estate at Dalswinton in Dumfriesshire, which seemed to him a suitable site for his experiments; on it there was a farm called Ellisland—it had no house, to be sure, but it ran to a hundred and seventy acres 'romantically [but also rheumatically] situated on the west bank of the Nith'.[8] This farm Miller offered to Burns; the lease was at £50 a year for three years, then £70 for seventy-six, but Miller was also ready to put down three hundred pounds to build the much-needed dwelling-house. Out of the proceeds of the Edinburgh Edition Burns had lent a hundred and eighty pounds to his brother Gilbert, which left him some two hundred of his own wherewith to stock and start the farm; it was cutting things fine, but as a whole the offer was markedly superior to any which had ever confronted the unfortunate William Burness. Burns, as was typical of him, procrastinated; for some reason he was suspicious of Miller—whom he was eventually to blame, with no great justice, for his Ellisland failure. He sent an old Ayrshire friend and experienced farmer, Tennant of Glenconner, to inspect the land; contrary to his expectations—perhaps to his hopes—Tennant was in favour. At Whitsun, therefore, of 1788 Burns entered upon Ellisland. There being no house (the local workmen were almost twentieth century in their delays over building one) he lived for some months alone in a hovel, with his newly-wedded wife forty-five miles away at Mauchline. Needless to say, he visited her a good deal.

Burns was in after days to talk bitterly about Miller's 'selfish craft', but there is no evidence that Miller was other than fair and open-handed. He knew the farm was in a poor way, but thought it could be recovered, and he made his offer on these lines. He was right, as it turned out—he sold Ellisland eventually for £2,000, and by 1879 it was fetching £170 per acre; where Miller was optimistic was in the amount of capital and the interval of time he estimated as necessary for the recovery. His new tenant, at any rate, could make small progress and became rapidly disheartened; in February of 1789 he had 'good hopes of it', but by March it was a 'very very hard bargain' and by July 'a ruinous affair on all hands'. Perhaps Burns had lost the appetite and the capacity for hard work which had distinguished him at Lochlie; perhaps, as Josiah Walker thought, he had too many diversions and left his servants too frequently unsupervised; perhaps the system of the day was hopelessly against him. At any rate, it soon became evident that Ellisland was to join that long and ancestral procession of failures, headed by Clochnahill, and in which the standard-bearers were Mount Oliphant and Lochlie. It seemed only a question of time till the Excise should claim its victim.

The Ellisland days seem to reveal a man happy enough, yet labouring to recover not only his exhausted farm, but also his exhausted self, and being equally unsuccessful in both. Except for the sudden and blinding flash of *Tam o' Shanter*, he wrote nothing at Ellisland that was of his best quality and much that was very far below it; nor could he, as he strove to do, break new ground; the songs, many of them excellent, which he now began to collect and rewrite for the Johnson and the Thomson volumes were no novelty. To speak plainly, he doddled and drifted. He had 'a hundred different poetic plans', but plans they remained; he thought of writing a drama about Robert the Bruce and, on the strength of what seems a very inadequate synopsis, ordered from Edinburgh the complete works of the British and French dramatists; but if this treasury of good example ever arrived, it did not write for him a single scene. A new ideal and exemplar swam into his mind—Quintus Horatius Flaccus dispensing cynical wisdom from his well-found Sabine farm. He began to 'philosophise', he turned more and more to politics, he wrote extensive letters on religion to his admirer and mentor Mrs. Dunlop—always a sign that he had no other mental occupation. He interested himself in the Monkland Friendly Society and its Subscription Library—probably the first institution of its kind in Britain and half a century in advance of its time; we may see here perhaps the mantle of William Burness the Educator descending upon his son. (But his subscribers disappointed him by insisting on 'damned trash'.) In these varied activities of mind and body he jogged along from his thirtieth to his thirty-second year, no more able to put one of his aspirations into effect than to make Ellisland pay. He was happy enough, and extolled—perhaps more loudly than sincerely—his domestic bliss; but already he was quite evidently not the man he had been, and a series of illnesses and accidents reduced him still further. Ellisland was certainly not one of the high-lights of his life; but if Burns's dream was to be a Horace, Ellisland was the nearest he ever came to realising it.

In fact, Burns was becoming an ordinary domesticated man with a hobby—the collection and rewriting of old Scottish songs; from this it was but a step to becoming an ordinary man with a hobby *and* a job. The Excise was not to be staved off and he applied for an appointment in the district. For a time, with characteristic courage, he attempted the impossible task of combining the duties of a gauger with the unremitting toil of the farm; then, Ellisland failing and abandoned, the Excise came into its own at last. At the age of thirty-two he became what he ever afterwards remained—a full-time Exciseman.

A fearful amount of nonsense has been written and talked about Burns and the Excise, beginning with Coleridge's celebrated 'Ghost of Maecenas! Hide thy blushing face! They snatched him from the sickle and the plough—To gauge ale-firkins.' As will have been seen, 'they' did nothing of the kind. It was part of the Victorian tradition to represent Burns the Gauger as a miserable wretch condemned to a hideous drudgery which he loathed and in which he took no interest, enduring its odium with none of its compensations and drawing for these services a pittance which left him in grinding poverty, while the inevitable associations of his duties thrust him deeper and deeper into a bath of whiskey in ever lower and lower company. It is customary nowadays to blame that universal scapegoat Dr. Currie, Burns's first serious biographer, for these misconceptions; but they are more justly attributable to those of Burns's admirers who begat upon their own imaginations a figure having little counterpart in reality. The ethereal cloud-riding unpractical genius they conceived *should* have felt thus, and so—in their imaginations—he did feel; but, then, Burns was not an ethereal cloud-riding unpractical genius. No doubt, in a dark mood of hypochondriacs or hangover, Burns could write as if the Coleridge version were true, no doubt he could say—as he said so many inconsistent things when it suited him—that he was a caged finch beating and fluttering; but the evidence is happily otherwise.[9] In plain fact, Burns had considered—nay, coveted —an Excise appointment for the best part of a decade; in Edinburgh he had written to Glencairn that he would 'leave no stone unturned' (happy phrase!) to secure it; it was a great day when certain exalted persons wrote

'reposing especial Trust, and conficence in the Knowledge, Skill, Industry, Integrity, Fidelity and Circumspec-
tion of Robert Burns Gentleman'. Burns was very pleased
with his Commission, he was reasonably proud of it, he
liked his duties as well as anyone ever likes his bread-and-
butter job, and he drew what was for those days a toler-
able remuneration. He worked very hard with a view to
promotion, and promoted he would have been; his next
junior on the list became supervisor in a vacancy shortly
after his death, and there is little doubt that Burns, had
he lived, would have been given the step. As an Exciseman
he probably drank no more than he did as a farmer, and
possibly less; and he associated, not with the scum of the
county, but with his fellow professionals in this and other
comparable avocations. There is no evidence for the
suggestion that he either despised his work or pitied
himself in it.

It was certainly, however, the very antithesis of that life
of Horatian leisure which had been his confessed ideal;
the cynic lounging in his comfortable house on his well-
found and productive farm and commenting idly upon the
passing show. The work of a gauger in the 1790's was
indeed a whole-time occupation. To begin with, there
was at that time no convenient code or manual of instructions—Collector Huis's 'Abridgement', which must have
been a godsend to his subordinates, did not appear till
the year after Burns's death. Burns was expected to
assimilate an indigestible mass of Acts of Parliament,
General Letters, Memoranda and Standing Orders; the
appalling bulk of these may be estimated from the fact
that Huis's 'Abridgment' ran to nine hundred octavo
pages of print. It must also be remembered that in those
days practically every conceivable human activity was
subjected to some sort of tax or duty which it was the
gauger's duty to scrutinise and check; the work of soap-
boilers, for instance, was theoretically to be inspected
every four hours. Add to this an area comprising ten
parishes and two hundred miles of riding a week and it
will be evident that the incumbent had little time to sit

down either with his 'Tuneful Sisters' or with his bottle of Falernian. Burns could—and by Herculean effort did—contrive to squeeze in an hour or two to keep up his songs for the Edinburgh collections; but he could have had little energy or leisure either for those projected dramas and 'hundred different poetic plans' or for general dissipation. To his credit, he largely shelved the Muses and threw himself into affairs and into the Government work for which he was paid.

Nor was the pay by any means despicable. Burns started on a salary of fifty pounds a year, which rose quickly to seventy—a sum which compared very favourably with the parish schoolmaster's twenty or the parish minister's thirty-five; but besides this solid bread there was the butter of many and varied perquisites. The detecting officer was awarded half the fines realised and half the produce of seizures; he might also draw fifty pounds for the apprehension of a smuggler—and the Ayr, Wigtown and Solway coasts were nests of these profitable gentry. There were possible prizes of well-nigh incredible richness; on two occasions, for example, illicit spirit stocks worth five thousand pounds were seized—though not, unfortunately, in Burns's jurisdiction. Still, it was not so bad; on one day, in Burns's own station, the fines totalled between fifty and sixty pounds and while the expenses of 'dining'—and that liberally—the magistrates, clerks and witnesses had to be deducted from the officer's percentage, a comfortable balance must have remained. It is not too much to suppose that in a reasonably good year Burns the Gauger netted a couple of hundred pounds—which rather disposes of 'grinding poverty'. And there was always the dazzling prospect of one day becoming a collector, 'a life of compleat leisure' . . . 'the summit of my wishes . . . a life of literary leisure with a decent competence'. Truly, as Macfadzean remarks,[10] 'the conviction of smugglers was a better paying business than farming'. Much better—for Burns.

That Burns threw himself into his new work with enthusiasm, that he was eager to shine in it and be promoted, can hardly be questioned. When Perry of the London *Morning Chronicle* made him 'a handsome offer of an annual stipend for the exercise of his talents in his newspaper', Burns declined on the ground, among others, that it might prejudice his prospects in the Excise.[11] He intrigued repeatedly (as is not common with ethereal geniuses) for advancement; with Mrs. Dunlop (who was thought to have interest with Corbet the General Supervisor); with Graham of Fintry, a member of the Board, and his good angel. (Credit, so far unacknowledged, seems due to his immediate local superiors for the way in which they put up with this going over their heads; for Burns the 'usual channels' did not exist.) If these appeals were naive and artless—he suggested to Fintry that one Leonard Smith might be ousted to create a vacancy, 'as the gentleman, owing to some legacies is quite opulent, and removal could do him no manner of injury'—they were usually successful; as witness his move to the lucrative Port Division in Dumfries. He was proud of these victories; he wrote post haste to Maria Ridell, his current correspondent and flame, to announce the Dumfries transfer in a letter that breathes satisfaction. Indeed, so certain was he of promotion that both Nicol in Edinburgh and Mrs. Dunlop believed from his letters that he had been made a supervisor, when in point of fact he had only been placed on the approved list for that position. He found time, among his multifarious duties, recreations and crises, to submit (again ignoring the usual channels) a scheme of departmental reforms which would secure substantial economies; it was adopted. He wrote long and careful reports and took great pleasure in a position which enabled him, while soaking the large-scale professional offender, to wink at the occasional old wife brewing illicit ale for a fair-day. To suggest that such a man was a fish out of water or a tortured genius grovelling in squalid and detestable toil is merely absurd. The Ghost of Maecenas had not done so badly after all.

But Burns was always a perplexing bundle of contradictions. We have already noted that curious aberration which persuaded him that he, Robert Burns, was privileged to say what he chose and do what he chose and that those who resented these liberties were incomprehensibly unreasonable; he provided a fine illustration of this in Dumfries. Eager as he was to rise in his service, vital as he knew his post and its income to be, he apparently saw no reason why he should not indulge in political speechifying and toast-drinking along what could only be described as highly subversive lines. Quite apart from his professed devotion to the House of Stewart (of which we shall hear more later) and his pungent comments on the reigning family, he quite openly and publicly proclaimed his sympathy with the principles of the French Revolution. He may or may not have sent the 'carronades' from the seized smuggler, the *Rosamund*, with his compliments to the French Assembly; he may or may not have joined in the singing of *Ça Ira* in the pit of the Dumfries theatre; but he left no doubt, from his orations and odes upon 'Liberty', from his extremely outspoken letters and from his general conversation, in which direction his sympathies lay. It was not the direction approved by His Majesty's Government. Yet when at last he was hauled over the coals and saw his whole livelihood jeopardised he was dumbfounded. He wrote to Fintry in bewildered terror; he had been 'surprised, confounded and distracted by Mr. Mitchel the Collector telling me just now that he has received orders to enquire into my political conduct and blaming me as a person disaffected to the Government . . . I adjure you to save me'. (It was a grovelling letter, but not so much so as is commonly made out by those who have not read it—though there is some unseemly whining about 'wife and babes'.) Jove was not 'adjured' in vain; Fintry presumably intervened and the affair blew over. It blew over, indeed, with such rapidity—within a matter of days Burns was able to write to Mrs. Dunlop that all was 'set to rights'— that one is left with the impression that the authorities were out merely to scare an officer on whom they set some store and who seemed in danger of going off the rails.

The row was apparently not taken seriously in Dumfries, for almost immediately afterwards Burns applied for and was granted free schooling for his children, and he was also given a leading part in the newly formed Dumfriesshire Volunteers, which was in some sense a *corps d'élite*. On the other hand, if Josiah Walker is to be believed, it forced Fintry to drop a plan he was nursing under which Burns was to be transferred to a 'respectable office' at Leith, with little work, two hundred a year and unbounded opportunities to renew acquaintance with his Edinburgh literary patrons; if this was really so, it was indeed a pity. That the affair was bruited abroad in a sense less favourable to its hero we know from his friend Adair's anxious letter; he had heard that Burns had been 'dismist for some political nonsense'. And it drew from William Nicol one of the most sensible letters Burns ever received: 'Dear Christless Bobby, What concerns it thee whether the lousy Dumfriesian fiddlers play "Ça ira" or "God save the King"? Suppose you *had* an aversion to the King, you could not, as a gentleman, wish God to use him worse than He has done.' Perhaps the recipient took this sound advice to heart; at any rate, "dear Christless Bobbie' lay low for some time, sang no more revolutionary ditties and wrote instead *Does Haughty Gaul* with its unexceptionable sentiments: 'Who will not sing "God save the King" Shall hang as high's the steeple.' Let it never be said that Robert Burns, ethereal genius or no, was so poor a Scot as to be unaware on which side his bread was buttered.

But all this time that fatal malady born of the malnutrition, exposures and overstrain of his early youth was creeping steadily on. His heart was—and long had been—mortally diseased, a fact of which both he and his medical advisers were completely unaware; his 'hypochondriacs' and palpitations, his 'flying gouts' and rheumatic fevers

and 'malignant squinancies' were but progressive symptoms.[12] To tackle such an affliction with cold baths and
Glauber's salts—that 'sour-faced old acquaintance'—
was like opposing a Sherman tank with a peashooter; yet
this was all he could do for himself and all that contemporary medical skill could do for him. The disease, of
course, had much in its favour; the life he led or was
obliged by the custom of the time to lead, loading with
wine and spirits a stomach ill adapted to either; those
weeks and months in that miasmic hut at Ellisland; even
the move to Dumfries, a town then set in a swamp and the
last place to which a man in his condition should have
gone.[13] For a long time he regarded his ailment with characteristic courage, joking about it to his friends; but as one
reads through his letters in chronological order one can see
the wings of the Terror spreading and darkening over his
head. His letters become sad reading, then terrible. At
Ellisland as early as December 1789 he is 'groaning under
the miseries of a diseased nervous system', scarce able to
lift his head; and the tale goes drearily on, ever downwards. He has not been able to leave his bed today; he can
'scarce hold the pen'; he has been brought to the borders
of the grave; he fears that his 'protracted slow consuming
illness' will arrest his sun before he has well reached his
middle career. We come to June of 1796 and 'Alas!
Clarke, I begin to fear the worst'; he is so emaciated he
can scarce stand up; Cunningham would not know him
if he saw him; he is going to that bourne . . ; he cannot
eat; and at last, in his final letter, written to his father-in-
law, James Armour, who had once so bitterly opposed
him, 'I think and feel that my strength is so gone that the
disorder will prove fatal to me'. He was not deceived.
Yet all the time his magnificent spirit fought on unbeaten;
he sent Thomson some of the best items in his collection;
in the very letters in which he wrote some of the words I
have just cited he wrote also the most lucid and elaborate
of his notes on Scottish song. If these letters make dismal
reading, they are not without their triumph.

But long before that he had felt himself on a downward

THE BURNS STORY

slope; a sort of desperation crept into his manner; throughout the whole of his last years in Dumfries he was unstable, almost wild. As his heart weakened physically his spirit became more militant and more military, his mind turned more and more to soldiers and battles, he blazed out into *Scots Wha Hae*. Unfortunately he blazed out also in more questionable ways; bravado at night alternates with apology by day. Few admirers of Burns can with equanimity see him writing abjectly to 'S. Clark Jr.'—a Dumfries lawyer ten years younger than himself—'I was, I know, drunk last night, but I am sober this morning', explaining that he would have fought Captain Dods (whoever *he* may have been) with 'a brace of pistols' but for his wife and family, and beseeching Clark to 'wait on every gentleman who was present' and assure them that Burns meant no harm by his somewhat equivocal toast of the previous evening. Nor was this the only instance of its kind—there is a second apology to young Clark and one to McMurdo begging him to overlook a little turbulence on the previous evening and to disregard the 'maniac ravings of a poor wretch whom the powers of Hell and the potency of Port, beset at the same time'. And that class hatred for which the 'Patricians' of Edinburgh were perhaps primarily responsible, and which was so ugly and unworthy a feature of his character, becomes now intenser and more bitter; he is increasingly anti-gentry—almost what would have been called in the 1920's 'Bolshie'. Some at least of his betterclass acquaintances began to draw away from him— perhaps they were not altogether to be blamed; there was a serious fracas or scandal of some kind at the house of one of his 'county' friends, the Riddells.[14] But if his balance in outside affairs was shaky, the balance of his inner mind remained sound; his faculties were never impaired; to the last he continued to work hard, to immerse himself in his hobby of song-collecting and— to beget children. His vitality in this respect at least remained unabated; Jean Armour Burns and Anna Park, the barmaid at the Globe tavern, conceived within ten days of each other, however unpleasant the implications of this fact may be. If Robert Burns had to die young he certainly died fighting.

Well served to the last, his disease was now vigorously aided by his medical advisers; he was put upon a course of treatment which should, of itself alone, have killed him, and which did in all probability hasten his demise by some weeks. He was sent to Brow Well, an insignificant little 'spa' on the Solway firth, to drink the waters, do no work and recruit himself daily by riding and sea-bathing. (Currie states that Burns took this course for himself, being 'impatient of medical advice'; this sounds most improbable, but then Currie was himself a doctor—the closest trade union in the world.) The prescribed rest would have been beneficial, the mild iron tonic in the Brow Well waters would at least have done no harm; but to send a man in an advanced stage of heart disease galloping about on a horse or wading through the miserable mud and 'sleech' and mud-and-water that constituted the sea in this forbidding locality, and all this in a cold wet Scottish July—it was murder! Fortunately for himself, Burns had now no riding-horse and could not obtain one, but he resolutely persevered with the sea-bathing; the wretched inn had but a single bottle of port with which he might warm himself afterwards. I know nothing more heartrending, nothing so quick to draw tears, as the picture of poor Burns, alone with the Enemy in these miserably depressing surroundings—forced on this hopeless course in which he was yet also forced, as are we all in such circumstances, to hope. His great heart was game to the last; on the twelfth of July 1796, nine days before he died, he sent songs to Alec Cunningham and Thomson, one of them set to a particularly tricky tune; asking Thomson for a loan of five pounds—because he had got it into his head, poor fellow, that a certain haberdasher of Dumfries (or his attorney) who had sent him a harmless routine bill would have him cast into prison, there to perish—he undertook to repay with five pounds worth of the 'neatest song-genius you have ever seen'. Two days later, the 'course' being over,

he wrote the calmest letter to Clark of Lockerwood for a
loan of his gig: 'I have a horse at command, but it threat-
ens to rain, and getting wet is perdition.' In Lockerwood's
gig he took his last journey in life, arriving home to the
Mill Vennel in such a state that as soon as his wife saw
him she knew it was all over. He had strength enough to
write one letter—to his father-in-law for help for Jean in
her imminent confinement; then he took to his bed.
There a merciful delirium crept out of the shadows and
took possession of his parched and fevered body; and
three days later he died. The details of that death-bed
have been told and retold, discredited and re-credited;
we need not pry too closely upon such a scene. Three
days later again his body was taken to the Town Hall of
Dumfries, and on the following day it was carried in
procession to St. Michael's churchyard and there interred.
The chroniclers cannot even agree as to whether the day
was fair or wet; but there is a contemporary picture
showing the cortège; a detachment of Volunteers precedes
the coffin-bearers, who are followed in turn by a long tail
of mourners; the whole is advancing down the High
Street between a double row of spectators on foot and on
horseback. So went Burns to his rest; and in the middle of
the funeral service Jean Armour Burns bore him his last
child, a boy. Like several of its predecessors, it was not to
live long.

'Is thy Burns dead?' wrote Coleridge, apostrophising
Lamb, 'And shall he die unwept . . . Who to the
illustrious of his native land So properly did look for
patronage?' Burns himself had deprecated, in the case of
a fellow poet, the erection of molehills over the ashes of
genius neglected while it still breathed; but with Burns
once safely in his grave, his countrymen began almost
immediately to discover what a wonderful person he had
been. To her lasting credit, it was Maria Riddell—from
whom he had been for a time estranged, but with whom

he was reconciled before his end—who took the first step; within a fortnight of his death she had published in the *Dumfries Journal* that 'Memoir' which she afterwards touched up for Currie (and which Currie touched up for himself);[15] as a clear-sighted estimate of its subject it will rank with anything that has been written. A subscription fund was promptly started for the benefit of Burns's widow and family and realised twelve hundred pounds in no time; the said Dr. Currie of Liverpool undertook to produce an edition of the poet's life and works for the same laudable purpose. If Currie was not the ideal selection for the task, he was at least preferable to any of the other candidates, with the possible exception of Dugald Stewart, who refused, and he did at least accomplish the task—which might have been done worse. At all events, his book was a best-seller, running into edition after edition; the first of these netted twelve or fourteen hundred pounds for the fund. The stricken consciences of the Scots absolved themselves in vast libations of cash, the interest on which would have kept their poet in comfort all his days; in 1815 the Mausoleum in St. Michael's church-yard went up (£2,000), and in 1823 the heavily criticised Doon Memorial (£3,300), and in 1831 that on the Calton Hill (£3,000). The Government moved, after the manner of Governments, more tardily, but in 1817 Lord Panmure procured for Mrs. Burns an annuity of fifty pounds a year; again after the manner of Governments, this was too little and too late; Jean was now the proud mother of two East India Company cadets, Messrs. William Nicol and James Glencairn Burns, and was in a position to renounce the annuity after a single payment—a gesture which must have given her great satisfaction. But, what with one thing and another, the 'wife and babes' whom their husband and sire had so often trotted out on suitable occasions, and for whose welfare he was at the end most genuinely concerned, were never in any danger of starvation or anything near it.

What next? Well, Burns, the great Burns, was dead, and his family was suitably provided for; there seemed, for the time being, nothing more to be done. It is customary to say that during the first fifty years after his death Burns suffered something of an eclipse; this hardly seems to consist with the score of authors—and their publishers—who came forward during this period to cash in on the great dead, to retail their recollections of him, good, bad and indifferent, with the anecdotes they could collect about him, authentic, dubious or manifest invention. Art demanded the embellishment of the recollections, and they were duly embellished; anecdotes meant good money and they were in ready supply. Between the years 1808 and 1841 there was a perfect procession of 'Lives and Works', attacks and vindications, equalled only by the parallel column of Ploughman Poets, Weaver Poets, Dairymaid Poetesses and what not. For a time Burns's reputation tossed uneasily on these turbid seas; Heron and Currie had been scarcely eulogistic, Scott and Jeffrey were but coldly complimentary. But the Idolaters were already well away with that 'enthusiastic partiality' deprecated by Josiah Walker; the shrill counterblasts of James Maxwell, Poet in Paisley, and of 'Peebles frae the water-fit' were borne away on the rising gale of popular acclaim.[16] Already, it seemed, Burns was dowered with the guerdon —and the penance—of immortality.

The seal was set upon all this, and the Idolaters won their Armageddon, by the anniversary celebrations held at Ayr in 1844. This was a stupendous occasion, and was thought so important that *Punch* sent up Douglas Jerrold all the way from London to see what fun he could get out of it. (He did not get very much, but his publicity value was immense; *Punch* gave him a full-page article with pictures of Tam pursued by witches and a serio-comic Burns musing head-on-hand at his plough.) Jerrold took as his text 'Scotland Repentant'—that Caledonia stern and wild who, he said, had 'nursed her poetic child' much after the fashion of Mrs. Brownrigg; and certainly the repentance was lavishly expressed. In drenching showers an enormous procession marched to the shrine at Alloway; the Mauchline box-makers carried a huge cardboard thistle which Professor Wilson ('Christopher North') seized with great *éclat* and pressed to his bosom. The Earl of Eglinton provided a spread and a speech; there was also a dinner at fifteen shillings for the *élite*—though Jerrold could only secure 'a piece of cold tongue, a plate of gooseberries almost ripe and a pint of some mystery called sherry'.

From these glories it was but a step to the Birth Anniversary Celebrations at Glasgow in 1859, which totally eclipsed them. Once again Mr. Punch was to the fore; it has been said that the space allotted in that gentleman's columns is a good measure of the importance of any event; if so, the Glasgow affair was outstanding, for *Punch* gave it two and a half out of his eight letterpress pages in the current issue, including a long poem in hexameters (excellent) on the £50 Prize Poem Contest at the Crystal Palace[17] and a comic picture of an exploding haggis on a Sassenach dinner-table. Nothing could now stop either Idolaters or Immortality; not even the yet more gargantuan celebrations of the death anniversary in 1896; the curious may find the magnitude and intensity of these reflected in Volume VI of the *Burns Chronicle*, a monument perhaps to enthusiasm rather than taste.

And so to the present day, when at ten thousand Burns Dinners the 'Immortal' Memory is proposed; and ten thousand eager orators rise to justify themselves in the use of the word. So far there is no apparent indication that their claims will ever be proven vain.

So the outlines of Burns's career, like the salient features of his character, are simple. He was a hard-working man who drifted from one aim to another, failing at most of them; in character he was warm-hearted, frank, loyal, passionate for fair play, self-reliant, self-conscious, unstable and temperamental. It is easy to generalise and simplify in this fashion; but as we shall see, there are contradictions and subtleties which cannot be ignored.

That Victorian caricature with which we started was at
least commendably clear; but the more one studies
Robert Burns, the more do his lineaments fuse and blur.
Always his own best biographer, he has clouded the issue
by writing of himself now in one mood now in another,
sometimes with real frankness, sometimes with false,
sometimes with deliberate duplicity or with his tongue
lodged firmly in his cheek. One must know the mood of
the moment and its contributory causes; otherwise it is
impossible to make sense of his writings. He has not made
himself an easy man to know; nor always an easy man to
like.

Even his appearance is a matter of conjecture rather
than certainty; not because contemporary portraits of
him are lacking, but because these contradict one another
so violently that if one of them be a likeness the next can
be no likeness at all. One must start, of course, with the
Nasmyth portrait painted in Burns's first Edinburgh
winter in 1786; few objects, it has always seemed to me,
can have done more to mislead posterity or to hamper the
conception of Burns as a human being—though in justice
to Nasmyth it must be added that few pictures have
suffered more at the hands of copyists. The face that
looks out at us is no doubt beautiful and fine, but it is
much too beautiful and fine ever to have been the face of
Robert Burns. This Eton-and-Trinity young aristocrat
accords with no single one of the contemporary descriptions; here is neither Scott's 'sagacious farmer' and 'douce
gudeman' nor Josiah Walker's 'master of a merchant
vessel of the most respectable character'; where are
Currie's 'coarse physiognomy', C. K. Sharpe's 'very good
countenance but coarse', Farington's 'black-complexioned
and his general appearance that of a tradesman or
mechanick'? Where those pockmarks on the forehead on
which Gilbert Baird and Mrs. Marion Hunter so resolutely insisted? Contemporary admirers of the picture
thought it lacked 'muscularity' or was seen 'in perspective';
it lacks, to be frank, guts. Even at that, however, it is
infinitely better than the several variants on or from it

made at the time or soon afterwards; Nasmyth's own first replica, done for Thomson and preserved in the London National Portrait Gallery, has become a soulful and pouting evangelist with eyes up-turning to some unearthly vision, while his second or Auchendrain version had advanced towards sheer imbecility and more resembles an anaemic gibbon than anything that could ever have written *Scotch Drink* or *Holy Willie*. If, as has been alleged, these two variants were touched up by Raeburn, one can only be thankful for the otherwise disappointing fact that though they lived in Edinburgh for a time together, he and Burns seem never to have met, and certainly never for professional purposes.

Unfortunately, leading the field, the Nasmyth has been more frequently and more disastrously copied than any other Burns portrait; a score of engravers have done their worst with it and appalling caricatures of Burns have littered the homesteads of Scotland. Only two have failed to make it worse: Beugo, who had sittings from Burns himself for the Edinburgh Edition of the poems, and Freeman who engraved the frontispiece for Hogg and Motherwell. The former has succeeded in grafting upon Nasmyth a toughness and pugnacity which accord much better alike with contemporary descriptions and with one's own first-principle ideas; Burns himself—who hated being 'took'—cannot have disliked it, for he ordered three dozen prints upon India paper. The latter—Freeman —has conjured out of Nasmyth a coltish unfinished tousel-haired countrified boy with the celebrated brilliant eyes. It is improbable that Burns looked like this in his Edinburgh days, but at least he *could* have looked like it shortly before them, at least the version is human. Nasmyth also executed a full-length of Burns; it is said to have been painted, forty years later, from a sketch made at Roslin after a heavy night, and perhaps this accounts for the fact that the face in it is quite unlike either the original Nasmyth or any other portrait of Burns made then or thereafter.

Nasmyth varied wildly on himself, but one encounters,

ROBERT BURNS

as soon as one leaves him, downright contradictions. True, the Skirving head—a very beautiful drawing in dark red crayon—has still something of that *exalté* and seraphic expression; so much of it indeed as to make the whole faintly reminiscent of a Joshua Reynolds cherub—whiskered, perhaps, but still essentially disembodied. But when one comes to the extraordinary production of Taylor, the coach-painter of Leith, one is fairly baffled. It is, of course, a very bad picture, but even allowing for the artist's incompetence, it presents another wholly incredible figure, whether *a priori* or by comparison with other versions—a long, heavy, expressionless, lifeless, dull-eyed face glooming and brooding under a huge-brimmed hat. The portrait has an extraordinary and suspicious history;[18] but more extraordinary still, it was readily recognised as Robert Burns—though admittedly many years after his death—by his widow, his brother Gilbert, his Clarinda, Scott, Hogg and Gray of Dumfries; while on the other hand, William Hall, Dr. John Mackenzie and William Tennant—all of whom knew Burns intimately at any rate by sight—could see 'not the smallest resemblance'. (Nasmyth, who still survived and was consulted, confined himself to the remark that Taylor had no pretensions to be other than a coach-painter.) Some have thought the oddity may have been a portrait of *Gilbert* Burns and the wan egg-shaped face has a curious parallel in Bonner's portrait of his sister Isabella; one can only say despairingly that if Nasmyth is right Taylor is impossible and vice versa.

The silhouette portraits—Miers, Houghton and Bruce —bear a strong family resemblance, and so far as silhouettes can go they are credible likenesses; they show well the forward thrust of the face, the pronounced eye-ridges, the firm mouth, the tied hair. They show, too, the extraordinary length and roundness of Burns's head—it was of average height, but six millimetres longer than it should have been; it is a head shaped like a *pickel-haube*. But the range of expression possible to any silhouette is limited. We are left, then, among these portraits accepted

47

as authentic, with the three-inch miniature on ivory done in 1795-6 by Alexander Reid of Dumfries, looking from right to left, taken from the Watson collection; this is, to me, the only credible portrait of Burns, and it struck me as credible at first sight. To begin with, it is a Scots face and a Scots *farmer's* face—which cannot be said of any of the others—solid and sensible; it has the firm mouth, the slightly up-looking nose but out-looking eyes; the square back to the head; that slightly aggressive, slightly quizzical, *appraising* look which one feels Burns must have had, but which has become in Taylor a glower and in Nasmyth and his followers the rapt gaze of a visionary with a tendency to phthisis. Here one feels—making allowance for an eight-year interval—is a man who in his prime could have conquered women and held his own at the Edinburgh symposia. But again, if Nasmyth is correct—and so on.

So Burns, unfortunate in his early biographers, was equally unfortunate in his artists; they *would* refine and beautify into nonsense what must have been one of the grandest of human faces. As his niece, Isabella Burns Begg, told A. K. H. Boyd, Burns was a far bigger and rougher man than his portraits would show him. 'They tried to make him look like a gentleman,' said Isabella, 'and he was not one.' It is all too true. But if the curious reader would care to see what posterity could do to Robert Burns when it really tried, let him consult the very vulgarly produced edition of his life and works edited by the Rev. P. Hateley Waddell and published 'in parts' in 1867-9, where he will be met *in limine* by a blue, pink and yellow technicolour of Nasmyth where all features are lost in a salmon-coloured plate of porridge, round as a moon and silly as a cheese. 'Poor Burns!' as Mrs. Montagu (*née* Benson) said. 'Misfortune pursues thee even to the grave.'[19]

48

FOOTNOTES TO PART ONE

[1] *p. 13.* There is much discrepancy in the spelling of this name, which appears also as Lochlea and Lochlee; the form I have adopted seems the best supported. Indeed, from the 'poems' of Sanders Tait, it would seem that the accent was upon the first syllable and that the place was really *Loch*-ly, cf. Tait in *Burns at Lochly*, where the scansion demands a trochee— 'To Lochly-ye came like a clerk, And on your back was scarce a sark, The dogs did at your buttocks bark, But now ye're braw. Ye poucht the rent ye was so stark, Made payment sma',' etc.

[2] *p. 13.* In this view of the Lochlie litigation I follow John McVie, whose exhaustive article (*Burns Chron.*, 1935) seems to me convincing. The opposite and till recently the popular version is, of course, indicated in the Sanders Tait quotation above.

[3] *p. 18.* Of the practising members, Richmond, who compromised Jenny Surgeoner, fled to Edinburgh, and Smith, who had contrived to impregnate a servant girl twice his age, to Linlithgow. Burns, with Jean Armour in like situation, stood his ground, but began to meditate upon Jamaica. Despite the activities of this formidable body (or perhaps because it was already broken up by the pusillanimity of its members), the Sessions Clerk of Mauchline could record rather plaintively in 1788: 'Notwithstanding the great noise, there are only twenty fornicators since last Sacrament.' Holy Willie Fisher's nose must have been failing.

[4] *p. 18.* Catherine Carswell, *Life of Burns.*

[5] *p. 20.* Tait, for obscure reasons, attacked the Burns family in three poems—*B--ns in his Infancy, B---ns at Lochly* and *B--ns's Hen Clockin' in Mauchline.* They are of very poor quality, especially the last—wandering and witless, with inept expressions dictated by the necessities of ill-handled rhyme. The stanza quoted in note [1] above is considerably above Tait's average.

[6] *p. 23.* The Rev. Archibald Lawrie, then a divinity student at Edinburgh University, son of Dr. George Lawrie of Loudoun. The 'nesty closs' was Baxter's in the Lawnmarket, where Burns shared 'half a small room and half a small bed' (Lawrie) with Richmond, the Mauchline deserter of Jenny Surgeoner. After Burns joined the establishment, the landlady, Mrs. Carfrae, charged an enhanced rent of—sixpence a week.

[7] *p. 25.* 'Robert Burns's poems had, he acknowledged, surprised him; his prose compositions appeared even more wonderful; but the conversation was a marvel beyond all.' Wm. Robertson, D.D., Principal of Edinburgh University, as recorded by Chambers.

[8] *p. 29.* Catherine Carswell, *Robert Burns* (1933).

[9] *p. 32.* On 14th January 1790 Burns wrote to Wm. Dunbar, W.S., that there were no 'mortifying circumstances' in the Excise so far; and to Cleghorn, just before he left Ellisland, 'the Excise is the business for me'.

[10] *p. 34. Burns's Excise Duties and Emoluments. Burns Chron.,* Vol. VII, to which article I am indebted for many of my facts.

[11] *p. 35.* Philip Sully, *Burns and London, Burns Chron.,* Vol. XXIII.

[12] *p. 38.* I follow here Sir James Crichton-Browne, as most writers on Burns have done since his *Burns from a New Point of View* was published in 1926. The endocarditis theory has had the support of other medical men; see also *infra,* p. 68 *et sqq.*

[13] *p. 38.* 'Consumptions and rheumatisms are frequent here'—Dr. Burnside in the *Statistical Account.*

[14] *p. 39.* For a detailed discussion of this complicated affair see *infra,* p. 231.

[15] *p. 42.* For instance, he altered Maria's 'joy-inspiring bowl' (*Dumfries Journal* article) to 'flowing bowl'. Joy from bowls was no part of Currie's creed.

[16] *p. 43.* Both Maxwell (*Animadversions on some Poets and poetasters of the present age, especially R——t B——s and J——n L——k* (1788) and the Rev. Peebles (anonymously) in *Burnomania. The Celebrity of Robert Burns considered in a Discourse* (1811) hit out hard. According to Maxwell, writing in anapaestic verse, 'He in the west who but lately has sprung, From behind the plough tails, and the raking of dung, A champion of Satan . . . is to this land and this age a disgrace. . . .' 'This hellish wight. . . .' 'Yes—B——; 'tis o'er; thy race is run; And shades receive thy setting sun.' Peebles in powerful (if rather sermonising) prose let fly at the 'irreligious profligate' with his verses 'sentimental, droll, abusive, personal, obscene,' who exposed the saints to delight the profane; who wrote 'vile scraps of indecent ribaldry' *and* on a Sunday; who indulged in 'impious cursing and swearing'. *The Whistle* is the most 'daring and abominable thing' Peebles has ever met, while *Tam* is a 'horrible story,' not only 'absurd and shocking', but 'indelicate and offensive'. Burns 'gibbets himself and his friends publish his exalted infamy'. And so on.

[17] *p. 44.* The contest was won by Mrs. Isa Craig Knox of Edinburgh from a field of six hundred. She used the name of 'Isa Craig', and this gave *Punch* a fine opening which was readily accepted: 'Dark as winter was the flow Of Isa rolling rapidly', and (because Mrs. Craig was backward in coming forward for her award when called upon) she was 'deaf as Isa Craig'. Phelps the actor read the prize-winning poem when, in the words of *Punch's* hexameter expert, 'all were agreed that the poem was what you may call a slapupper'. The hexameter poem is really very good and will bear reading today. (*Punch*; 29/1/1859).

[18] *p. 47.* The picture purports to have been painted from life in the winter of 1786-7, Burns giving Taylor three sittings; but Burns never refers to it at all, and the only person who professed to have been present besides artist and sitter was Mrs. Taylor, the artist's wife. Taylor (who *was* mainly a coach-painter by profession) died shortly after the picture was completed, whereupon Mrs. Taylor locked it away in a room and would show it only as a special favour. From this retirement it emerged as a rare discovery sixteen years after the poet's death, when, as has been mentioned in the text, it was

'recognised' by several of his family and friends—Clarinda being enthusiastic and Gray rapturous. It was later engraved by Horsburg and published by Constable in his 1830 edition, when the topic in Edinburgh was whether or not Constable—or his partner Aitkin—had been fooled. Those with a gift for story-making may concoct their own theses from these odd events; there are at least half a dozen possible versions. The layman would say—with Mackenzie and Tennant—that the portrait *cannot* have been Burns, but the experts profess to recognise affinities between its outlines and those of Nasmyth, and so far it holds its place—though perhaps somewhat precariously—among the authentics. For informed articles on the Burns portraits see D. W. Stevenson, Alex. S. Mackay and others; *Burns Chron.*, Vols. I, II and V.

[19] *p. 48*. Waddell, whose publishers had the effrontery to claim that their edition was 'enriched' by its portraits, also included two engravings from what he called the 'Kerry Miniatures'. These repellant objects purported to be (*a*) Burns, (*b*) his eldest son Robert at the age of nine. Waddell bought them from an Irishman in Listowel calling himself the O'Connor-Kerry; judging by their correspondence (which he publishes in full) the general ignorance of the O'Connor-Kerry was the one thing comparable in magnitude to the credulity of the reverend editor. (The O'Connor sold the 'miniatures' because he had become destitute through a fire in his house which, oddly enough, had destroyed almost everything he possessed *except* these two paintings; he had obtained them, in exchange for a 'valuable old marine picture', from a Major Maunsell of Scallaheen—who was now deceased; he was 'certain' they were Raeburns, or Nasmyths at the least.) The atrocities were crudely painted on slabs of wood eight inches by seven and seven inches by five respectively, so how was it possible, in the first place, for Waddell to persuade himself that they could be the 'small miniature' of Burns's letter to Thomson, which was going to Edinburgh in May of 1795 to 'get itself be-crystallised' and which Burns thought the 'most remarkable likeness' ever taken of anybody? He did however so persuade himself, using some of the most wonderful logic ever printed. The pictures are utterly hideous; 'Burns' is a head-and-shoulders—a long, narrow, high-cheekboned, cadaverous, agonised and—one would say—essentially *Irish*

face. The boy is at full length; he is in 'full-dress schoolboy costume of green corduroy suit with bright "bowl buttons" and an elaborate white "point" French Revolution collar'; I hate to think that Burns would have put his eldest son into such a rig, or to believe that Jean would have passed his truly terrible trousers. The head could never possibly have been Burns; the boy—'a pretty bagatelle, a family bijou', as Waddell calls the object—might just conceivably have grown into the bloodhound face we see in the elderly photographs of Robert Junior; but, then, he might as easily have grown into Ally Sloper or the Cham of Tartary. Waddell's edition has merits as well as defects; but it is monstrous that a Scots editor and a Scots publisher should have collaborated to produce this intolerable outrage.

PART TWO

PORTRAIT OF THE ARTIST
BY HIMSELF

It is strange that the early enthusiasts on Burns should have found it necessary to concoct a figure so little resembling, in many ways, the object of their veneration, when Burns himself had provided them with the material for an almost complete and genuine portrait. It is true that a good deal of this material has only been made available by the patient research of recent years; but this might well have been compensated, in the case of the earlier biographers, by their much greater proximity to their subject. The subject himself was positively garrulous; never was any genius so self-revealing; never did any genius take such delight in spreading out his viscera, duly ticketed and labelled, on the dissection table; no member of the Oxford Group Movement ever so much enjoyed talking about himself. Of course, in a sense he talked too much; we have already noted that he could, consciously or unconsciously, distort himself according to the mood of the moment, and his moods were, like the habits of Mr. Salteena, many and various. Yet a little practice will render these fairly readily identifiable even in the written lines themselves, while the spaces between the lines fill up most revealingly. It was not, however, the method of Burns's annalists to go back very often to their sources.

It has been customary to fall foul of Burns's earliest biographers—Heron and the scapegoat Currie—for the establishment of these false ideas. Certainly they set the ball rolling—though Heron's *Memoir* has always seemed to me fairer and less anti-Burns than is generally made out. As for Currie, it must be remembered that he undertook a task which otherwise would not have been done; if he carried it out according to his lights, which were not the best lights, that could not be helped. Currie was a Burns fan; he admired the works, but was not attracted by

the man; as a teetotaller and a moraliser, he hardly could
be. He was reluctant to assume the editorial mantle—or
did he just, like the Victorian drawing-room miss with
her music, want pressing?—but this once assumed, he
laboured untiringly at that disconcerting mass of 'sweepings'[1] that was hurled upon him. He drew not a penny
from the enormous earnings of his work, but gave his
labour gratis. His attitude towards his task may be
illustrated by his own naïve confession; 'It has been found
necessary to mutilate many of the individual letters
and sometimes to exscind parts of great delicacy'; these
last were not only the unprintables, as one might have
supposed, but also the 'unbridled effusions of panegyric
and regard'. Further, 'the Editor' (complacent gentleman!)
'has found some correction of grammar necessary'. In
point of fact, the Editor 'found necessary' some quite
substantial rewriting. Currie was about as much in
sympathy with Burns as he would have been with a witch-
doctor from the Congo; he had only met him once—in
Dumfries in 1792—had clearly not formed a high opinion
of him at that brief encounter, and ever afterwards was
predisposed towards whatever was relevant to the adverse
impression he then recorded. The villain of the piece here
is really brother Gilbert; given a great chance, as editor
of the 1820 eighth edition, he funked it pitiably—'it
would ill become me to do anything which I knew to be
disagreeable to Dr. Currie's friends'. In the name of God,
why? Presumably, one imagines, because Gilbert, still
struggling with Mossgiel and aiming just then at an
advantageous marriage, was desperately in need of the
money; and as the publishers were piping a solid two
hundred and fifty pounds, they—and he—thought they
were justified in calling the tune. (The edition failed, and
Gilbert lost the second two hundred and fifty he had been
promised if it ran to a second printing; I think he deserved
to.) Currie therefore went gaily on, uncorrected.

But it was not all Currie; Jeffrey and Scott are far from
blameless. The former, reviewing Cromek's unsatisfactory
Reliques, gave authority to the notion of the 'unlettered

ploughboy', comparing Burns with such oddities as
Thomas Dermody and Stephen Duck (*seu quid ineptius!*);
the latter, a trifle patronising throughout, harped unnecessarily on the poet's humble origins.[2] (Jeffrey accused
Burns of 'vulgarity'—from which, oddly enough, he was
almost entirely free.) At all events, Heron, Currie and
Cromek became the standard-bearers of a procession; the
contribution of most of their immediate followers may be
summed up in the acid remark of Charles Kirkpatrick
Sharpe: 'When authors die, what *lies* people who *might*
have seen and known them tell.' In one of the formulae he
developed in his Letters, which he repeated more than
once with minor variations, Burns wrote: 'A damned
Star has all my life usurped my zenith and squinted out
the cursed rays of its malignant influences'—and so forth;
many of those early star-gazers would seem to have
walked within its beam.

Burns's cardinal accusation against himself was that he
lacked an aim; but as any psychologist could have told
him, he was split between two aims, equally powerful and
mutually destructive. The one was hereditary—to be a
successful farmer; the other was personal—to be a
successful writer. These inevitably clashed; the lure of
creative writing rendered more than commonly distasteful
the hard grubbing manual labour without which no farm
can be made to pay its way; while the drudgery of a
working farmer's day brought him tired and disgruntled
to his verses. We have already noted his self-confessed
dream of bliss—to be a sort of Dumfriesshire Horace; and
Horace is an attractive figure to all of us who, like Burns,
are constitutionally lazy. This may seem a strange thing
to say of a man who worked so hard that he killed himself;
and indeed Burns was not physically lazy. Yet he displays
time and again the vacillations and the dallyings of the
mentally lazy man; he disliked taking decisions and put
them off as long as possible; it was something of a 'sooth

boord' when he wrote that the supporters in his coat of arms should be a pair of sloths and the crest a slow-worm. 'On *reason* build resolve', as he was so fond of quoting to his correspondents; but Burns could 'resolve' one thing one day and its contrary the next; and in either case he took the word for the deed, the resolve for the accomplishment, and there left it. With characteristic self-revelation he wrote to Muir; 'I am still undetermined as to the future and as usual never think of it'; the first part of this was true, the second false—he *thought* of the future a great deal too much. We have already noted that projected, and only projected, drama which progressed just as far as the 'pretty large poetic works' of which, as he told Peggy Chalmers, he had been laying the foundations. The 'Poet's Progress', a 'fragment of the intended whole', which was to be (in a letter to Dugald Stewart) 'the work of my utmost exertions, ripened by years', remained a fragment, never ripened at all, and was finally fobbed off upon Graham of Fintry nearly three years later as an original 'epistle'.

The subscribers to the unworldly genius theory delighted to represent their idol as impetuous and hotheaded, dashing impulsively into action ruinous or beneficial; the truth is that Burns had more than the normal measure of good Scots canniness. It was a canny Scot who conveyed his property to brother Gilbert in order to dodge the Armours' warrant; it was a canny Scot who wriggled with that same Gilbert into Mossgiel under the noses of Maclure's bailiffs; it was a canny Scot who played safe and dropped from the Kilmarnock edition the Twa Herds, Holy Willie, Hornbook and the Ordination, and who conveniently—and quite incredibly —'forgot' that he had ever written the Jolly Beggars. He was so canny over the move to Jamaica and the post in the Excise that the first never materialised at all and the second only at the eleventh hour. There is no earthly reason why this prudence should be held against him—as many of his critics appear to think it should; he had to make his way in life with nothing but his own gifts and his own judgment to rely on; the few cards dealt him must be slowly and carefully played. Yet perhaps—though this he would never have admitted—he did lack faith in himself; perhaps he did believe in that squinting star and the quotation he attributed to an unspecified Hebrew Seer—'Whatsoever he purposeth it shall not come to pass, and whatsoever he doeth, it shall not prosper'; perhaps, with prophetic instinct, he saw that, do as he liked, he must eventually fail. 'What proves the hero truly great Is never never to'—shilly-shally; but we cannot all be heroes—not always.

Burns was intensely interested in *quicquid agunt homines,* but he was even more intensely interested in *quicquid agit* Robert Burns. Just as he could not write six lines about a woman without posing himself as her lover, so he invariably centred any given set of circumstances upon himself. He dramatised himself tirelessly—and at times tiresomely. He had a magnificent sense of theatre—so much so as to suggest that we have indeed lost something in those projected but unwritten dramas, even the one based on the seemingly unpromising theme of the shoemaker who ran his awl into the Bruce's heel. How superb he must have been when Maria Riddell sent her carriage for him to Brow Well and the emaciated figure with its tumbled hair said, entering her sitting-room: 'Madam, have you any commands for the next world?' Or as the hero of the less well-authenticated story of the contemporary tea-party at the manse of Ruthwell; the afternoon sun blazed in at the window and the daughter of the house, stricken by the ravaged face so cruelly floodlit, made to pull down the blind. 'Let him shine!' said Burns—and really one cannot resist the adverb 'dramatically'—'He will not shine long for me.' He loved to take the centre of the stage, now in one character, now in another. At Mossgiel (Commonplace Book)—age twenty-five!—he has been 'all along a miserable dupe to Love', and has

59

been 'led into a thousand weaknesses and follies by it'. At Irvine (letter to his father) he is a man dying long long before his prime; about to bid 'ere long and perhaps very soon' an eternal 'adiew' to a weary life: 'as for the world I despair of ever making a figure in it'. (But the letter perks up at the end to practicalities—'my meal is out, but I am going to borrow'.) In Edinburgh he is the bright, doomed, fluttering butterfly; I have already quoted from his letter to Greenfield—how he stands 'unintoxicated, with the inebriating cup in my hand', awaiting 'the stroke of envious Calumny' which must surely come. In Dumfries: 'Here I sit, altogether November-ish, a damned melange of Fretfulness and Melancholy; not enough of the one to rouse me to passion, nor of the other to repose me in torpor': his soul is flouncing and fluttering like a wild finch 'caught amid the horror of Winter and thrust into a cage'—the fact being that a spate of Excise work has forced him to postpone a meeting with Maria Riddell. I do not wish to seem heartless on the subject of these outbursts; but I would suggest that while shedding a tear for the tormented man, one should remember at the same time to applaud the artist. The artist at least was enjoying himself.

This sense of theatre, this passion for self-dramatisation, is best illustrated in his Letters; it is interesting and at the same time pathetic to see how he can lash himself up into the most terrific crescendo. A good example is the letter to Glencairn written on 13th January 1787, which, beginning quite calmly and sensibly with a request for permission to publish, works itself up into the wildest rhodomontade. The same over-excitement is to be seen in the celebrated letter 'from the regions of Hell amid the horrors of the damned' written to one or other of the Riddell ladies after the scandalous affair to which allusion has already been made;[3] the tone rises steadily to the impressive climax—so often quoted misleadingly out of its context—'Regret! Remorse! Shame! Ye three hellhounds that ever dog my steps and bay at my heels, spare me, spare me!' An overdone apology, perhaps, for a *bêtise* however gross. . . . Or in a letter to Peggy Chalmers in 1788, which again begins quite reasonably—and again has been frequently quoted out of context—'God have mercy on me! A poor damned, incautious, duped, unfortunate fool! The sport, the miserable victim of rebellious pride, hypochondriac imagination, agonising sensibility and Bedlam passions!' Miss Chalmers must have been a little puzzled to note that the cause of all this —or the only cause emerging in the letter—was that Creech the publisher was paying up less promptly than he should. And the damned squinting star—at full length, complete with Hebrew Prophet—seems rather an excessive and extravagant comment on the fact that he had just received all his ordered copies of the London *Star* except the two he really wanted, which were those containing his own verses. There is no need to multiply examples; rhetoric and self-dramatisation, going hand in hand, were a passion with Burns; at some times they fairly ran away with him; at all times, and in whatever he writes, allowance must be made for them.

But well indeed might Maria Riddell record that Burns was 'candid and manly in the avowal of his errors'. He was much more than that. There are times when his 'avowal' is not so much 'manly' as the jubilant roar of a self-accusing—and at the same time self-admiring—Jove.

Naturally, with all this self-dramatisation, one finds a certain amount of small-part posing, of everyday disingenuousness. There is no accusation in this; some degree of pretence—be it bluff or evasion—is a component in all of us, and indeed civilised society could not get along without it. It is of interest in Burns because it fits in so well with his 'canniness' and his staginess; and because it shows that a man almost fanatically honest in larger matters may still have his own small and personal affectations and tarididdles. It is necessary, of course—and sometimes not easy—to distinguish what is pure prose or disingenuousness from the fluctuations of mood in which he really believed for the time being what he said; but when this has been done, there remain a number of instances where he could *not* have believed his own statements and where his tongue must have been quite consciously in his cheek.

Many of his poses, of course, arose from feelings genuine enough at root, but magnified and exploited and exhibited; some of them were the converse of these feelings. I have already insisted that Burns was no more a 'Ploughman Poet' than Dr. Blacklock was a bricklayer poet, and that he was perfectly well aware of the fact and would have resented very bitterly and justly being classified with the artisan poets and poetesses of the day, the Stephen Ducks and the Janet Littles. Yet there are times when it obviously paid to be the Ploughman Poet and when it would have been sheer bad business not to live up to that label—for instance, in his earliest days at Edinburgh. As a Ploughman Poet, Edinburgh had taken him up; if he had ceased to be a Ploughman Poet he would no longer have been a curiosity and Edinburgh would have dropped him; so he did not cease—for some time—to be a Ploughman Poet. There are stories of his tramping up and down Smellie's printing-room, in boots and a driving-coat, cracking an enormous whip—the complete rustic. He had prepared the way for this reputation himself; we have seen the sententious preamble of the Mossgiel Commonplace Book, and there was more than a suspicion of mock humility in the Preface to the Kilmarnock Edition. He could write some claptrap to Moore about aiming to please his 'compeers, the rustic inmates of the hamlet', and could offer to the Editor of the London *Star* the 'Productions of a simple ploughman' simply because his Scots sense told him they were thereby made more readily saleable to the Sassenach. But in his heart he knew that the Ploughman Poet, like his rustic compeers and his 'simplicity' were so much stage effect.

There was another set of poses in which he liked himself so much that he may at times have believed in them.

These were originated by *The Man of Feeling*, that book which he 'prized next to the Bible'; the soft-hearted (and soft-headed?) Harley of that somewhat treacly novel was continually being moved to tears; he sighed; he went into ecstasies at the sight of quite ordinary objects; he sat for long periods in silence with his head on his hands gazing at God. Burns therefore—long before ever he saw Edinburgh or The Man's creator—began also to do these things. He enjoyed it; he developed it; after apostrophising Fergusson's neglected grave, he prostrated himself and kissed the uncommemorated turf;[4] on his Border tour he knelt down upon the frontier of Scotland and with uplifted hands prayed for and blessed his country. (This last, however, is according to his companion Ainslie, who may have embellished; Burns's *Journal* says only: 'Coldstream—went over to England—glorious river Tweed—fine bridge—dine at Coldstream.') Again at Blairathol, coming to a small hut and waterfall on the banks of the Tilt, he 'threw himself on the heathy seat and gave himself up to a tender, abstracted and voluptuous enthusiasm of imagination'; so that his cicerone, Josiah Walker, could hardly get him in to his supper with the Duke. All of which, of course, must have been very effective.

It was said some time ago that Burns 'learned French' in a week's study with Murdoch at Ayr; he also took lessons, along with Beugo the engraver, from a Frenchman in Edinburgh, and one of his poses—one of the most harmless and amiable of them—was a certain Francophile pretentiousness in that language. With his more favoured correspondents—especially with Peggy Chalmers—he loved to interlard his letters with little French tags, generally of a somewhat elementary order. It was this same Peggy Chalmers who put a period to this particular vanity, for one day—so the story goes—she introduced him to a real French lady, and Burns, to his chagrin, found she could not understand a word of his nor he a word of hers. Worse still, his maladroitness in the language landed him in some sort of *bêtise*—so easy to do in French —and the lady, translated no doubt by Miss Chalmers, who must have been enjoying herself, rapped his knuckles for it smartly. One can imagine the fury Burns, who was normally much too canny—or too lucky—to be involved in such contretemps, must have felt.

Finally, there were the poses which became not poses at all, but grew into his nature. For a long time his favourite hero was no doubt the Man of Feeling; then, after his return from Edinburgh, a quite different figure usurps Mr. Harley's place—the Miltonic Satan. Quite probably he announced that Satan was his hero—it was to James Smith in his letter from Mauchline in June 1787— as a joke, certainly as a conscious bit of posing. But the idea ingrew; the picture of that defiant angel, expelled and fallen so frightfully from—Edinburgh—began to assume a personal value. If he could not be the Lion Rampant at 'Scotia's darling seat', let him at least be the Devil Couchant at Ellisland. The Miltonic Satan became just a little true. So also with Burns's class hatred, which began as a pose, conscious or otherwise, a piece of adolescent bravado, away back in the days of the Tarbolton Bachelors, but in time soured into fact. It *was* a pose in essence, because when he actually met the aristocracy, he liked them; he paid Lord Daer a handsome tribute in verse, which it is to be hoped his Lordship appreciated as he should have done; he even liked 'old Q.', whom he had abused so bitterly for political reasons and, meeting him in the flesh, discovered in him 'first taste' and 'first manners'. The class hatred pose, which like the Miltonic Satan ingrew and turned to reality, was, also like it, a product of the Edinburgh disappointment; the 'stateliness of the Edinburgh Patricians' had a good deal to answer for. But for these aristocrats we should not have heard so much about 'lobster-coated Puppies' in Dumfries, nor would a perfectly harmless gentleman's carriage have appeared as the 'rattling equipage of some gaping blockhead, contemptible puppy or detestable scoundrel'.[5] And what is more, poor Burns would have been a happier man.

As to disingenuousness, almost all Burns's Letters are

disingenuous, because they were written with an eye to the immediate recipient and his tastes, and also with an eye to copying and circulation among his own personal friends. At times the desire to please his audience led him into caddishnesses which one would prefer to forget: to display as the Mauchline Buck, the 'Tarbolton Satan', he could write of women he professed to love with a quite revolting brutality. This sort of exhibitionism is not endearing, and there are other disconcerting sophistries. It was perhaps venal to say that the 'feelings of a father' caused him to abandon the Jamaica venture—when it was really the death of Mary Campbell and the prospect of the Edinburgh edition; less so to give Dr. Moore an entirely false account of the Armours ('some ill advised ungrateful people had uncoupled the merciless legal Pack at my heels'.) There seems to have been something worse than mere disingenuousness, and more like plain cheating, in his dealings with Daddy Auld, the parish minister of Mauchline, over his 'single man certificate' in 1786 and his eventual marriage to Jean in 1788. And when he copied for the Glenriddell MS. one of his love-letters to Clarinda and explained in a marginal note that it was 'the fustian rant of enthusiastic youth', he knew quite well that it was nothing of the kind. In such cases disingenuousness comes a little too near to deceit.

Burns could be disingenuous, too, about his writings. He could 'forget' the Jolly Beggars, as we have seen, and could write 'the author has not the most distant mercenary view in Publishing', while all the time 'the author' was pestering his friends to canvas for subscriptions. 'Never blow my songs among the million,' he wrote to Niven, 'as I would abhor to hear every Prentice mouthing my poor performances in the streets': he may have believed this—or not. It was hardly playing fair to send the 'Poet's Progress' to Graham of Fintry as an original composition hot from the anvil; or to present the gullible Mrs. Dunlop with a Clarinda poem, slightly altered, as if it had been written for herself alone. On the other hand, it was perhaps pardonable to flatter an Edinburgh theatre audience by telling

them that Home had formed wild Shakespeare into plan
—which, let us hope at least, he could not have believed:
and when we come to his rapturous reception of the
'poems' of his lady correspondents—Clarinda and Mrs.
Dunlop—we may raise our eyebrows, but must at the
same time admit that we have done precisely the same
thing ourselves and will do it again. Burns's only fault
was that he *over*did it; one wonders that the ladies did
not see as much, but then, few budding authoresses have
ever shared the Carpenter's complaint anent the thick-
ness of the butter. Still, when he professed that he would
put Mrs. Dunlop's *Address to a Young Lady* 'against any
as many lines in our language'; or when he told Clarinda
that parts of her '*Talk Not of Love*' 'would have been
worthy of Sappho', then surely he was going an unnecessary distance beyond what Dugald Stewart called his
'extreme facility and good nature in judging the compositions of others'.[6] However, they did not see it; and
since he described himself as one 'who never cares for
speaking anything else but nonsense'—in itself a fairly
disingenuous remark—we may leave it at that.

True to his Horatian ideal, Burns had a great notion of
being what he called a 'Philosopher'; and he was so
perhaps to the extent that we all are. But, as with most of
us, his 'Philosophy' too often ran along hack and well-
worn lines. These rather jejune speculations he took very
seriously and as his life progressed 'Philosophy' began to
some extent to oust his verse; it can at least be said that
much of the one was as good as much of the other. He
thought and wrote a great deal about religion and the
life after death and an honest man's hopes of heaven—
more especially when the *Timor mortis conturbabat*; but he
struck out no more original idea than 'God's a good
fellow and 'twill all be well'. (Though, perhaps, for those
days and in Scotland, that *was* rather an original idea.)
Sociologically, he could not improve on the doctrines of

the Jolly Beggars and the Epistle to Davie. Liberty is all that matters; the free peasant and the free beggar are happier and better off than the nobleman. (But what about the free nobleman?) The implications of the words he threw off so dashingly were something he never thought out. On the other hand, there is no reason to suppose that his correspondents—especially Mrs. Dunlop—ever tired of his discourse; Clarinda indeed wrestled with him about religion till she gave him up, but Mrs. Dunlop never gave him up—at least never because he bored her. Mrs. Dunlop was capable of absorbing indefinitely such profound thoughts as 'little does the fond Mother think, as she hangs delighted over the sweet little Leech at her bosom, where the poor fellow may hereafter wander and what may be his fate.' . . . Or again; 'I have often observed in the course of my experience of human life that every man, even the worst, have [*sic*] something good about them': 'let any of the strictest character for regularity among us examine impartially how much he is indebted to the World's good opinion, because the World does not know all.' These extracts from his First Commonplace Book are not unfair samples of Burns the Philosopher; he never really outgrew them.

This is not to say that he did not reflect seriously on the current topics and problems of the day; he did—and to some point, for he brought to them an alert mind and a judgment, considering his opportunities, quite remarkably acute. It is interesting to speculate just where this interest might have led him; for it is certain that for the last ten years of his brief life he was more a publicist than a poet—perhaps, indeed, he always was. It is a thousand pities that Ellisland broke up—where he was shaping so well towards turning the Nith into a second Bandusia; or that he could not live to earn that 'life of compleat leisure . . . the summit of my wishes' enjoyed by those demigods the collectors of the Excise. Then indeed we might have known, in addition to Burns the Poet, Burns the Novelist, Burns the Essayist, Burns the Critic. But alas! it was not to be.

It is necessary now to enquire what was the mental equipment on which Burns based the Horatian hope. In the first place, this must evidently have been largely conditioned by his physical equipment, which was none too good—which, in fact, would have defeated any man with a less indomitable courage. The theory—put forward with great authority by Sir James Crichton-Browne over twenty years ago—that Burns suffered from and perished of endocarditis, a disease of the heart brought on by his excessive labours as a boy and aggravated by constant therapeutic blunders, is now, I think, generally accepted.[7] 'He died,' says Sir James categorically, 'of endocarditis, a disease of the substance and lining membrane of the heart'; it was initiated by rheumatism which 'attacked him in early years, damaged his heart, embittered his life and cut short his career'. The trouble declared itself early —as heart troubles usually do—in those headaches, palpitations and night faintings which made his life at Mount Oliphant a burden to him, in the 'vapours'and glooms at Irvine, in the cold-bath-beside-the-bed period at Mossgiel. This form of heart disease, says Sir James, is mild and 'insidious', and may run over a span of twenty or thirty years; during intervals the patient may live his life as if nothing ailed him, but every now and then will come a feverish attack which marks a milestone—and these attacks will worsen. Burns had one on his first arrival in Edinburgh; others in early 1788; others all through the winter of 1789-90 and in the winter of 1792. There was a characteristic rally in 1794-5 which but served as a prelude to the final crash in October of the latter year. The spasm of energy in which he is said to have actually expired is typical of the disease. Thus Sir James Crichton-Browne; and other medical opinion has supported him. Dr. Harry B. Anderson of Toronto speaks of 'auricular fibrillation' and a 'bacteriological endocarditis which developed in a terminal infection', while as recently as 1944 Dr. S. Watson Smith of Bourne-mouth considered that 'Burns's last long illness, for many months gradually worsening . . . would seem to be, on the scant information available, subacute infective endocarditis—microbic inflammation of the heart which usually ends fatally in septicaemia'; he adds that a 'painful arthritis' (poor Burns's 'rheumatism' and 'flying gout') is a not rare complication.[8] Little doubt therefore seems to be left as to the cause of Burns's death; nor is there any at all that, if he could have had better understanding and better treatment from his doctors—if Lister had lived a hundred years earlier than he did—his life might have been certainly eased and probably considerably prolonged.

I have dealt with this subject at some length because, as we have seen, it was a cardinal item in the accepted picture of Burns that he drank himself to death. This was not really a very intelligent suggestion. In order to drink himself to death, any man must first drink himself half to death and then three-quarters to death; that is to say, he must reduce himself to a state in which both body and mind become partially paralysed, in which he totters on his feet, shakes, sees strange objects, wanders in his mind and flounders in his speech. It can hardly be said that this was the case with Burns, who was writing good songs within a week of his end and who appeared to Maria Riddell at Brow Well as clear-headed and sensible as ever he had been. There is no mention of any of the symptoms of dropsy or of the other kidney troubles of the chronic soak; there was none of that cirrhosis which carried off his friend Willie Nicol. It may be less romantic to die of heart disease than of disappointment and drink; it is certainly a less dramatic gesture; but heart disease, not drink, is what finished Robert Burns.

There is a further suggestion that, in his latter days at least, he suffered from venereal disease. This idea may have originated from the statement that Maxwell, who attended him, was dosing him heavily with mercury (a treatment for which it seems difficult to account), but is more probably attributable to some veiled and ambiguous hints thrown out by Currie, whose delicacy on this occasion went so far as to disable him even from writing plain English. Currie wrote of an 'accidental complaint' which 'from October 1795 till the January following . . . confined Burns to his home'. This, taken by itself, is practically meaningless; but Currie also wrote of 'the succeeding part' (of the 'convivial scene') 'over which uncontrolled passion generally presided. He who suffers the pollution of inebriation, how shall he escape other pollution?' If Currie, as a medical man, meant anything by this, it is difficult to see what else he could have meant but venereal disease. But 'let us refrain', says he, 'from the mention of errors over which delicacy and humanity draw the veil'. These 'errors' cannot be drink, which Currie has been 'mentioning' lavishly; he does not seem to realise that he *has* 'mentioned' the other thing, and with all the damaging effect of innuendo; he had better have been more explicit or held his tongue. Crichton-Browne scouts the venereal disease as 'a vile and groundless insinuation' and Snyder advances two sound arguments against it. In the first place, he says, Burns never infected his wife or any of his other women, and in the second he never mentions it in his letters. One can readily believe that Burns's first action on receiving a dose of the pox would have been to announce it with loud delight to Ainslie or Cleghorn or some other of his more Rabelaisian acquaintance. Nor is it very obvious where he could have picked it up; drunk or sober, he did not affect the sort of company from which venereal disease is normally contracted. There is, in a word, no evidence whatsoever that he had it.

In the light of these researches poor Burns's own comments on his health, written in ignorance and often in hopefulness, make painful reading. He wrote, of course, of what he called his 'hypochondriacs'—'a constitutional hypochondriac taint which made me fly solitude'; he is driven to the Muses, after a night of thunder and a morning of 'lurid fogs', 'for refuge from the Hypochondria which I fear worse than the devil'; 'I feel that horrid hypochondria pervading every atom of both body and

soul'; my 'deep incurable taint of hypochondria'. In the
Mossgiel Commonplace Book 'my body too was attacked
by that most dreadful distemper, a Hypochondria or
confirmed Melancholy', and this is followed by a pathetic
'prayer' to be used when 'fainting fits or other alarming
symptoms of a Pleurisy or some other dangerous disorder
. . . first put Nature on the alarm'. Reading all this,
both above the lines and between them, how is it possible
not to be fired and exalted by Burns's lifelong courage?
'Burns,' says Mrs. Carswell, 'a melancholic who was
swung by love, by drink, by congenial converse or by
poetic composition into a brief glory of defiant optimism';
it does not seem to me that the glory was so brief as all
that.

I have always thought that one of the meanest things
ever written about Burns was Stevenson's attack upon
poor Robbie's 'hypochondriacs'. He 'suffered', said
Stevenson, 'like a fine lady from sleeplessness and vapours
. . . at a touch of sickness he prostrated himself before
God, in what I can only call unmanly penitence'. Alison
Cunningham's petted baby might well have spared
himself these comments.

To this constitutional weakness Burns, of course, added
his own peculiar vices—drink and women. They were not,
needless to say, peculiar vices in his day, nor have they
been so in any other. But whether or not he made them
peculiar by indulging in them to a degree above the
average, he certainly wrote about them with unwonted
frequency and zest. Currie and subsequent biographers
took him at face value on these subjects; for this they were
perhaps not to be blamed—it would be easy, by extracting
the relevant passages from his letters, to show Burns as a
chronic and self-confessed drunkard and womaniser. But
we must, I think, be very chary indeed how we do this.
Burns was always something of a braggart and boaster,
and never more so than on these two subjects; it was a

maxim in my young days that a man who was always talking about his wine and his women probably *did* very little in either. Burns no doubt did a great deal in both; but—how bad really was he?

Not nearly so bad as—with characteristic self-dramatisation—he made himself out. He was not promiscuous; his women are really comparatively few and but for his unfortunate gift for procreation we should never have heard of some of them at all. 'Dear-bought Bess' has immortalised the uncomely Elizabeth Paton; without their fertility it seems improbable that history would have recorded the names of May Cameron or Jenny Clow. His affairs of any consequence can be reckoned on the fingers of a hand. For this there was good reason. He had the aversion to the professional harlot which is shared by most intelligent men; on the other hand, as brother Gilbert has recorded—and as one might have perhaps guessed!—he was 'no Platonic lover'. Burns agreed with Donne as to the 'right true end of love'; he aimed never short of possession; but it must be the private and preferably clandestine possession of something not common to the herd. This involved him in the pursuit of those who had to be won before they were wed; in the long period of siege and capture, the further period of possession and enjoyment—which must also be long if it is to compensate for the effort expended, and the inevitable slow diminuendo when the fires begin to fade. In the case of Burns all three of these stages were perhaps more rapidly traversed than is normal; but a life much longer than Burns's will not afford time for a very great many of these studied and serious affairs. Of course, just as 'what's done we partly may compute, but know not what's resisted', so we may know for certain the acknowledged amours, but remain in ignorance of the unmentioned—which may have been many. They *may* have been, but in view of Burns's character and the requirements posited for his sexual interest, it does not seem probable. We should have heard of them—and from the horse's mouth—all too fully.

When we turn to the drinking, the story is somewhat similar. God knows he drank, but God also knows that he was a convivial drinker, not a sodden, and that he drank no more than his associates. In those days everyone drank —except Currie. And as Linklater well says, 'His strong emotions were like the addition of proof spirit to his every glass, while in the majority of his companions their lack of feeling was a repeated diluent.' 'Burns', said the honest Ettrick Shepherd, 'has been accused of inveterate dissipation and drunkenness. Nonsense! Burns was no more a drunkard than I am; nay, I would take a bet that on an average I drink double of what he did; and yet I am acknowledged, both in Scotland and in England, as a most temperate and cautious man; and so I am.' Hogg's view of his reputation in this respect may have been a little rosy, but he is a useful counter to Currie's teetotalling estimate of Burns's potations. Burns took the intelligent view of a night's drinking. 'I love drinking now and then,' he wrote in the margin of his copy of Sterne, 'It defecates the standing pool of thought . . . a now-and-then tribute to Bacchus is like the cold bath—bracing and invigorating.' But a night of carousal and even the resultant hangover are matters for mirth—if they are not so, then they are unpardonable; and Burns liked to have such matters to write about. Certainly, for the benefit of his correspondents, he made the most of his *noctes ambrosianae.*

Perhaps this was because drinking, to Burns, was always something of a conscious feat; he knew perfectly well that his stomach was ill adapted to strong liquors, and he probably envied those with more accommodating entrails. At any rate, stomach or no, he must show himself as good a man as they; if there was, or had been, a bottle in sight, it must be brandished before their eyes. But he confided his real troubles to Dugald Stewart on one of those early-morning walks on the Braids; 'he told me indeed himself that the weakness of his stomach was such as to deprive him of any merit in his temperance'; and to Mrs. Dunlop in a letter containing one of his best phrases—'Hard drinking is the devil with me, but they will not have me if I do not drink with them, and every time I give them a slice of my constitution.' And he admitted in Dumfries that he could not drink 'gentleman's weight'—few men with work to do and a livelihood to earn could be expected to.[9] I am not pretending for a moment that Burns did not heartily enjoy an evening's debauch—I might as well call him a teetotaller and be done with it; but it was more of an effort, more of an event for him, it called up more of his energies than in the case of most of his *sympotes*, and he probably paid for it more painfully. He fought, however, with his weak stomach as he fought with his weak heart; he could and he *would* drink 'gentleman's weight' or as near it as he could manage. Oh, a fine free roystering bottle-emptying no-heeltapper was Robert Burns—and the world must hear of it.

Of Burns's boasting that he was intoxicated or nearly so, when he manifestly was not, his letters afford many examples. Perhaps the earliest symptom of this curious sort of *panache* is in the autobiographical letter to Moore; Burns would have Moore believe that as far back as the Kirkoswald days he 'learned to look unconcernedly on a large tavern bill' and to 'mix without fear in a drunken squabble'; as his emoluments at that time amounted to seven pounds a year, a very small tavern bill indeed would have rendered him bankrupt; much to the point is Rule V of the Tarbolton Bachelors—'No member is to spend more than threepence on drink.' Thereafter he never misses an opportunity of showing how gloriously he could imbibe; he is at pains to explain that they were all 'bitchified' at the time of the riding accident on Loch Lomond side; he tells Peter Hill he is 'miserably fou'—and writes a very good business letter about the subscription lists; writing to Nicol his only Braid Scots letter—and a masterpiece at that—he must needs assert (obviously mendaciously for no 'bitchify'd' man could have composed such a thing) that he 'gat myself sae notoriously bitchify'd the day after kailtime that I can hardly stoiter but and

74

ben'; Lawrie is told of a 'bottle of good old port' at his elbow; Cunningham that he is 'completely nettled with the fumes of wine'—when there is no obvious sign of it; Mrs. Dunlop gets a 'shocking scrawl' made so by the fact that he has just 'dined and supped' with a gentleman— and the letter and its enclosed poem are excellently written if perhaps with a slightly heavier hand than usual. Poor Clarinda came in for quite a lot of this; he is 'unfit to finish my letter . . . pretty hearty after a bowl which has been constantly plied'; he is 'miserably stupid this morning. Yesterday I dined with a Baronet' (observe that the title is *not* omitted for a' that!); he is 'just risen from a two hours' bout after supper with silly or sordid souls, who could relish nothing in common with me but the Port'. Clarinda, reading with some surprise the lucid and reasoned discourse on religion contained in this last letter, wondered naïvely that 'you could write so distinctly after two or three hours over a bottle'. This should have taught Burns a lesson; it didn't.

If one is to take all this stuff at face value and not as an ill-advised but on the whole harmless bravado, then, of course, Burns was never sober. Currie—who knew nothing, good man, about drinking—did take it so, and he cannot be altogether blamed if he pictured a drunkard reeling downwards into a dishonoured grave. The persistence of Currie's version is a good illustration of the advantages of getting in first; defenders of Burns were not wanting but—like Peterkin, for instance—they came forward only after Currie held the field and they never quite caught him up. It is conceivable that one or two of these champions, outraged by the tar in Currie's portrait, went rather to the opposite extreme and overdid the whitewash; but they were respectable men of position and certainly would not have lied outright, not to save the reputation of their own mothers. Findlater, Burns's superior in the Excise, was categorical; 'the superintendence of his behaviour was my special province . . . I never saw him—which was very frequently while he lived at Ellisland and still more so after he removed to

Dumfries—but in the hours of business he was quite capable of discharging the duties of his office, nor was he ever known to drink by himself or seen to indulge in the use of liquor in a forenoon . . . I never beheld anything like the gross enormities with which he is now charged'.

The suspicious may say—if Findlater had the 'superintendence' of Burns's behaviour, he had to say this, otherwise he would show himself neglectful of his own duties; and at best Findlater is fairly guarded—forenoons and hours of business only. But another witness comes forward—Gray the Rector of the Dumfries Academy, a disinterested witness and one who deals with hours other than those of business; Gray had, he said, often come upon Burns explaining to his little boy 'the English poets from Shakespeare to Gray, or storing his mind with examples of heroic virtue, as they live in the pages of our more celebrated English historians. I would ask any person of common candour if employments like these are consistent with habitual drunkenness.' We may dismiss Jean and Gilbert as partial—though indeed Gilbert confines himself cannily to his brother's earliest days before he 'commenced author'; but there are still Dugald Stewart and Mrs. Montagu. The former said: 'Notwithstanding various reports I had heard during the preceding winter of Burns's predilection for convivial and not very select society I should have concluded in favour of his habits of sobriety, from all of him that ever fell under my own observation'; follows the poet's plaintive confession anent his stomach. Mrs. Montagu in her turn wrote to Jane Welsh Carlyle, 'during the Carnival of the Caledonian Hunt, "when universal Scotland all was drunk", I never saw Burns intoxicated, though the Member for Dumfries and the Laird of Arbigland (and many others) were much more tipsy than Tam o' Shanter, for he could see witches and warlocks, but they could neither see nor stand and were brought home in a state of inglorious insensibility': she goes on to recount how Burns, at any dinner-party where there were women, invariably joined the ladies long before any other man. Against all these apologia must be set Syme's statement that on one occasion Burns insisted on their getting 'hopelessly drunk' (what of it?); and a rather disconcertingly circumstantial and credible account by Josiah Walker of an evening at the Globe at Dumfries when Burns, after laying down the law and firing off 'epigrams'—with pause for acclamation —for some time, eventually became a bore and a nuisance, sitting on and on till three in the morning, becoming 'unnecessarily free in the avowal of his excesses', and alternating 'coruscations of genius' with repeated calls for more and more liquor, which—as he was Josiah's guest—was considered ill-mannered. All this, however, happened in November of 1795, and November of 1795 was late in the day for poor Burns. The reader may make what he cares of all these conflictions; perhaps the whole position is best summed up in the simple words of Alec Cunningham which so annoyed Mrs. Montagu—'he drank as other men drank'. Those who still believe otherwise must do so, it seems to me, because they so desire.

The investigation of Burns's physical condition has led us some little distance from that question with which we started it—what was the mental equipment on which he based his Horatian dream and hope? Very well, then, what *was* it? In the first place, it is absurd to represent Burns—as has often been done—as a *lusus naturae,* a solitary brilliant flower in a cabbage patch of illiterate blockheads. Burns was bred in a household which may or may not have been so full of a divine content as Murdoch supposed it, but wherein, under the leadership of William Burness, self-improvement was pursued with a zest verging on fanaticism. It was said—though probably in jest—that the Burness family were so eager for knowledge that they ate their meals with a spoon in one hand and a book in the other; if Robert had the touch of genius and the predilection for a special line of self-expression which carried him farther and higher than the rest, he was

THERE WAS A LAD

certainly no lone intelligent among boors. Old Burness could be called a self-educated man and brother Gilbert a well-educated man; Gilbert could write an excellent and easy prose, often more pleasant to read than the studied flamboyance and 'antithetical' counterpoint of his brother. The girls, after the custom of the time—or after the custom of girls?—were less instructed; but Isabel at least was in after life to display an acute intelligence. A young genius, therefore, desiring to sharpen his wits, had no lack of whetstones.

Into this earnest-minded family was presently introduced John Murdoch, a young man of eighteen, almost equally intense in the acquirement and propagation of learning. As a preceptor in literary style Murdoch had drawbacks; he was the sort of man who could describe his new home as the 'argillaceous fabric' (*Scottice* 'clay biggin' ') or the 'mud edifice'—anything, in fact, except plain 'cottage'; if he wanted to say that his pupil returned from school to the farm he had to make him 'exchange the grotto of Calypso for the field of Ceres'. But stripped of his pedantic absurdities, Murdoch was quite evidently a man with a real vocation for teaching. He could not induce young Robert (then aged, be it remembered, six!) to do anything in Latin,[10] nor could he make a musician of a boy who seemed to have neither ear nor voice; but in any subject in which he had a fair chance he was most successful. He was no mere teacher by rote, he saw to it that his students understood what they were learning and could express it in their own words; he was successful because he was intensely happy in his work. He did an enormous deal for Robert Burns; certainly he was well worth the sixpence or so a day he received as salary—plus, of course, his keep. It is a queer commentary on the manners of the times that this gentle paragon should have ruined himself locally by taking a glass too many and uttering slanders about the parish minister; a melancholy foretaste of the ruin and poverty in which his blameless sun was eventually to set.

Something has been said already of the books with

which this teacher and his pupil had to work; I say 'had
to' because the resources of the Burness household were as
limited as those of the book-shops of Ayr and Irvine; they
had to work with such tools as they could get. The volumes
available made up in solidity what they lacked in inspiration, but they might easily have been worse; it was not a
period when very much light reading was produced in
Scotland. And 'no book', wrote Gilbert, 'was so voluminous as to slacken [Robert's] industry or so antiquated
as to damp his researches'. Burns's literary feeding was
miscellaneous and haphazard; his course of reading was
not one that would ever have been prescribed by a
university syllabus or an editor of a *Hundred Best Books*;
and the result was a wideish but curiously unbalanced
knowledge with marked lacunae and a somewhat perverted standard of taste. He was strong, for instance, on
the sentimentalists—Shenstone, Beattie, Sterne and the
drivelling verses prefaced to Harvey's *Meditations among
the Tombs*, which he read with 'a rapture beyond expression'; but on Shakespeare, again for instance, he was
almost a blank; he had apparently at least glanced at
Lear, Othello, Hamlet and *King Henry the Eighth*, but when
he wrote from Ellisland for a complete edition of Shakespeare's works he was still adventuring into largely
unknown country. He found Addison unexciting (though
he liked *Mirza*), preferring Blind Harry's Wallace and a
Life of Hannibal, the tone of which, says Hecht, was
'heroic'. On the top of the gloomy Harvey and the weepy
Man of Feeling, he fogged his groping mind with much
Deistic and theological controversy. He possessed Allan
Ramsay's *Tea-Table Miscellany*, but on the Makars—who
were indirectly to mean so much to him later—he was
weak. (Here I think Murdoch was to blame; Murdoch
would have thought the Makars low.) Thus, while he
was certainly anything but 'unlettered'—was indeed, for
his class and time an exceptionally well-read young man—
his literary background was limited and lop-sided. As a
natural result of all this book-learning his work was
derivative if not directly imitative; and, like all self-

educated men, he was inclined to overvenerate his models. Had he not possessed his genius, he might have become—like so many of his predecessors and contemporaries—a mere copycat and rewriter; under Murdoch, he was heading hard to be a second Dr. Blacklock. Yet his taste was at heart sound; the moment he came across Fergusson he knew the shams for what they were. For the rest, his genius saved him; if he must rewrite, he rewrote, almost invariably, better.

Simultaneously with all these impeccable works I have been citing, some of them highfalutin, some of them merely preposterous, he encountered—and absorbed— the rich human indigenous indecent vein of country humour. Few Scots songs of the period were other than highly indelicate, not to say abominably obscene; his own mother's favourite ditty told him that sexual intercourse was 'the best thing That e'er a young thing got', and it may be assumed that many of 'Aunt' Betty Anderson's anecdotes bordered on or traversed the drawing-room Rubicons.[11] He delighted, as would any normal young man, in these 'Cloaciniads'; he was torn between them and the majestic purity of Thomson or the academic elegance of Gray. What shall we say of Burns's bawdiness, which theoretically disgusted the Victorian gentlemen and quite practically intrigued their inquisitive ladies? Well, Burns enjoyed Bawdry—which of us does not? He might protest to Mrs. Dunlop that it was a 'contemptible baseness', but there is twice as much life and verity in his letter to Provost Maxwell of Lochmaben a few months later; there Bawdry is 'the turtle-feast of the sons of Satan, and the delicious, secret sugar-plumb [sic] of the Babes of Grace'. He would not have been human if he had not contributed to the turtle-feast a few 'Cloaciniads' of his own—like the 'bagatelles' he sent to Johnson 'which the world have [sic] not seen, or perhaps, for obvious reasons, cannot see'. But the plain fact remains that, considering the broad licence in speech he allowed himself, his published writings which the world *can* see are remarkably free of it.

McNaught has done Burns a service by his careful examination of *The Merry Muses of Caledonia,* a collection piratically published after the poet's death by means of a dishonest subterfuge and containing—in its later editions at least—such obviously Burnsian titles as 'Paudieen O'Rafferty' and 'Sheila-na-Guiry'; McNaught concludes that Burns's disclaimer of most of this rubbish was justified and that perhaps a score of the items in the only trustworthy edition are his.[12] Burns saw this coming; as early as November 1794 he wrote to Thomson that he had heard ballads sung in the streets of Dumfries 'with my name at the head of them as author', though it was the first time he had ever seen them; and he told Maria Riddell at Brow Well that he was alarmed and worried at the thought of what might be posthumously published under his name. Examination of his acknowledged 'Cloaciniads' shows that Burns, as a writer of bawdry, was not at his best—the 'Court of Equity', for instance, is shoddy stuff—but still his touch has a certain authenticity and merit; examination of the incompetent drivel contained in the later editions of the *Merry Muses* convinces on its own evidence that he could never have written it. That the scrawlings of the feeble-minded on lavatory walls have often been attributed to Burns is not his fault; it is a penalty of successful versifiers which he shares with Byron, Stevenson, Kipling and many others—and will doubtless continue to share with whoever may be the popular poet in any given era to come.

In these reflections upon Burns's bawdiness I am not really wandering from the present point—his mental make-up and equipment. The Fescennine lays of the Ayrshire countryside were as much a part of this as the elegant numbers of Pope, the thundering antitheses of Junius, Blair's dismal *Grave,* or the theological contortions of a dozen dreary Scots divines. All these and more he had read—often with marginal annotations—all these he had appraised and digested by his seven-and-twentieth year. It was with this background in his mind that he launched the Kilmarnock Edition, stood fire at the symposia of the Edinburgh bigwigs, embarked, as guide, critic and censor, on the Monkland Friendly Society, and —hoped to be a Horace.

That his ambitions were never fully realised was due to other qualities in Burns besides his physical condition and his mode of living. One of these we have already noted—his complacent belief or assumption that he himself could say and do what he liked without offence and that those who took offence from it were tiresome fools. This defect had another side to it, as unsatisfactory as itself; Burns was as absurd about his pride as the most preposterous Highlander in *Waverley*; he had an Alan Breck readiness—which increased in his later years—to be 'insulted'. A snub he never forgot or forgave—and in the nature of things he received several. Rushing in with 'twenty couplets' on the death of the great Dundas and transmitting these by hand to the house of his son, he was given not even an acknowledgment; the Dundas family and faction, hitherto uncultivated, to say the least of it, now became *bêtes noires*. He met with identical treatment from Glencairn's sisters, and in similar circumstances; this time rather inexplicably, though the ladies may well have liked the pretentious and windy verses he sent them as little as their brother had enjoyed his more fulsome flattery. The classic snub, of course, is that administered by the Lass of Ballochmyle; the 'Lass' was the thirty-year-old Williamina Alexander, whose brother—a 'Nabob'— had just bought the estate from the ruined Sir John Whiteford; Miss Alexander, first offered a complimentary poem and then approached for permission to include it in the printed collection, took no notice whatsoever, then or thereafter. There is something to be said for the Lass; the verses *are* fairly oncoming, and were, indeed, condemned by Burns's Edinburgh censors as libels against Poesy and Taste; while Burns's letter was one of his worst—a mass of clichés about the 'vernal year' the 'verdant spreading leaf', even the 'feathered warblers pouring harmony'. Miss Alexander was, moreover, a newcomer to the locality; she saw no more than 'a stranger whose personal appearance was not very prepossessing' and on enquiry heard only of 'a village poet of indifferent character'; neither young nor specially 'bonie'—and knowing it—she may even have suspected a leg-pull. However that may be, Burns never forgave her; he got his own back, in annotating the poem for the Glenriddell MS., by some sarcastic remarks about herself and a pungent 'epigram' about her brothers—who had done him no harm: 'When Fate swore that their purses should be full, Nature was equally positive that their heads should be empty.'

Burns in this mood is not very likeable; Angellier, with some justice, thought his spitefulness worse and more regrettable than his bawdry. We all know the venom with which he turned for a time on Maria Riddell and with which he pursued the luckless—and deceased—Mrs. Oswald of Auchencruive, whose precise cause of offence has never clearly emerged. (If it was really, as he pretends, that he was turned out of the inn at Sanquhar by her funeral cortège, then surely the resultant Ode ranks with the 'damned duped unfortunate fool' and other gross overstatements.) We know, too, of his rages when the first Edinburgh printer he interviewed had never heard of him; when Mrs. Miller of Dalswinton, having exacted praise 'over the belly of my conscience' for her 'couplets', took no notice of 'Raving winds around her blowing'; on the 'scab and hunger' occasion when the inn at Inverary was too busy to receive him with honours; when the 'pedant frigid soul of criticism' insisted on certain omissions from the Edinburgh Edition; when he nearly dropped the Excise idea (or so he told Clarinda) because of the 'great person, Miss ——'s friend' who 'questioned me like a child about my matters'. *Per contra*, at the height of his fame and what should have been the height of his *hybris* (if he had any) he could send a good-natured if slightly contemptuous letter of thanks to an old busybody in Alnwick who had rebuked and 'advised' him on his immoral and dangerous tendencies. In his sober senses Burns was not at all a vain man; but there were times when he acted, to his own detriment, as if he were.

He could also be most terribly tactless. The letter and verses on Dundas which I have just mentioned were a case in point—for he had been consistently and openly anti-Dundas; so, of course, were his idiotic bravado toasts at Dumfries. He could write to an Earl (who was trying to befriend him) on the 'venal contagion of the titled tinsel courtly throng'; and he could allude to the late King and Queen of France as a 'perjured Blockhead and an unprincipled Prostitute' in a letter to the mother-in-law (Mrs. Dunlop) of two French *émigré* aristocrats. He made the same poem serve for the almost simultaneous deaths of the sons of two ladies who lived no farther apart than Craigdarroch and Afton and who were likely to compare notes. He had a positive genius for getting names—and names important to him—wrong, calling Patrick Miller 'Peter' and Findlater 'Findlayter'. He was weeks in Edinburgh before he had the sense to call on Dr. Blacklock, who had done so much to get him there; he dropped an appalling brick at Dr. Blair's table by bursting out in ecstatic eulogy of the Reverend gentleman's colleague—and rival—'in a tone so pointed and decisive as to throw the whole company into the most foolish embarrassment'. He offended his patron and champion Mrs. Dunlop, 'as I had got a slap in the face', by asking if he *must* read the verses of her protégée Janet Little. To these known instances we must add the many unspecified examples hinted at by Dugald Stewart, who wrote of his partiality for making remarks 'shrewd and pointed through frequently inclining too much to sarcasm' with that wit that was ready and vigorous, but 'not often pleasing and happy'. So altogether—whether from swelled head or sheer thoughtlessness—Burns did not go out of his way to smooth the path before him.

Finally we must consider here a quality on which Burns himself set superlative value and which many of his admirers have rated equally high—what he called his 'Independence'. 'Independence', like 'Liberty', was a word he often used, but whose implications he was never at pains to trace to their logical ends. The 'sturdy beggar' in Burns's writings is invariably 'independent'; in life, of course, he is not—he is constantly on the look-out for the police. The honest craftsman is 'independent'; he is not—he is conditioned by the laws of supply and demand, and by the caprice of employer and customer. The 'intrepid independence' of that (post-Edinburgh) hero the Miltonic Satan was rather an idle boast in a Lucifer strictly incarcerated in hell. If a man is to live agreeably in the society of his fellows—as Burns above all things desired to do—complete Independence, whether of speech or action, is impossible; and in the hands of a man uncertain of himself—as Burns very often was, despite his gift for carrying things off—Independence can be a very dangerous doctrine. Nobody in his senses is going to quarrel as to the merits of standing on one's own feet, looking the whole world in the face and owing not any man; but it is not always and to everyone a practical proposition. Nobody was more ready to place himself under a patron than Burns; there is again no accusation in this, for it was a necessary consequence of the social conditions under which he lived and the aims he was endeavouring to achieve. But there were times—as has so often happened with others than Burns—when his 'independence' took an uglier form and began to bear an unpleasant resemblance to the uncomfortable boorishness of a fish out of water. It is not independent to be ungracious; it is not independent to be rude; or bumptious; or aggressive; although many men—among them occasionally Burns—have confused these adjectives. Josiah Walker, who was in many ways the shrewdest and most perspicacious of Burns's contemporary critics, wrote of a 'boastful sturdiness not unusual in his original rank': Burns's 'independence was less perfect than he wishes it to be supposed and his dread of incurring obligation proceeded partly from the necessity . . . of supporting a character to which his claims had been so numerous and decisive'. A man who 'dreads incurring an obligation' is apt to be a churl: Burns could not accept the occasional fiver from Mrs. Dunlop without ponderous letters in which, as Wallace says, he 'reasoned himself into toleration' of this affront. When Thomson, greatly daring, sent him a well-earned present of five pounds, he replied grumpily about the 'pecuniary parcel' and 'the cold unfeeling dirty Ore', but—he kept the five pounds (because to return it 'would savour of bombast affectation'). Either, 'Dear Thomson, Thank you very much' or 'Dear Thomson, Take back your beastly money' would have been a more honest and more dignified acknowledgment—and the former would certainly have been more gracious.

No doubt Burns, if put to it, would have excused on the ground of 'independence' what was really a good deal of unnecessary boorishness. No doubt he called the Rev. Whoever-he-was a damned blockhead in order to show his independence; no doubt it was for the same reason that he wrote to the Edinburgh lady who, without an introduction, had invited him to a party that he would be pleased to attend if she would invite also the learned pig from the Grassmarket. And his 'independence' was fully in command at his first visit to Mrs. Dunlop—who, however exasperating she may have been, had shown him kindness, stood his good friend and unquestionably wished him well. Mrs. Dunlop had made great preparations and was looking forward to an enjoyable evening; Burns was snappish while he stayed and at the first opportunity rode off without even a civil farewell. His hostess got back at him in a very amusing set of verses, in which she made her servants tell each other that Burns had brought his 'havins'—i.e. his manners—from the plough; 'He may write books but by his gate, He's little sense and verra great conceit.'[13] If this was independence it would have been better modified—or wanting.

Enough has been said on a very ticklish subject. But, beset by such foibles, is it any wonder that Burns made enemies? Indeed, it is the best proof of his great personal charm that he made so few, and that so many of those with whom he fell out for a time were ready—like Mrs. Dunlop and Maria Riddell—to forgive him.

I may seem to dwell too much on the less satisfactory aspects of Burns's character; I do so because a man's failings are humanising things, and without some allowance for them it seems to me impossible to make Burns into a round and credible figure or to explain the disappointments and failures in his life. But, of course, he had magnificent endowments which should have—and have in fact—obliterated all these from memory. He had in the first place an abundant gift for identifying himself wholeheartedly either with a cause or with an individual. This expressed itself in two ways. The first was his glowing patriotism, local and national; the second his lovely loyalty to his friends.

On the former of these it cannot be necessary to descant at any length; pick up a copy of his verse and it will not be long before the heartfelt and impassioned words spring at out you. Burns's love for Scotland was no pose; it was something that he felt in the inmost parts of his being—though no doubt he expressed it better in *obiter dicta* and asides than in his full-dress efforts. We are all of us tongue-tied on the subjects that lie nearest to our heart and it was so with Burns; when the patriotic fervour chose its own moment and forced itself out it was good, but in this—as indeed as in all else—he could not write to order. Not even to his own order; how poorly that pretentious and unsatisfactory poem *The Vision* compares with the vigour of 'But, Willie, set your fit to mine, An' cock your crest; We'll gar our streams and burnies shine Up wi' the best.' Or even with the plain prose of the Commonplace Book—that moving passage about 'my dear native country, the ancient Baileries of Carrick, Kyle and Cunningham'. Syme's note on this passage says: 'The above may furnish a remark on the Bard'; it may indeed—several of them.

Burns's patriotism, whether for Caledonia or for Kyle, was an affair of the emotions neither requiring nor capable of reasoned defence. It was the same with his more personal loyalties. I doubt if it has ever been generally realised how much Burns did to help his family. Quite apart from the way he crippled his hard-won Edinburgh capital by lending Gilbert two hundred pounds to 'save' Mossgiel—and that, too, at a moment when he needed his every penny for the start at Ellisland—he regularly paid five pounds a year towards the maintenance of his mother, who long survived him; and according to bills produced by Gilbert at the time of his death, Dear-bought Bess's keep, washing, clothes and school were costing Burns over seven pounds a year. (The mother's annuity and the Dear-bought Bess charges were to be deducted by Gilbert from the 5 per cent interest on the loan; an elementary piece of arithmetic will show that they more than washed it out.) When his rather feckless uncle Robert Burness died, his family of two sons and a daughter were taken into the household at Ellisland without question and the daughter was to be kept there 'till she be quite woman grown'. And Burns could write a letter to his young brother William—an unsatisfactory creature who was always out of work; was he perhaps unemployable?—a letter which should have warmed the cockles of that young gentleman's heart and led him to thank his gods for such an elder brother; 'if ever you be . . . in a strait for a little ready cash, you know my direction. I shall not see you beat while you fight like a Man.' (Brother William might have fought like a Man or he might not; but he died of the 'putrid fever' soon after reaching London, Murdoch being resuscitated there to help bury him.) It is perhaps worth noting in parenthesis that despite all these outgoings Burns's debts at his death amounted—according to the estate trust documents unearthed by McNaught—to no more than £14 15s.; his assets were £180 plus moveables; figures which dispose alike of the current allegations whether of extravagance or destitution.

As to his friends outside the family, it may be true that he eventually quarrelled with most of these—very few of them go with him through his life; but while they were his friends they were so indeed, and they could have the whole of him for the asking and anything he had to give. At a moment when he was himself none too flush of cash he subscribed for eleven copies of David Sillar's poems— a work in which he had no belief at all; and it was with genuine regret that he had to refuse him a loan some years later. (Sillar repaid this by refusing to contribute to the Doon Memorial—though by this time he was well off, owing to fortunate casualties among his relations; he did, however, take a leading part in starting the Burns Club at Irvine—which cost nothing—and he wrote a rather faintly-praising memoir on his dead companion.) Burns's friends, while they were his friends, could do no wrong— just as, when they lapsed, they could do no right; the patient way he bore with Nicol on their highland tour is a shining example. If one version of the story is correct, his self-denial when the two stayed with the Duke of Athol was wellnigh superhuman; Fintry, from whom Burns had the highest hopes, was a guest, and the great Dundas was expected; but the impossible Nicol, imagining himself neglected, had to make a silly scene and demand instant departure; Burns, with the greatest good nature and at the cost of his own expectations, went off with him. If this be true it was, it seems to me, a remarkable exhibition of loyalty and friendship.

And there were other lame dogs besides brother William who owed him gratitude; the classical case is of James Clarke the schoolmaster in Moffat who had been handed up to the Patrons for 'harshness to some perverse dunces under his care' (Burns to Alec Cunningham, enlisting his help for Clarke). Clarke was no specially close friend of Burns, but Burns threw himself into his little war with the Patrons with something like frenzy; he wrote him encouraging letters, he pulled every string he could reach, he lent Clarke money—which there is some evidence that Clarke repaid. In the end Clarke won and Burns wrote: 'Huzza! Io triumphe!' Burns could find time in a busy hour to write to Mrs. Dunlop soliciting her patronage for a young bank clerk, John Drummond; he wrote John ('Hornbook') Wilson a most careful and helpful letter of advice and introduction when that middle-aged ex-shopkeeper thought of trying his luck as a clerk in Edinburgh; when the widow of the old family friend William Muir was left in difficulties over his estate, he wrote eagerly to Gavin Hamilton offering to get her, through his Edinburgh friends, the best legal advice free of charge. It is pleasant to think that these loyalties—or some of them—were repaid in kind; Richmond, with whom Burns lodged in Edinburgh—and who must have had a good deal to put up with now and then—would read to him and soothe him when he lay awake at night worrying in his 'hypochondriacs'; the exacting Mrs. Dunlop, hearing him on one occasion decried as a 'scandalous free liver in every sense of the word', defended him with such vigour that ' 'twas observed I was too warm'. 'I wish to God', she wrote, 'somebody that could serve your interest thought of it half as often as I do.' But what need to multiply instances? If there be a type truism in the world, it is the statement that Burns had a warm heart; and it would have been strange had it not met with reciprocating warmth in others.

And besides this endearing loyalty to the cause—whatever and whoever that cause might be—he had in full measure Barrie's 'lovely virtue' of courage. He was a fighter of superb and indomitable quality. Syme has a story—more acceptable, on face value, than many he told—that on his death-bed, when Syme took him by the hand, he made a 'wonderful exertion' and said in a strong voice: 'I am much better today—I shall soon be well again.' It is credible; that is the sort of man he was. Burns's life was a long and losing battle with stupefying toil, ill health, disappointment and balked ambition. Yet he is remembered as the prince of good fellows, the very king of

ROBERT BURNS

companions, the man whose wit and charm and brilliance
of talk could hold his hearers spellbound and colour for
the time being the drabbest of environments and the
most dismal of days. If that is not an example of sheer
transcendent victorious courage, what in history is?

Lastly, what was Burns's attitude to the two most
important topics of his day: religion (a much more
living force then than now) and politics? As to religion, it
has been said—he may even have said it once himself—
that he was an atheist; but, of course, no Scot of his
upbringing in the latter half of the eighteenth century
could be an atheist. Nor—as Dr. Macintyre has well
remarked—would any Scot be such a fool as to call
himself an agnostic, thereby implying either ignorance
on a fundamental issue or the inability to make up his
own mind. In truth Burns was a sincerely religious man,
though—as always—without any great profundity of
thought.[14] He was equally disgusted by both the alternative doctrines set before him by his spiritual preceptors—
the bitter Christless Calvinism of the Auld Lichts, and
the Moderates or New Lights with their pratings about
'common sense'—Burns saw clearly that common sense
can have nothing to do with religion. But he was unable
to devise for himself any *tertium quid* to take their place.
He could not join Clarinda in her conventional rejoicing
in Christ's atonement, which seemed to him rather a
cowardly way of creeping out of one's responsibilities.
(Clarinda talked a lot about her 'conscience', but Burns's
was really far the more active and acute.) He was, indeed,
accepting no pigs in pokes. 'I am a sincere believer in the
Bible,' he told Mrs. Dunlop, 'but I am drawn by the
conviction of a Man, not the halter of an Ass.' On the
other hand, 'A Mathematician without Religion is a
probable character' (a curious foretaste of Jeans's and
Eddington's mathematical universe!), 'an irreligious

Poet is a Monster'. It was necessary to believe in Something or Somebody, but when he asked himself just What and Who? his answers became vague. Somewhere there was a God the Father, kind and omnipresent, but neither to be taken for granted nor grovelled to; anthropomorphic, not unapproachable and actuated by Love. He was led to the fairly obvious corollary that hell was nonsense and the Devil an old wife's bogle. Christ puzzled him; he was a 'great Personage' related in some incomprehensible way to Godhead; by some equally vague direction God had entrusted Christ with the 'administration' of our earthly affairs. Placing himself boldly in God's shoes, he concluded that God's heart must be at least as big as his own, in which case Auld Lichts and New were alike imbecile; 'every upright honest man of whatever sect will be accepted of the Deity'.

Clarinda, quite off Burns's rails, as usual, and struggling vainly to get him transferred to hers, exclaimed: 'Sylvander, I believe nothing was a more impracticable task than to make you feel a little of genuine Gospel humility'. She was right. Burns was no great dealer in humility at any time; his God was an 'upright honest man' who could be treated with on equal terms and depended upon to stick to any bargain He laid down. And there was always at the back of his mind an idea that religion might be a joyous thing, freed alike from the hypocrisies of its professional exponents and the lamentations and groanings imposed upon their flocks. This perhaps derived originally from the *Manual of Religious Belief*, where Son requests, rather with the air of one laying a trap, 'to hear you at large upon religion giving pleasure to animal life', and Father responds—heartily and at the length of several pages—completely justifying this (for the day) unusual outlook. With Clarinda—most of his religion was with either Clarinda or Mrs. Dunlop—he developed vigorously his 'religion of the bosom', which did not really take him much further than it took old Omar; Clarinda's response was: 'My God! Sylvander, why am I so anxious to make you embrace the Gospel? I dare not probe too deep for an answer.' The religion of Clarinda's bosom at the moment was perhaps not far to seek.

For reasons which will readily suggest themselves Burns was much preoccupied with the question of life after death; his views here will be well seen in a letter he wrote to Muir in 1788—much better than in the exhibition piece on the same subject he sent to Ainslie a year later. Writing to Peter Stuart on Fergusson, he thought that poet, so unhappy on earth, would be assured of future happiness 'if there be a life beyond the grave, which I trust there is; and if there be a God presiding over all nature, which I am sure there is'. If his views on admittance into Heaven were correct, the almost insane squabbles of the contemporary theologians were beneath his notice; but he could not help being drawn into them by his love of a battle in which one could take sides. He did not subscribe to the absurdities perpetrated by either of the 'Lights'; it is curious that a man who fell so readily for the slogans of political parties should have remained impervious to the war-cries of the contesting godly. He did not believe in one sect or the other; yet when Dr. McGill produced his *Practical Essay on the Death of Jesus Christ* and found himself before a Presbytery Committee on a charge of vitiating doctrinal purity, Burns leapt into the fray with 'Orthodox, Orthodox', and would doubtless have gone to much further lengths but for the necessity of keeping one eye upon his job in the Excise. (McGill, a weakling, recanted in any case; here was no Clarke of Moffat.)What one may call the political side of Burns's religion was half-hearted; his was ever the attitude of Gallio or of that cynical spectator at the Holy Fair. This did not save him from violent accusations of impiety. Here, too, just as with the drinking, a defender came forward after his death; here again, just a little too late.[15]

In religious politics, as between sect and sect, a man's choice even in those days was reasonably free; with state politics it was another matter. Burns, like many another, was to great extent obliged to take his political colour from the colour of his patrons. Scotland was at that early stage in party politics—the United States are still in it—where a man voted not for a principle, but for So-and-so, or So-and-so's agent, or the still lesser flea upon that lesser flea's back. Snyder pertinently reminds us that out of the 65,000 inhabitants of the Burgh of Ayr in 1782 only 205 had votes; these could be—and of course must be—carefully nursed by the prospective candidates, and any signs of slipping from the fold must be instantly checked. Burns early assumed the colours of Fox and the Whigs—it was one of the Rev. Peebles's charges against him that he even 'reprobates the measures of Mr. Pitt'; he was not allowed to swerve from that allegiance. It is difficult nowadays to make very much of those political verses which to Blair 'smelt of the smithy', and to James Maxwell of the infernal sulphur—and which now smell merely of must; the 'Election Ballads' on which he prided himself and which he recited with such gusto to Josiah Walker have become tediously unreadable, and his 'Ballad on the American War', as Snyder says, would 'tax the learning of any annotator'. If any interest is to be got out of Burns's politics nowadays, it must be sought elsewhere than in the Whig—Tory—Heron—Gordon—Johnstone—Miller battles of the day, however thrilling these may have been at the time for a poet who loved fighting.

Burns was keenly interested in politics, as in anything presenting two warring alternatives with one of which he could identify himself. He had no illusions as to their moral value—as witness the 'What is Politics?' 'What is a Minister'? catechism he sent to Cunningham; and after he was appointed to the Excise he was equally well aware that politics was no place for him. 'Politics is dangerous ground for me to tread on,' he wrote to Mrs. Dunlop in 1794, 'and yet I cannot for the soul of me resist an impulse of anything like Wit.' It was true; he could not keep out of them, and in them he could not keep silent; and we have seen into what trouble this led him. That the local Dumfries elections were meat and drink to him may be

seen from the 'Election Ballads', from the quite excellent
report on the candidates and their characters he sent to
Graham of Fintry (incidentally enclosing 'Thou lingering
star'!) and the rather unfeeling letter he wrote Mrs.
Dunlop on her son's death, in which he is much more
concerned to describe an election fight than to elaborate
his condolences. And no one can follow Burns through his
life story without noticing that the attractions of politics
become ever more tempting and that—as he always did
with temptations, bless him—he succumbs to them more
and more.

Burns made a fool of himself in politics in two respects—
his occasional outbursts of what one might call 'Stewarting' and, of course, the French Revolution. With characteristic want of logic he gave rein to these notions simultaneously as the spirit moved him; as Rosebery said, he
was both Jacobite and Jacobin; he seemed to want *both*
a British Republic *and* the King to Enjoy his Own Again.
Burns's 'Stewarting' is a characteristic and constant
feature of his life which perhaps I should have noticed
earlier; it seemed to attack him, like an intermittent
fever, at irregular—sometimes at long—intervals. The
conviction that his ancestors had fought and suffered for
the exiled dynasty went very far into his roots; it took
origin probably in a tradition, current in his family and
no doubt told him by his father, that his original forbear
was a certain Walter Campbell of Burnhouse (hence, of
course, 'Burness'), 'a small domain in Argyleshire'; the
said Campbell was driven out by the Duke of Argyle for
his Stewart sympathies, and migrated to Kincardineshire,
where he founded that long line of unsuccessful Burness
farmers. One would like as much as did Burns to believe
these stories, but one lacks his gift of self-persuasion—as,
for that matter, did his own brother Gilbert, who discredited the Jacobite traditions entirely. There is no
evidence whatever that any of his Kincardineshire
ancestors were occupied, whether in the '15 or the '45, in
any other pursuit than wrestling with their unhappy
holdings; Burns's grandiose letter to Lady Winifred

Constable, 'What they could they did and what they had they lost', was only true in so far as the unbridled foraging of the rival armies in the '45 and the economic blizzard which followed it were contributory causes in their ruin. The fugitive Campbell is no better authenticated—indeed, rather worse.[16] It was not, however, Burns's way to collect possible objections to anything he desired to believe, and so, every now and then throughout his life, the thought of his dispossessed ancestors and the dispossessed monarch for whom they suffered returned and rankled in his blood. Nor—as was again his way—did he hold his tongue about it. His letter to the *Star* in November 1788, fired by some anti-Stewart sneering in the local pulpit, was moderate and sensible enough—it is, incidentally, a brilliant example of the 'antithetic' style he so earnestly and mistakenly cultivated. But we all know the 'idiot race to honour lost' lines indelibly inscribed on the window-pane in Stirling, which were much less innocuous. Whether or not he joined in the toast of 'Awa' Unkies' (which no Scot will need to be told means 'Out with the Outsiders'), he certainly informed one of his correspondents that the House of Hanover was 'an obscure beef-witted insolent race of foreigners whom a conjuncture of circumstances kickt up into power and consequence'. The injudiciousness—to say the least of it—of this leaves one gasping.

Nor was he any saner on the subject of the French Revolution. To this continental eruption Scotland was on the whole well disposed until the invasion scare, when she turned her coat with some rapidity. The wise or worldly got out of the entanglement early; Burns, with his heart genuinely engaged, stayed in too late. He would have done better to heed the advice of Mrs. Dunlop, who warned him more than once that he was playing with fire. We have already seen the scrape that this dangerous game got him into. His open activities seem to have gone no farther than subscribing to an Edinburgh periodical of supposedly French sympathies and proposing at least to attend a Friends of the People Conference with similar views. But he talked much and foolishly; he was evidently known to belong to a pro-French clique in Dumfries (against whom the 'Loyal Natives' launched doggerel broadsides); if he was lucky enough to escape actual harm, it did him no good.

Burns's Jacobinism was a symptom or offshoot of a much more serious feature in his political life—his growing bitterness against the 'upper classes'. This class-hate, by Tom Paine out of the Edinburgh Patricians, becomes very marked towards his end, and probably contributed a good deal towards any dropping of him by his 'county' friends that actually took place. In his surly ungracious gloom one can imagine he would become an awkward guest at a country-house party; embarrassment was probably averted all round by striking his name out of the invitation list. This was a pity, because it still further embittered a life already sufficiently burdened with unhappiness and because class-hate accords so ill with that 'unbounded good-will to every creature, rational or irrational' which he professed in himself and which we have all so delighted to acclaim in him. Those in-growing Edinburgh snubs have a lot to answer for.

However that may be, there is no doubt that, towards the end, Burns's interest in politics and affairs was ever quickening and deepening; and this leads to the interesting speculation—how far would it have gone had he lived? I am personally convinced that from Ellisland onwards he was on a change of road which would have led him into another country. I will wager the guess—as Professor Masson did before me—that if Burns had lived under present-day conditions he would have deserted verse-writing in his middle years as a plaything and would have concentrated his gifts and his energies upon public life. He would have turned his steps along the inevitable avenue for such as he of journalism, disdaining no longer that offer from Perry of the *Morning Chronicle* which he in real life refused. He would have become first a columnist, then the editor of a 'progressive' weekly, then, almost certainly, a Socialist member of Parliament. There his easy superficial judgments, his assured uncritical certainties and his gift of the gab would have marked him out early for Ministerial rank; he had just that sort of mind. *Quo non ascendam*? He might have become Prime Minister of Britain. Some of these things I am convinced he would have done even in his own day had his life and faculties continued and so far as opportunities were open to him. He would far have outgrown the 'Ploughman Poet' that he never was.

Let me perhaps attempt to sum up the picture, the self-portrait, we have been assembling. A man of ambitions; a hard worker struggling with physical adversities and a dislike of work; inclined to vacillation and an unacknowledged self-distrust; canny and in many ways prudent; a self-dramatist and something of a *poseur*; prone to the pleasures of the bottle and the bed; bawdy and genial; touchy and tactless; superficially religious; vitally interested in all human affairs; loyal; patriotic; intrepid. There are—and have been—millions of such men. The truth is that Burns was a far more ordinary man than his admirers have ever allowed. Discount his genius and he remains a family man who managed his domestic finances with care and skill, and was interested in the future of his children; who did his job efficiently and well; who enjoyed equally his hobby of song-writing and an evening's argument over a glass or two. There perhaps is the secret of his immortality and of the undying affection in which his countrymen hold him—that an ordinary man should be a genius and a genius, after all, an ordinary man.

FOOTNOTES TO PART TWO

[1] *p. 56.* Syme was supposed to have done some preliminary weeding-out and arrangement, but he slung at Currie a 'huge and shapeless mass . . . the complete sweepings of his (Burns's) drawers and his desk . . . even to the copy-book on which his little boy had been practising his writing . . . the sheep were not separated from the goats; and—what had perhaps not happened before since the beginning of the world —the manuscripts of a man of genius, unarranged by himself, and unexamined by his family or friends, were sent with all their sins on their heads, to meet the eye of an entire stranger.' —W. W. Currie; *Memoir of James Currie.*

We learn from the same source that Burns's Commonplace Book—and some other MSS.—had a narrow escape: 'My father took all that was good—I know he told me a little while before his death that I might as well burn the whole, which however, I never did.' Thank God! Lamb, writing to Coleridge, said that Currie's 'Life' was 'very confusedly and badly written, and interspersed with dull pathological and medical discussions.' . . . 'Do you know the well-meaning doctor? Alas! *ne sutor ultra crepidam.*'

[2] *p. 57.* Actually Burns's first reviewers—(1) Sibbald in the *Edinburgh Magazine* and (2) Mackenzie in the *Lounger*—started this pernicious nonsense; (1) 'Extracts from the Poems of Robert Burns, a ploughman in Ayrshire'; and (2) 'this Heaven-taught ploughman from his humble and unlettered station'. Stephen Duck, the 'Poetical Thresher', was made a parson by his admirers, but liked it so little that he went mad and killed himself. The *Edinburgh Advertiser* of 28th November 1788 pointed out to its readers how wise Burns had been in reverting to the farm and so avoiding all risk of this unpleasant fate.

[3] *p. 60.* For some discussion of what can be known about this episode see *infra*, p. 231.

[4] *p. 63.* To do Burns justice, he did after a long struggle get a stone put up up at his own expense on Fergusson's grave. The stonemason had also rather a long struggle for payment.

[5] *p. 64.* The length to which Burns could go in this mood can be seen in a generally blood-and-thundery letter to Peter Hill; here a harmless prostitute is ridden down by a 'Coroneted Rep . . . hurrying on to the adulterous assignation—she who, without the same necessities to plead, riots nightly in the same guilty trade.'

[6] *p. 66.* The reader may judge for himself. Mrs. Dunlop's lines were "Be all a Mother's fondest hopes can dream, And all you are, my charming girl, seem.' (Mrs. Dunlop, like Burns, gave full value to her 'r's'—as in 'gir-ril'.) Clarinda's 'Sappho' lines were 'He bound me in an iron chain, And sunk me deep in woe.'

[7] *p. 68.* According to Sir James Crichton-Browne, Currie had endocarditis himself and died of it; yet he never suspected it in Burns. If so, it was an odd coincidence.

[8] *p. 69.* 'The Disease that Killed Robert Burns'. S. Watson Smith, M.D., *B.M.J.*, 30th December, 1944. Reproduced in *Burns Chron.* 1946.

[9] *p. 74.* What was considered 'gentleman's weight' may be gathered from the statement of Macmurdo, judge at the Whistle Contest at Glenriddell, that Craigdarroch, who won, drank 'upwards of five bottles of claret'. This is, perhaps, a little disappointing; one feels that William Hickey, out in Calcutta at the same time, could have done better. Was Burns present at the Whistle Contest? Did 'William Hunter the butler', whose colourful account of the poet's behaviour was relied on by Sir James Crichton-Browne, ever exist, or was he Scott Douglas's 'drivelling old blacksmith' who told nothing but a string of lies? This is a keen but minor controversy into which I have not the space here to enter.

[10] *p. 78.* Burns told Maria Riddell that he had all the Latin he needed—*omnia vincit amor.* Gilbert says he could not stomach *The Rudiments of the Latin Tongue*, but used to go back to the book 'on chagrin or disappointment especially in love affairs'. Hence an early (and unsurviving) humorous poem with the burden 'So I'll to my Latin again.'

[11] *p. 80.* Betty's anecdotes must have been told when William Burness's back was turned, for Murdoch records that

one of two occasions when he saw Burns's father really angry was with an old man on the farm who was using 'smutty inuendoes and double entendres'. A curiously natural—and modern—phrase for Murdoch.

[12] *p. 81*. See McNaught's article in the *Burns Chron.*, Vol. III, p. 25. See also—if you can!—his edition of *The Merry Muses*. This authoritative publication, sponsored by the Burns Federation, was also of service to Burns, as it put a limit, at least thenceforward, to the garbage which might be pitchforked into subsequent editions. The piratical publication was specially hard if 'Christopher North' is to be believed; according to him, Burns, when very hard up, 'repelled with horror' the offer from a 'miscreant' of fifty pounds for his MS. collection. Alas! there were other 'miscreants' to come.

[13] *p. 86*. Mrs. Dunlop's poem deserves to be better known than it is. It begins—

> 'Five months of expectation past,
> The long-wish'd hour arrived at last.
> A face peept in just at the door' . . .

Mrs. Dunlop saw in the face genius, humour, good sense, manly spirit—and several other qualities which she expected to see; but alas! Burns was like a sweet milky coconut in an 'acid husk'. Mrs. Dunlop had 'a thousand questions' to ask and an 'evening walk' planned; but 'you were cross and would not stay'. ' . . . My crowquill wants strength to tell what joy was murdered when you bade farewell.' Some of those present thought Burns too 'fat and fair', others missed the 'waked loof'—the hardened palm—and took him for 'college-bred', getting his mice, lice and daisies from books. Then—

> ' . . . goes the cook to warn for dinner.
> "Faith, lads," (quoth she) "as I'm a sinner
> Yon chiel gade in wi' spurs an' boots,
> Is daft Rob Burns that prents and shoots,
> Does nought but cast about quire clashes
> And rant and rin and chase the lasses." . . .
> "Losh keep's, is't him? What like's his horse?
> I'm sure his book's no' worth a curse.
> Trow ye there's siller in his purse?" '

The entire staff gaped in horror at Burns's unceremonious departure and thus expressed themselves—

'Giff that be Burns, he may hae lear
But faith! I'm sure he has nae mair.
He's brought his havins frae the plough,
Ne'er touched his hat nor made a bow;
Lap on his horse an' pu'd his coat thegither,
Clashed to the Major's gin he'd been his brither.
He may write books but by his gate
He's little sense and verra great conceit.'

And even on the next day there was 'sober, serious sorrow
That he who knew to please us all Should find his pleasure
here so small'. Quite evidently Burns's manners throughout
were deplorable and—with a less pertinacious admirer—
might have cost him dear. See *Robert Burns and Mrs. Dunlop*;
Correspondence edited by William Wallace. Mrs. Dunlop,
like her illustrious guest, was much better in this vein of poetry
than in her 'Addresses to Young Ladies' and the like. I think
she was certainly one up on this occasion.

[14] *p. 91.* One must agree here, I think, with Dean Stanley
(Burns a 'wise religious teacher') rather than with Principal
Rainy. For an interesting discussion of Burns's religion—to
which I am here indebted—see Dr. McIntyre, *The Religion of
Burns*; *Burns Chron.*, Vol. XXII, and Tonny Daar, *The Religious Development of Robert Burns*, in the same issue.

[15] *p. 93.* The Rev. Hamilton Paul, *The Poems and Songs of
Robert Burns with a Life of the Author.* Air [*sic*]; 1819. Paul said
that Holy Willie's Prayer was precisely the view of 'those who
call themselves the pure reformed Church of Scotland'. Paul
was censured for this, but not dismissed from the Ministry.

[16] *p. 96.* The Stuarts of Inchbreck, the proprietors of the
estate since 1547, were positive that Burns's ancestors had been
in Bogjorgan and Brawlinmuir since the time of Mary Queen
of Scots. Walter Burness, the traditional ancestor and thereputed son of the fugitive Campbell under his new name, quite
certainly died in 1670, which would put the Campbell's move
to Kincardine somewhere a few decades before that date at
most. Not nearly early enough. We must conclude that—like
so many ancestors—the Campbell was interesting but apocryphal. For a good account of Burns's paternal ancestors to
which I am here indebted, see H. J. Rennie, *The Burns Family
in Glenbervie; Burns Chron.* (1931).

PART THREE

BURNS'S WOMEN

LOOK at it how you like and how leniently you like, this is
not an aspect of Burns's character in which his admirers
can find much satisfaction—though owing to the aura of
romantic tushery in which he has been enveloped, many
of them have contrived to do so. There is no getting away
from the fact that in his sexual life Burns was something
of an animal. For Burns women existed for one end and
for one end only; and though this may be a sound and
practical view of the sex, it cannot be called a lofty one.
Almost anything with the requisite physical concomitants
could be exalted for the time being—and sometimes for
quite a long time being—into his darling. He coupled
himself mentally with every woman he saw. Even in his
mortal illness and even with Jessy Lewars—who was a
good girl, no doubt, but no romantic beauty—his heart
must be 'rent' and he must seek 'a mutual faith to plight'.
At the time which his apologists have chosen as his most
spirituel—the hour of nostalgia for Highland Mary in
which he wrote 'Thou Lingering Star'—he was carrying
on with Anna Park of the Globe tavern in Dumfries, who
was probably no more than what Mrs. Carswell calls her
—'a hearty gay and lavish Scotish barmaid'. Park or
Campbell, Miss Lewars or Miss X, he is always the
'swain'; the successful and rather boastful swain in his
earlier poems, and in the later a 'hopeless' lover with a
frequency of ill success that becomes more than a little
boring. But the goal of the swain, successful or otherwise,
was always the same—possession. There is no doubt as
to which part of a woman Burns would have selected as
the most interesting.

His technique must, of course, have been first-class.
Gilbert tells us that in his very young days he was bashful
and awkward with women; but a very little practice
overcame these early inhibitions. Sillar, in their adolescence, was green with envy over his 'facility in addressing

the fair sex'; the sight of a skirt on the horizon was invariably a 'death-blow' to their conversation. We have already seen that Miss Logan of Cumnock found him 'coarse and boisterous' in his address; but he soon overcame that—or perhaps Miss Logan was finicky—for by the Edinburgh days his methods had been perfected. Scott's tribute has already been mentioned, and even Currie had to admit his 'sorcery' with women when, by restraining the 'vehemence and exuberance of his language', he could give his manners 'an impression of taste, even elegance', seldom seen when he was in male company. A man who could adapt his approach to Jane Duchess of Gordon and to Jean daughter of Armour was a dangerous fellow to have around. On his own showing, however, his method was the old—and remunerative— one of going straight for the objective. 'Pay your particular assiduities,' he advised young brother William, 'and try for intimacy as soon as you feel the first symptoms of the passion; this is . . . the best preservative for one's peace.' He adds a hasty rider against 'guilty amours', which are bad everywhere, but in England 'the very devil'; but it is the first part of the advice that comes from the heart—and very sound it is. It was at any rate a clear statement of the lines on which Burns himself conducted his campaigns, and from all the evidence he never had to 'pay his particular assiduities' for very long without fruit.

Yet I have already repudiated the suggestion that Burns was promiscuous and I do so again now. Peebles of the Water-fit lamented his 'succession of Dulcineas'— passable perhaps in a heathen Horace or Ovid, but *this* was a Christian; 'love-making was his fort [sic]: he made love from vanity'. This is Peeblesque nonsense; there was not a very long succession, they were not Dulcineas, and he made love not out of vanity, but because his body urged him. And Josiah Walker showed less than his usual acumen when he wrote: 'His excessive subdivision of this exhaustless article [love] reduces any single portion of it to a very insignificant value'. True,

Burns himself noted in the margin of his Sterne: 'Is love like a suit of ribbons that one cannot share it among womankind without lessening the quantity that each should have?' And this was his theory as exemplified in his verses, where no specimen of womankind can appear without immediately participating in the dividend; but he did not put this into practice. His real affairs were comparatively few, and each in turn had a reasonably prolonged run—one indeed lasted him for the most of his adult life. If we neglect the mere utilities—the Clows, Camerons and Parks—the number of love-affairs in his life was probably below the ordinary male average rather than above it.

Where he was unfortunate was that these affairs were made conspicuous; firstly because he was the notorious Burns and secondly by his embarrassing gift for fertilisation—a serious drawback in an age when contraceptives were practically unknown. As a result his liaisons were not only costly, but also scandalous; they became the food of gossips and the ammunition of his enemies. Nor did he display even the most elementary prudence in the satisfaction of his desires; he 'tried for intimacy'—and normally with success—from the word go, and his 'dearest member' was more unruly than the scriptural tongue. And—this is less pleasant to record—by his dearest member he was guided and actuated; he could extol the 'tender passion' and so forth almost *ad nauseam*, but the impression remains that with him 'love' was a carnal need carnally satisfied where it could, at the moment, be got on the terms he enjoyed. In this pursuit he was tireless to the end. He could run concurrent affairs with Jean Armour and Mary Campbell, and with such vigour as to put one of them in the family way and quite probably both.[1] Four years later he could still beget a child on his wife and another on the barmaid of the Globe within ten days of each other, however distasteful this may be to his apologists. In fact, the only thing to do is to abandon the apologist attitude altogether and take Burns as he was— the animal rather than the spiritual lover; with a passing regret for his unselectiveness and an aghast admiration for his total disregard of what the Victorians alluded to as 'the almost inevitable consequences'.

Josiah Walker—I apologise for citing him so often but he did, I think, have a remarkable insight into Burns—observed over a hundred years ago that Burns was habitually drawn to 'females in that condition of life where the effects of sensibility are generally overcome by a certain coarseness of sentiment, and sturdiness of character'; in other words he preferred, all through his life, women of his own original station or below it. That was no fault, but it may have been a misfortune; for if one is casting round for reasons why Burns failed to rise, one must not forget this one. Dr. Lauchlan Maclean Watt has written of Burns's 'condescension' in noticing lower-class girls; this seems to me as unperceptive as Peebles with his string of Dulcineas and love-making from vanity. If there was any 'condescension' it was in the literal sense of the word only; they 'went down' together. The plain fact is that—to his ultimate loss—he preferred them. The perspicacious Josiah attributes this to his fear of snubs from the better-class, whom he suspected throughout his life 'to an excess inconsistent with the excellence of his understanding'; this last, God knows, is true, but in the main I think Josiah is for once at fault. Burns was ready enough to approach the Edinburgh ladies on quite familiar terms, but they would have nothing to do with him; and this it was in the last resort that stuck him in the Edinburgh adventure and sent him back crestfallen to Mauchline. Burns could boast, in one of his caddish moods, of bringing down a lady who had 'seen the politest quarters of Europe . . . from her aerial towerings pop at my feet like Corporal Trim's hat'—but did he ever do any such thing? If so, when and who? If, as many have thought, the 'Miss' referred to was Peggy Chalmers, the boast was a boast and no more. With one exception Burns was never on intimacy—in the sexual sense—with any woman of better class than his own or any woman who was in any degree his mental equal. They simply could not care for him 'in that way'—not even Maria Riddell, unconventional and acutely interested as she was. The exception, of course, was Clarinda—who was, however, not the kind that comes down with a pop.

This is, when one comes to think of it, a rather extraordinary thing. What was it that put them off? His manners were apparently unexceptionable; that aggressiveness and law-laying that did him harm occasionally with the men has never been a quality repugnant to women—not, at least, in the case of a male to whom they are otherwise attracted. He could take his food at table like a gentleman; he could dance and not romp; he dressed with taste and was adequately equipped with soap and clothes-brush. Yet they would not have him. Why not? No doubt he drank and sang low songs in low taverns, but—who didn't? No doubt he had unsuitable—and, of course, fecund—passages with servant-girls and the like, but who cared? Clarinda, for all her conscience and all her kirkiness, thought nothing of them; she took Jean Armour in her stride, confining herself to an admiring surprise that Burns could remain fond of the girl 'after enjoyment; few of your sex have souls in such cases'. (An illuminating comment, perhaps, on Mr. McLehose!) No; a bastard or two would not have stood between the Ploughman Poet and the Patrician ladies. Making all allowances for the rigid class distinctions of the day (and, after all, Burns was a genius with prospects, and no clodhopper), it does seem very strange that in the emancipated atmosphere of the Edinburgh of 1786 a brilliant and handsome young man with unlimited sex appeal could find no young lady to love him; could he have married, say, even Peggy Chalmers, to look no higher, what a new world would have spread at his feet; how rapidly what were mere talents and prospects would have been translated—by interested relatives—into an appointment and cash. Was his technique at fault—was it too well adapted to 'females' of 'a certain coarseness of sentiment'? It may have been so, but I do not believe that the man who could adapt himself into the salons of

Blair or Erskine or the Duchess of Gordon could not—an he would—have modified his approach *ad libitum*; let him be but his natural self, avoiding crudities, and he had really no more to do. One is left with the conviction that he did not try; and not because he feared snubbing, but simply because, the better offering, he was drawn to and preferred the worse. And *if* he showed this—as in his transparent way he probably did show it—then, of course, he was damned.

To begin the survey of Burns's women at their lowest level, let us consider poor Anna Park, the barmaid of the Globe at Dumfries, who was certainly among the least of his lights—though even she drew some verses which at face value set her in a higher position. If Alec Cunningham is to be believed—always a question—she was more or less common property, and some corroboration of this is suggested by the easy manner in which all concerned took her 'disgrace'. It was, at any rate, the simplest thing for Jean Armour, Mrs. Burns, to take the infant—first harboured for a time at Mossgiel—into her own house and suckle it with the contemporary but lawful brother her husband had provided. Opinions will vary as to this act of Jean's; it can be represented as Madonna-like magnanimity or as the acquiescence in the inevitable of a nature broke to a purely animal existence and resigned to anything that Burns might do; as Clarinda once put it, Jean must have been either an angel or a dolt. At all events, she has more credit out of the incident than has Burns. Chambers has endeavoured to whitewash his hero by recording that Jean was 'imprudently' away on long visits to Ayrshire at the times of Burns's intimacy with Anna; such visits no doubt would have been imprudent if Jean valued her husband's fidelity, but in plain fact the records show that they did not take place. Jean can be traced more or less continuously at Ellisland from the summer of 1789 right through 1790; she must certainly at any rate have been accessible within ten days of the crucial enjoyment of Anna. There is really no excuse for Burns in the matter of Anna; the girl was willing and coarsely attractive, Burns was willing and completely unfastidious. The only bright feature in the story is the child—named, by some curious error, Elizabeth, a name already patented by Dear-bought Bess at Mossgiel. Anna Park's Elizabeth, being recognised on the same terms as her namesake, drew, as she did, her two hundred pounds from the Subscription Fund on her twenty-first birthday married a respectable ex-soldier weaver called Thomson, and gave birth to two sons and five daughters, three of whom were present at the Glasgow Anniversary celebrations in 1859. Anna's own fate is uncertain; it is thought that she must have died at the birth of her child or very soon after, but this is by no means proved.

With Anna Park, whatever her fate, must be lumped the other mere used animals—May Cameron, Jenny Clow and Elizabeth Paton. The first two of these, neither of whom was in an exalted social position, were Burns's Edinburgh mistakes; I have already said that these errors were probably not regarded by the *élite* so seriously as to damage Burns's credit, though no doubt they did little to advance it. The poet treated both ladies cavalierly; they differ from most of his other victims in that they had to pursue him for their dues. Miss Cameron wrote Burns a letter which he passed on to Ainslie (this was before Ainslie turned pious) with these words: 'Send for the wench and give her ten or twelve shillings, but don't for Heaven's sake meddle with her as a *Piece*—I insist on this.' Cameron, however, was not to be put off with ten or twelve shillings, for presently she took out a writ against Burns and obtained some legal satisfaction. As to Jenny Clow, she was apparently forgotten till November of 1791, when Clarinda—whose current desire to annoy Burns was probably much greater than her interest in the erring Jenny—officiously brought to his notice the misery and penury of 'Your old acquaintance Jenny Clow who, to all appearance, is at the moment dying'. Clarinda

signed herself—such was their relationship at that time—
'I am, sir, your sincere well-wisher, A.M.'; but Burns
hastened, if thus tardily, to do something for Jenny. It
was in thus bringing Burns and Clarinda together again
that the creature achieved her principal importance. The
fates of Jenny Clow and May Cameron are as obscure as
those of their children—if they survived—who were *not*
recognised among those on the sinister side of the family;
in fact, mothers and infants, they all disappear. So dim
are these figures that some have even supposed that
Cameron and Clow were one and the same; but they do
seem to have been separate if similar entities.

Elizabeth Paton, the servant-girl at Lochlie, is of rather
more interest as illustrating the attractions which were
sufficient to lure Burns into his first essay in paternity.
Isabella Begg, Burns's niece, had heard of her as 'rude and
uncultivated to a great degree . . . with a thorough
(though unwomanly) contempt for every sort of refinement'. The family—Gilbert and the girls—thought that
the faults of her character would soon have disgusted
Burns, and they encouraged him to resist the importuni-
ties of his mother that he should marry her. If a household
so upright and godly as that at Lochlie could adopt this
attitude, then Elizabeth Patron must have been pretty
dreadful. She is said to have been very plain-looking,
though she owned a 'handsome' figure; indeed, for a time,
while Jean Armour was out of favour, her legs replaced
that lady's in verse eleven of *The Vision*. Burns could hail
the resultant offspring as 'Wee image o' my bonie Betty',
and write elsewhere 'My handsome Betty by my side', but
even he could hardly pretend that poor Paton was a
figure of beauty or romance. Probably her chief virtue in
his eyes was her accessibility; she was on the spot, and
according to Isabella the 'poor creature' loved him with a
'most beautiful devotion', which is always a help to
young gentlemen attempting procreation for the first time.
The disconcerting thing about the incident is that it was
to this animal creature, the servant in his own house, that
Burns turned in the first flush of emancipation after his

father's death;[2] to Paton the rough-and-ready maid from Largieside—and nothing better. Paton would do.

So much for Park, Clow, Cameron and Paton. But there is another group of lights, lesser no doubt, but still by no means such farthing-dips as these; Kilpatrick, Thomson, Lorimer, Lewars, Begbie. We may dismiss the first two of these as juvenilia, though no doubt they played an indispensable part in Burns's development; in every young man's life there has to be an awakener, but as the awakener rarely persists for any length of time, it matters little whether her name be Nelly Kilpatrick or not. Nelly's importance was that she associated love in Burns's mind with two interrelatable things—poetry and autumn harvest weather; the August moon always thereafter saw him full of power and danger. His much later relations with 'Chloris' Lorimer, of which much has been made by the romancers, would appear to have been as artificial as the name he gave her, of which—coming to his senses some months before he died—he eventually saw the absurdity. The Lorimers were people who came to the farm of Kemishall near Ellisland from somewhere on the Moffat side; and Burns's interest in 'Chloris'—her real name, curiously enough, was Jean, though she spelt it 'Jane' in the copy of Collins he gave her—was at first vicarious. She was sixteen years his junior, and in 1791 at any rate he was still trying to enlist her affections for his colleague in the Excise John Gillespie, whose name was inscribed with hers on the Ellisland window-pane. (The Excise people had a good deal to do with Kemishall; other Excisemen, Lewars and Thomson, were also in pursuit of Chloris, but made no headway; and Burns had to visit the place in the course of his duties.) But at some stage—possibly between the writing of the yearning 'Poortith cauld' and the satisfied 'Come let me take thee to my breast'—Burns forgot about Gillespie, as Chloris had done long since, and stepped more successfully into that gentleman's shoes.

How far this affair was ever really serious, how far Burns and Chloris went before, as Scott Douglas says, it 'suddenly collapsed in gloom', are matters on which there is no good evidence; the fervour of Burns's verses is, of course, nothing to go by. Nor is the inscription in the book of poems he gave her with its reference to 'so many fictitious reveries of passion'; this may only represent expediency or a change of mood—or the recrudescence of Maria Riddell. It was, perhaps, also in one of these moods that, in writing to Thomson, he cast her in the role of Sterne's Eliza—'a mistress, or friend, or what you will, in the guileless simplicity of Platonic love'. Thomson was not to put a 'squinting construction' on this; others have squinted pretty obliquely since. Chloris met an English gentleman called Whelpdale at a ball in Moffat, ran away and married him at Gretna Green and lived to repent it after the most approved traditions. Whelpdale was a wastrel and Chloris had to come home again to Kemishall; her father lost his money and she had to go into service—though there seems no good evidence for pursuing her with the horrors of prostitution and vagrancy to which Mrs. Carswell condemns her. Alec Cunningham, of course, would have her a liberal believer in the 'dispensing power of beauty' in which dispensation Burns was more than ready—with many others—to join; Jean Armour, on the other hand, told that persevering enquirer McDiarmid that Chloris came often to Ellisland; 'she had remarkably fair hair and was perfectly virtuous'. But then, Jean was a kind woman and Cunningham was a tattler. Poor Chloris had not the best of chances; her mother drank; Burns, hauled over the coals for some excise slackness in respect of Kemishall, replied: 'I never found anybody but the lady . . . and one of the times it would have rejoiced all Hell to see her so drunk.' But Burns, in his weather-cock way, was by then turning against Kemishall and Chloris for unknown reasons; Chloris's brother likewise fell from favour. The Lorimer episode is rather an obscure story altogether; one thing, however, does seem to emerge— that Burns 'loved' Chloris, as Chloris 'loved' Burns, only in either a purely practical or a purely figurative sense.

Still less romantic is that final recipient of Burns's

versified passion—Jessy Lewars; even the poet himself perceived the absurdity of this pretence, which is more than can be said for some of his admirers. Jessy Lewars was a young girl, nearly twenty years his junior this time, the sister of that Exciseman Lewars who vainly pursued Miss Lorimer; the Lewarses and the Burnses were neighbours in Dumfries, and when Burns took mortally ill, his wife being many months gone with child, Jessy came about the house to help, and did help very competently and kindly. Kind and competent she may have been, but a figure of romance never; there is a picture of her in middle age or a little later which shows a heavy solemn spherical face almost inhumanly devoid of expression; it is a matron's face, yet one can see from its bones that she could not have looked much otherwise as a young woman. It is a criminal libel both on Burns and Jessy to suggest a love-affair. Three years after the poet's death Jessy married—as Burns had said she would—a Dumfries lawyer called Thomson, whom she presented with five sons and two daughters, all apparently as blamelessly uninteresting as herself; the Thomsons, says Elizabeth Ewing,[3] lived that happy life which has no history. In view of her services to the poet Mrs. Jessy Lewars Thomson was buried close to Burns's mausoleum, and Scott Douglas tells us of a 'pilgrim'—was it perchance Scott Douglas himself?—who was thrilled to observe that, under this 'beautiful arrangement', Jessy's tablet remained dry throughout a blast of north-westerly rain. 'My plaidie to the angry airt, I'd shelter thee, I'd shelter thee.' Ah me! what things Burns's 'pilgrims' have seen and heard, to be sure; but this one, I think, would have pleased him.

The final member of this group of lesser lights is placed last here, though in actual fact she came on very early, because she is the only candidate meriting serious attention as a possible influence in the poet's life—Alison Begbie,[4] the supposed original of 'Mary Morison'. Burns is thought to have written her, presumably in the Lochlie days, at least five letters, in the course of which, with a great many words, he proposed marriage to her; after some initial encouragement she either turned him down or, having first accepted him, then backed out of it; Burns thereupon wrote to her sadly, 'Sharing life with you, would have given it a relish that, wanting you, I can never taste.' On this many assumptions have been based. I have heard it said by serious students of Burns that had Alison Begbie not refused or jilted him, Burns would have been spared a bitter and lasting disappointment, would have settled down in his early twenties and would have led an entirely different—and of course a better—life. I doubt it. To begin with, it seems improbable that he would have allowed this or any other rejection to sour his future; 'ne'er break your heart for ae rebute', he himself wrote, for 'gin the lassie winna do't, Ye'll find anither will, jo'; this seems a much more likely attitude to Miss Alison Begbie. Nor is there any reason to suppose that marriage with Miss Begbie would have transformed him into a model householder and citizen; certainly marriage with Miss Armour did not. But worse still, there is very little evidence that Begbie ever jilted him at all; and worse yet again, there is but dubious evidence that he was ever in love with her or asked her to marry him. The former point—the jilting—is based on two statements: his own, in the Autobiographical Letter to Moore, that in his twenty-third year *some*body—'a belle-fille whom I adored'—jilted or refused him 'with peculiar circumstances of mortification', and that of his sister Isabel that the person here referred to was Alison Begbie. The second point—the proposal—relies on the said five letters of which only one original MS. survives, the others being drafts found by Currie among the poet's papers; in these the suitor 'recommends himself' in phrases so incredibly stilted and in periods so frigidly polished that one doubts if even Burns at two-and-twenty would have thrust them upon any girl in whom he had an interest. There is much about 'universal benevolence' and the 'sacred principles of virtue and honour'—in which no young woman, hoping to be told she was lovely and loved, could take much interest.

The style, turgid and argumentative and complete with Pope quotation, certainly resembles that of Burns in his efflorescing mood; but the question is, did he write these letters to Begbie, and if so, did he write them on his own behalf or—as he sometimes did—for one of his less accomplished fellow farmers? Their impeccable and lifeless phraseology finds a suspicious echo in another model love-letter which *was*, on Burns's own admission, written for a friend. Professor Ferguson,[5] who is our best authority on Burns's correspondents, is very doubtful about the whole thing. The theory that Begbie embittered and ruined when she might have salved and regenerated Burns's life is intriguing; but on the available evidence one dare not, I think make too much of Begbie.

We must turn now to a gallery of women of quite another type; women who closely affected Burns's life because of an intellectual or even spiritual intimacy, but in whose case there was no question of sexual complications at all. Or if this last be thought impossible in Burns's attitude towards any woman whatsoever, let us say that sex considerations were, in these cases, kept under strict control. First there comes—perhaps as a border-line case, because Burns would have liked to interest her sexually very much—that vivacious common-sense and friendly creature, Peggy Chalmers. It is not quite clear where Burns first met her; it may have been in Ayr quite early in his life—she was Gavin Hamilton's cousin and a bosom friend of his sister Charlotte; Burns himself says it was in the Ochils; certainly they knew each other in Edinburgh in 1786-7, where Peggy used to read and sing to the blind Dr. Blacklock. She was the kind of woman he was bound to encounter sooner or later—the balanced, sensible Scots type who could be as amusing and lively as you please, but yet had no nonsense about her; it is a disconcerting type for those whose method is to 'try for intimacy', because they are always seen through immediately and put gently but firmly back where they started. Nobody has contended that Peggy Chalmers was a beauty—plainness is a concomitant of the type; but according to one of her relations, her bright hazel eyes and neat shining little teeth gave her face 'a charm not always the result of fine features'. She was a small creature, compact and svelte; a reader who kept her reading to herself, a good listener. In her sisterly way she was very good indeed for Burns; he felt at ease in her company, whether face to face or on paper, and showed himself accordingly at his very best. He had a high opinion of her and sought her high opinion of him; after his marriage in 1788 she received one of his fullest and most careful apologia for that astonishing act, complete with the French tags he now more or less reserved for her. According to Cromek, Cousin Charlotte Hamilton—was she perchance a little jealous; she was much the better-looking of the two, but Burns was all for Miss Chalmers—threw all his letters to Peggy in the fire; many of them are certainly missing, and this is a pity, for those that have survived were among his best letters and often enclosed excellent snippets of verse such as Glenasp and the Wabsters' Grace; and she could inspire him to such fine phrases as 'when you whisper, or look kindly to another, it gives me a draught of damnation'. Burns told Clarinda that Peggy was 'divine', but 'surrounded by the blandishments of flattery and courtship'; Clarinda, who had been shown Peggy's letters and knew herself for the time being perfectly safe, replied: 'Why did not such a woman secure your heart?' Why not indeed? If Peggy would have married Burns it would have made a cataclysmal difference to his life.

Was the question of marriage ever broached between them? It is not very certain. Long after Burns's death Peggy—then Mrs. Lewis Hay—told the poet Campbell, who told Dr. Carruthers, who told Scott Douglas, that Burns had proposed to her and that she had rejected him; she didn't say why. But by this time Peggy had reached that stage of life when ladies like to look back upon a besieging army of ardent admirers and are ot wholly to be trusted in their reminiscences. Yet there is some good corroborative evidence. On the 7th of January 1787 Burns wrote to Gavin Hamilton that he had met a 'Lothian farmer's daughter' (which Peggy incidentally was) whom he had almost persuaded to accompany him to the west country; this may seem an odd way of writing about the girl to her cousin, but is not inconsistent with Burns's arch third-person allusions. If his third tour—to Harviestoun, the 'shade of the Ochils' and 'Devon banks'—was not undertaken in pursuit of Peggy, there seems no reason why it should ever have been undertaken at all. Adair, Burns's travelling companion, landed his fish—Cousin Charlotte; Burns was less fortunate; Peggy, it seemed, like all other women of her class, just could not care for him in that way. Besides, there was Mr. Lewis Hay of Sir James Forbes's bank in Edinburgh, a gentleman carrying social and financial guns of a calibre that blew poor Robbie's out of their sockets. Hay won; Burns lost; perhaps Miss Chalmers lost something, too. Hay died twelve years after the marriage, leaving her with six children; twenty years later she went to Pau for her health and died there at an advanced age in 1843; life with Burns might have been shorter and harder, but it would almost certainly have been more exciting. Burns— it is a testimony to his regard for Miss Chalmers—took his rebuff with unaccustomed quietness; the correspondence naturally dropped, but without acrimony. It is an odd thing that Burns's very last song, sent from the horrors of Brow Well a few days before he died, was 'Fairest Maid on Devon Banks'; if this was indeed newly written at the time—which seems doubtful—and if it indicates a final nostalgia for Peggy Chalmers, it would show how much she meant in his life and how much he lost by her obduracy to his 'assiduities'.

Next comes an entirely different character, who has already brought herself several times into these pages— Mrs. Francis Anna Wallace Dunlop of Dunlop. I have always thought that great credit is due to Burns for the way in which he bore, over a long period of years, with this kindly, well-intentioned, occasionally bountiful, but consistently exacting and tiresome old woman. The phrase 'old woman' is not fair; but she was almost thirty years older than Burns and became a grandmother during the correspondence more than once; moreover, the role she assumed from the outset was explicitly elderly, being that of Voltaire's old-woman critic who read his MSS. and passed them—or did not pass them— for publication. (That Voltaire's 'old woman' was neither so old nor so innocent as Mrs. Dunlop seems to have thought need not trouble us.) From the first she took every advantage of her self-imposed authority. Mrs. Dunlop was *imprimis* a fan, and the type of fan of which every successful author collects at least one specimen; the type which begins with admiration, advances to criticism, and develops into a censor and mentor with quasi-dictatorial powers. She was first drawn to Burns by the *Cottar's Saturday Night*, which rescued her from the doldrums consequent on her elderly husband's death and her son's financial incapacity; the latter had sold the ancestral estate of Craigie to pay for his debts, and Craigie belonged to Mrs. Dunlop's father Sir Thomas Wallace, who claimed descent from the great William— 'a fact,' says Ferguson, 'which she neither forgot nor allowed others to forget'.

With the Cottar—to which last Mrs. Dunlop would have had Burns stick indefinitely instead of indulging in such 'childish levities' as *Tam o' Shanter*—began a correspondence which ran for ten long years and in the course of which Burns wrote seventy-nine letters and Mrs. Dunlop a hundred and seven.[6] This voluminous exchange has been very fully preserved; lacunae suggest only four missing Burns's and perhaps twice as many Dunlops; at fourpence for a 'single' and eightpence for a 'double', the Post Office must have done well out of it. Mrs. Dunlop was so moved and delighted with the *Cottar* that (*teste* Gilbert) she sent 'a person express to Mossgiel, distant fifteen or sixteen miles', with a 'very obliging letter' ordering several copies of the *Poems* and extending an eager invitation to call at Dunlop House as soon as was convenient. (Burns replied—cannily—that he would look in on his return from Edinburgh but he did not, in fact, present himself for a considerable time.) She began lecturing him almost at once on his 'undecency' and opining that Edinburgh would turn his head; he proceeded therefore with the correspondence on a clear preview of what he was letting himself in for. That correspondence—far too voluminous to be tackled here in any detail—is invaluable to any student of Burns; apart from the opportunities it gave him for airing his 'philosophical', critical, political and above all his religious views, it is a most useful barometer both of his mental condition and his outside activities. When Burns is busy or preoccupied with affairs of the heart, it languishes; when he is in a Horatian mood of leisure—as at Ellisland —and is for the moment unshackled to any of his charmers, it flourishes. He wrote to her with complete— sometimes with a reckless and tactless—freedom; without Mrs. Dunlop, we should have known much less about Burns.

Given enough time, all authors must end by disappointing their more enthusiastic fans, and Burns certainly disappointed Mrs. Dunlop. We have already seen how sadly he let her down on the occasion of his first and belated visit to her house; at a second visit he did little better, for the correspondence immediately thereafter suffers from a definite chill. He was constantly resistant, too, to her diligent advices and proposals; he would not look at the military career she envisaged for him—on the lines of her own sons the 'Major' and the 'Captain'; he replied with practical sense that he lacked the money for it. He was lukewarm towards the Chair of Agriculture for which she put forward his name; he would not even go and see Adam Smith about the Salt appointment on £30 to £40 a year. He wrote beautiful disclaimers to her accusation of his bawdiness—but went on being bawdy. He invited her criticisms and accepted them—in tones so humble as to suggest to the outside observer a tongue in a cheek, but he did nothing about them; if she asked him to emulate Thomson and drop his horrid plebeian Scots dialect, his response was to send her *Tam o' Shanter*. He hurt her deeply by marrying his Jean without consulting or even informing her in advance; and he would *not* be interested in the poems of her protégée Janet Little. Often he ignored the points she raised in her letters; often, indeed, he ignored the letters themselves and did not reply for weeks or months; hence irritating and repeated queries—did he *read* her letters? had she offended him? The true answer to these would probably have been in the first case 'No' and in the second 'Yes'; quite probably he often did not or could not read her letters, which were of vast length, closely and not too legibly written, ill spelt and wholly innocent of punctuation; while there were times when her tiresomeness reached so aggravating a pitch that a reply could only have been couched in language which would have terminated the correspondence. It did not terminate, however; with frequent frictions, with blanks and bumps, it went staggering on; because in truth neither of them could quite do without the other.

Burns treated his self-constituted manageress somewhat casually; it is difficult to believe that he was not at times deliberately insincere—as when he grovelled in acceptance of her criticisms or larded her 'Verses to a Young Lady' with such fulsome flattery as 'above anything of the kind done by any Author now living'. He was deliberately disingenuous as to the authorship of the *Auld Lang Syne* he sent her and, as we have already seen, he could fob off on her, as for herself, a second-hand poem belonging to quite another lady. Once or twice she did see through him, as in the case of the 'mendicant insincerities' in his 'plaintive epistle' of 1794; but normally she seems to have swallowed him all, hook, line and sinker. Burns's reply to an accusation of leg-pulling would probably have been that the plain truth would have wrecked the friendship and that flattery was the only way to keep the old lady in a good temper. In which, no doubt, he would have been right and wise; for, like Peggy Chalmers, though in quite a different manner, she did him a great deal of good.

The Burns-Dunlop correspondence has provided Burns students with its own problem—why did it suddenly drop in 1795? It *was* dropped—and at the Dunlop end. Why? Wallace, who has great authority on this subject, thinks it was mere inadvertence on her part; she had gone to London, she was preoccupied with her affairs and her daughter's long illness; she would have written again in time. This theory seems to me quite inconsistent with the belief that Mrs. Dunlop still retained any affection for Burns; for during the year he had written her letters which no friend could have ignored. Mrs. Dunlop might have filed *Does Haughty Gaul*—though it was a recantation on the very lines she had been urging; but his pathetic letter of 31st January 1796 announcing his grave rheumatic fever and the death of his daughter Elizabeth (the *third* or lawful 'Elizabeth') should have drawn a reply from a stone. He wrote her a final letter of farewell—a very dignified and moving composition it is—on the 10th of July; there is some confusion as to whether even this was acknowledged and whether, if it was, the letter reached Burns before he died; the only certain communication from her is her letter to Gilbert replying to his intimation of his brother's death. But if she received and did not reply to that letter of 31st January, she must already have been offended with Burns beyond hope of remedy, yet there is nothing to show why this should have happened. Her last letter to him, on 12th January 1795, was a chatty and friendly narrative about her stay in London; thereafter silence falls. There is no evidence of any missing letters. It has been suggested that the cause of offence was to be found in Burns's letter of 12th January 1795 (which would have crossed hers of the same date from London) in which he let fly about the 'perjured Blockhead and unprincipled Prostitute'—Louis Capet, that is, and Marie Antoinette; this was not only a sufficiently tactless remark to the mother-in-law of two French *émigrés*, but was in flat rebellion to her counsels of political caution. Yet it hardly seems to be enough to justify the guillotining—and that, too, in circumstances of such special cruelty—of a correspondence which had gone on so usefully and so long. There must, one feels, have been some much more grievous cause of offence; Burns could offend royally and Mrs. Dunlop could sulk in silence like Achilles; but what it was, no man knows— or in all probability ever will. It is one of the minor Burns mysteries and so remains.

If Burns reveals himself in this candid and intimate correspondence, so does his partner. She was the typically Scots blend of sentiment and shrewdness, magnanimity and pettiness, humour and dudgeon;[7] all through her letters one sees the intelligent quizzical eyes looking out under their high-arched eyebrows as they do in Gilbert Mosman's portrait of her as a girl of seventeen. (They remain alert and watchful in another picture fifty years on, though the loose mouth of the girl has tightened.) If she exercised a strictly maternal control over her protégés, who had a better right than the matron, descended from Wallace, who had reared to adolescence at least the majority of her own seven sons and six daughters? Thirty years older than Burns, she was to survive him by nearly twenty. And if it were indeed Burns's ill-guided Blockhead-and-Prostitute outburst that ruptured the friendship, it had a strange pendant. Mrs. Dunlop's elder daughter, Mme Perochon, was one of those who had brought the *émigrés* into the argument; and Mme Perochon was to be, for many years, the close friend and associate of the widowed Jean Armour Burns. As a result, Jean gave her as a last resting-place the original grave in St. Michael's churchyard which Burns had occupied till his body was removed to the Mausoleum; there in God's good time Mme Perochon was indeed interred, and there, by curious circumstance, Mrs. Dunlop's daughter still lies.

Lastly, in this particular group of Burns's women, comes that bundle of espièglerie, Maria Riddell—at once the only English 'foreigner' and the only really first-class woman with whom Burns ever went any distance.[8] Maria is a creature so interesting and so attractive in herself as to tempt one into interminable digressions; I must forego these and stick to her points of contact with Robert Burns. It is only necessary to say by way of preamble that Maria was born Maria Woodley, daughter of William Woodley, twice Governor of the Leeward Islands—a place Maria, however, did not see till she was sixteen. There two years later, in 1790, she married Walter Riddell, the widower of an Antigua sugar-princess—handsome, dissolute, extravagant, everything the widower of a sugar-princess and the husband of a sugar-king's daughter should be. In the following year Riddell brought his bride home to his native country of Dumfries and bought or half-bought an estate there which he renamed Woodley Park. Maria was no great stickler for class distinctions—she had not inherited the fastidiousness of her mother's cousin, Lord Lavington, who was wont to use gold tongs in taking anything from the hands of one of his negroes—but even so it would have seemed unlikely that she would come into intimate contact with the local Exciseman. This she did, however, because Walter Riddell had a brother Robert who lived at the neighbouring mansion of Friar's Carse; he was an amateur musician and antiquarian (and a man who has been of inestimable service to us by his commissioning from Burns copies of many of his writings.) Robert Riddell had taken up Burns from the time of his first arrival in Dumfriesshire and Burns, Exciseman or no, was in and about Friar's Carse a good deal. There Maria presently met him; she made a point, indeed, of doing so; she had written a book about her West Indian travels and thought Burns might help her to a publisher. She had also written poetry since the age of sixteen (it was part in those days of any young lady's accomplishments, but Maria's was above the average) and was considered to have scored, at the same early age, off Jekyll, the famous London wit. She had been rather disappointed in Walter Riddell and in marriage generally;

the Dumfriesshire society, whether at Friar's Carse or at Woodley Park, was dull. Burns was not.

Maria at nineteen was not one to let grass grow under her feet, and by the 22nd of January 1792 she had Burns sitting down to write an introductory letter to his old friend Smellie, the Edinburgh printer and publisher. Burns was still sufficiently undazzled by Maria to refrain from that fulsome praise he bestowed on Clarinda and Mrs. Dunlop; Maria was 'a votary of the Muses' whose verses 'always correct and often elegant, are very much beyond the run of Lady Poetesses today'. (They might easily have been that.) Smellie was not interested in Maria's verses, but he did publish her book—*Voyage to Madeira and the Leeward and Caribee Islands*, by Maria R—— which was well reviewed; on sight of the authoress he was captivated, for he wrote to her later: 'Why did you grapple with a soldier? We *two* should have made a COUPLE of figures in the literary world.' On this satisfactory basis the Burns-Maria relationship was founded; presently they went, together with some friends, to visit the lead-mines at Wanlockhead, where Maria made a nuisance of herself by insisting on going down a shaft and Burns suffered from claustrophobia and was very uncomfortable. (But his conversation on the journey was fascinating.) From this good beginning matters progressed merrily; by April of the following year Maria was 'thou first of Friends and most accomplished of women, even with all thy little caprices'; a few months later Love is conquering conscience and thoughts are 'rioting wanton in forbidden fields'. Burns brushed up his French again, which had been rusting since the days of Peggy Chalmers: he presented a copy of his poems as 'un gage d'Amitié le plus sincère'. And presently Maria became the recipient of a number of verses such as 'The last time I came o'er the moor', in which, needless to say, Burns was already the impassioned if hopeless lover and 'the wretch of love, unseen, unknown'; we have seen in the case of Chloris and Jessy Lewars how much these dramatisations might be worth in solid fact.

Nevertheless, a very pleasant little affair was developing when that obscure and unhappy incident occurred which has already been mentioned—the fracas at Friar's Carse or Woodley Park at the close of 1793 in which Burns, under the influence of drink, insulted *à outrance* one *or* other *or* both of the Riddell ladies. I shall endeavour to remove some of these alternatives in a later section of this book;[9] meantime we are only concerned with the fact that some such occurrence took place and that as a result a coolness developed between Burns and Maria. Such coolnesses with Burns were apt to turn to heat, and so they did now: he wrote some vicious and abusive verses about his former 'first of Friends'; he sent these to Clarinda —who was still faintly in the offing—commenting bitterly on Maria's 'scandalous conduct to me, and two or three gentlemen here as well as me', as a result of which she 'steered so far to the north of my good opinion that I have made her the theme of several ill-natured things'. How ill-natured those will see who read the *Monody* and the verses *Pinned to Mrs. Walter Riddell's Carriage* and the *Epistle from Esopus to Maria*, where the bludgeon becomes an acid-dipped stiletto. He also referred to Maria sneeringly, to Mrs. Dunlop, as a 'fantastical fine-fashioned dame of my acquaintance'; and just as Paton's legs had once displaced Armour's in *The Vision*, so now 'Eliza' ousted 'Maria' from her dwelling in *The last time I came o'er the moor*. Like the brothers of the Lass of Ballochmyle in like circumstances, Walter Riddell also came under the ill-tempered fusillade. For some time there was a complete estrangement; but at the New Year of 1795 Maria apparently held out an olive branch which was grudgingly accepted. Reconciliation followed, and by the middle of the year they were friends again. And it was Maria who invited him to dinner in the last days at Brow Well—a bolder and more unconventional act then than it would be now—and who wrote his obituary, generously and sympathetically, in the *Dumfries Journal*. However vehemently one may be disposed to take sides with Burns over the offending fracas, one must admit that Maria's forgiveness of his very disagreeable verses was magnanimous in the extreme.

Life would be easier for the historian of Burns if any two contemporary chroniclers would agree even on external appearances; he encounters this difficulty once again in the case of Maria. The portrait of her by Sir Thomas Lawrence shows us a reasonably charming if rather intense young woman with her head posed on her hand and upward-gazing eyes; she has dark wispy tousled 'wind-blown' hair with short-cut ends, a long nose with an inquisitive point, a large mouth rather than a small. White throat and bosom are candidly displayed. It is, as Mrs. Carswell says, a 'keen, piquante face'; lit up by eager interest in, say, the lead-mines, or by the flashing mischief of that caprice for which Maria was famous, it might well be captivating. But now hear Charles Kirkpatrick Sharpe, who knew everybody there was and disliked almost everybody he knew. 'She was an affected —painted—crooked postiche—with a mouth from ear to ear—and a turned-up nose—bandy legs—which she however thought fit to display—and a flat bosom, rubbed over with pearl powder, a cornelian cross hung artfully as a contrast, which was bared in the evening to her petticoat tyings, this pickled frog (for such she looked amid her own collection of natural curiosities) Burns admired and loved. . . . Burns wrote a copy of satirical verses on the Lady—which she afterwards kindly forgave, for a very obvious reason—amid all his bitterness he spared her in the principal point, which made her shunned by her own sex, and despised by the rest of the community.' And in his copy of *The Metrical Miscellany*, which contained nineteen items by Maria, Sharpe wrote 'she was . . . a worthless profligate woman'. Once again the reader must choose between contradictions; Sir Thomas Lawrence had the reputation of being a good painter with a fine eye for a likeness; on the other hand, there is no known reason why Kirkpatrick Sharpe should have gone out of his way to libel Mrs. Walter Riddell. What he meant by his hints on the 'principal point' I can translate

no more than I can elucidate some of the darker insinua-
tions in *Esopus*; the thing is a mystery. It is not, however,
of crucial concern for our immediate purpose; Burns, at
least, did not see Maria as a 'pickled frog', nor would he
have described her as either profligate or worthless. He
does say in a letter that he knows her credit with her own
sex is not high, but as he offers no reason, that takes us no
further.

I have no doubt I shall be censured by many for the
inclusion of Maria in this group of Burns's women instead
of among his avowed and reciprocating loves. Snyder,
'reading between the lines', believes Maria to have been
in love with Burns, and many others have considered that
Burns was in love with her. Where the lines are so irregular and so widely spaced as they are in this instance—and
indeed in most instances relating to Burns—it is possible to
read almost anything; my own reading is that there was
no love in it. Of course, Burns in his verses said he was in
love with Maria; but in that case, with whom was he not?
There will be quoted against me Maria's 'Stay, my
Willie' reply to 'Canst thou leave me thus, my Katie?'
and still more forcibly Maria's *To thee, lov'd Nith*—'For
there he roved that broke my heart, Yet to that heart, ah,
still how dear', with its 'altars of ungrateful love . . .
cold as my false love's frozen heart'. Admittedly Maria
wrote these pieces; but I simply cannot believe that she
wrote them about Burns. They 'go' with the tone of
nothing else she wrote about or to him: I would rather
believe that they were the products of that imagination
which, as she tells us in her diary, enjoyed the 'regions of
sentiment and romance'; I would rather even believe that
she wrote them about Walter Riddell—who did 'rove'
by the Nith and who would have broken anyone's heart
several times over. No doubt Burns wrote to her 'God
grant that you may live at least as long as I live, for were
I to lose you, it would leave a vacuum in my enjoyments
that nothing could fill up'; but Burns in love was wont to
write more fierily than that. And on the other side, I find
it difficult to believe that any young woman could have

written of a lover but ten days laid in the grave as Maria wrote of Burns in the *Dumfries Journal* within that time; her 'Memoir' is a fine tribute generously paid, but it is quite dispassionately appraising and critical; it is not written with the pen and ink of love. Nor, on first principles, was love between these two very probable. Maria was capricious and wilful; quite probably she was morally easy-going; but her head was screwed on tight and she never lost it. She had the sense to see that she was dealing with a very remarkable man who, as a man, was impossible; and he that he was dealing with a reasonably remarkable woman who, as a woman, was quite beyond him. Their relations fluctuated; doubtless they flirted, perhaps even played with fire; there may have been moments of close and tempting approach—sometimes perhaps too tempting to withstand; but that Maria was in desperate love with Burns or he with her I simply cannot believe.

Nor is it necessary to believe any such thing in order to enjoy the sight of Burns at long last meeting and making friends with a woman who was his peer in vitality of spirit and adventurousness of mind. Maria was Somebody; she had been Somebody before she ever came to Dumfries and she was Somebody after she left it;[10] she was a woman of the world as remote from Clarinda's suburban gentility as Clarinda was from the Cowgate of Mauchline; for once Burns met in what he habitually called the 'fair sex' an intelligence that equalled his own. Maria must have been an inestimable comfort and advantage to his closing years. That such a woman came into his life so late was a misfortune and we may sigh for it; but—better late than never.

And now, not without fear and trembling, we approach the Three—Clarinda, 'Highland' Mary Campbell and Jean Armour Burns. Objection will be raised, no doubt, *in limine*; by what right does Clarinda trespass upon this holy ground? Was she not a mere flirtation, a comic

interlude, a piece of artificial nonsense, a bogus Dulcinea,
a silly philandering, an Arcadian antic? The answer is—
she was not. She was not—to Burns, at least, which is
what matters—comic or bogus or artificial or silly. It was
Alec Cunningham—who had been refused access to the
Burns-Clarinda letters and probably never saw them—
who started all this nonsense about 'stage postures and
picturesque positions'; his cynicism has been followed
too long and too uncritically. For this there is reason; to
understand properly the relations between Burns and
Agnes McLehose it is necessary to read laboriously
through a protracted and somewhat wordy correspondence; it is easier to pick up a prepared label and call the
whole affair a comedy of errors. There were errors
certainly—but little comedy. Clarinda's own grandson[11]
had no belief in the Cunningham version; and no more
have I.

Clarinda was born Agnes Craig—'Nancy' to her
friends—the daughter of a surgeon in Glasgow; she was
just three months younger than Burns. The Church was
more strongly represented in her ancestry than medicine;
her father's brother was a minister and her maternal
grandfather was 'a model of evangelical piety and pulpit
eloquence'. As a child she seemed—characteristically—
unable to make up her mind about living or dying; but,
her life having been despaired of once and for all, she
naturally lived to be eighty-two. Her affair with Burns
occupied the last decade in the earlier half of her life—
from the ages of twenty-eight to thirty-seven, he being, of
course, coeval; but though she never entirely vanished
from his ken, all of the business that counted took place
during a few months at its outset and the last five years
were negligible. She had a scrappy education and was
probably what would now be called 'common'; but a
fluffy and bosomy prettiness made her, in her teens, a
Glaswegian toast. Among others attracted by these
endowments was a plausible rogue called McLehose, a
Glasgow law agent; discouraged from calling by her
relatives and friends, this gentleman had the enterprise

to book the entire Glasgow-Edinburgh coach by which
Clarinda aged seventeen was travelling; this excellent
piece of staff work—an indication of talents which were
to carry him far and profitably—succeeded as it deserved;
Miss Craig married McLehose in 1776. She might well
have sung, in the words of her future admirer, 'I'm o'er
young to marry yet', though even by this time, poor girl,
she had no 'mammy' from whom she could be taken. In
any case, the marriage was not a success. Her own girlish
restlessness combined with her husband's unsatisfactory
behaviour to bring about a separation in 1780—but not
before Clarinda had produced three children, two of
them surviving, and a fourth expected. Clarinda fell back
on her father till he died two years later when she went to
Edinburgh, where her uncle, Lord Craig, was a Lord of
Session, to improve herself and to live on a small annuity.
McLehose had so far abstracted the surviving children
and forbidden her to see them; now—curious coincidence
with Burns!—he announced his imminent departure for
Jamaica[12] and landed the children back upon his wife in
her tiny quarters on the first floor of Gerard's Entry off
the Potter Row. McLehose promised to support them in
lavish style, but never sent a penny, though he throve in
Jamaica from the word go.

This, then, was Clarinda's situation when Burns met
her in December of 1787; the equivocal rank of a grass
widow in straitened circumstances, dependent very
largely on the charity of Lord Craig and closely watched
by the neighbours; saddled with children, one of them a
very sickly boy, and tied to a husband who for sheer
unsatisfactoriness left Walter Riddell standing. She was,
however, trying hard to improve her neglected education;
she was 'cultivating the Muses' and in the intervals of art
and learning giving very good and memorable parties.
The Burns episode ran at heat from December 1787 till
March 1788; and by fits and starts at long intervals till
1794. Half way through it, to be exact in 1790, McLehose
unexpectedly sent twenty pounds from Jamaica—not a
great sum, but all he ever did send—with a warm invita-

'CLARINDA'
(Mrs. Agnes McLehose)

tion to join him there; Clarinda shilly-shallied over this for some time, but eventually decided to accept, and sailed for Jamaica in February 1792, bearing with her the memory of a touching farewell with Burns two months earlier and the manuscript of *Ae Fond Kiss*; she travelled by the *Roselle*, on which Burns had once booked that berth he never occupied.

Clarinda had written a beautiful letter to Lord Craig about the 'path of duty' and the blessing of God which she might expect to attend her prayers along it; her expectations were disappointed. McLehose met her only tardily and then in a vile temper and perhaps slightly intoxicated; presently she discovered a negro lady in possession and several mulatto children—a circumstance, which as her grandson rather quaintly says, 'could not be otherwise than a source of mortification and annoyance'. It was so much so that she sailed for Britain by the same boat as took her out, and arrived back in the late summer, somewhat draggled in health and spirits. As McLehose continued to send no money, she instituted proceedings before the Court of Session and was at last awarded an aliment of £100 per annum—one-tenth of what McLehose was then making as an attorney in Kingston; even this inadequate sum could never actually be extracted from him, and when at last he died in exile—and in affluence— twenty years later, his entire possessions were carried off by his 'friends' on the spot and not a penny came home. Clarinda went on living on her annuity, her friends and some hundreds of capital belonging to her husband which were discovered in Coutts's Bank—where they had all along been lying *perdu*. She went on living till she had outlasted all her friends and even all her grandchildren except one—and even herself. Lady Moodie, who saw her in the year of her death and attended her death-bed, found her deaf and uninterested in external happenings; asked if she feared death, she replied 'Not so much now.' Compared with her life, it really offered little to fear.

Clarinda has been constantly blamed for her hot-and-cold, backing-and-filling treatment of Burns; but in assessing this it is necessary to bear in mind her situation in Edinburgh as outlined here. She has been described by an unprintable hyphenated word of which the second component is 'tormentor' or 'teaser'; it seems better to say that, like Burns himself, she was rent by a sort of schizophrenia. One part of her nature urged her to have a good time and damn the consequences; the other, begotten by those Calvinistic ancestors and her 'sainted mother', said to her: 'You have obviously been given a poor deal in this world; your hope is wholly in the next; *make sure of it*.' She lived thus in a perpetual torment, first of indecision— 'dare I or daren't I?'; then—if indeed she had dared—of remorse and the terror of hell. She clung to Christ, but was half afraid he would fail her when it came to the bit. And she was overshadowed by two grim and towering figures; one was Lord Craig, on whom she very largely depended for bare subsistence, the other was the Rev. John Kemp of the Tolbooth Church, on whom she depended for spiritual stiffening and consolation. The Rev. Kemp strove with her manfully and perhaps enjoyed it; he was at least sufficiently interested in her to offer to pay her son's school fees. Obviously she walked upon a razor's edge where a false step—and she did so enjoy false steps!—might have the most grievous consequences.

Into this delicate situation burst the conquering Apollo Burns, immediately making everything ten times worse. In came Love—with all his disastrous promises and threats and dilemmas. What was Clarinda to do? She loved Burns—as she had prepared herself to love him—at sight; McLehose was a mere name on a small island in the Caribbean Sea; the windmill was before her and her cap in her hand. And yet—what had Burns to offer? Love, no doubt, physical sensations the most delectable; but, leaving out all question of sin and Divine vengeance— what about a home? Burns had no income and no apparent prospect of any; he had no employment nor was he trying very hard to find one. If she ran away with Burns—a logical conclusion they were both too terrified ever to face—Lord Craig would certainly disown her; and

as for the Rev. Kemp——! What then would happen to
the children—to whom she was genuinely devoted? The
knot was, of course, unresolvable; it had to be—and should
have been—cut. One or both of them should have said:
'This will not do; it can only lead to damnation and
misery; let us end it right now.' But when in history have
lovers accomplished these so simple, so desirable and so
impossible acts?

Lovers they were from the start. As everybody knows,
they met on 6th December 1787, by design of Clarinda's,
at a tea-party given by her friend Miss Nimmo, Burns
being lured there partly by the consideration that Nimmo,
his hostess's brother, was an officer of the Excise who
might help him towards that post with the idea of which,
in the cross-currents of the Ellisland project, he was idly
dallying. But if Nimmo appeared at all, he was completely
neglected. Clarinda, almost swooning, saw before her the
great-eyed, black-browed master of her dreams; Burns
saw at his feet a plump, frilly, fluffy little woman, roundly
feminine in her contours, with a face full of invitation and
a huge chiffon bow in her hair. A soft voice proceeded to
explain to him what her bright eyes were already saying.
It was all over in five minutes. Clarinda went straight
home and invited him to tea on the Thursday; the date
was unsuitable, but he would come on the Saturday.
Whereupon the Devil, seeing his opportunity, stepped in.
Burns, who was due to leave Edinburgh for Ayrshire in a
few days' time, had his leg badly damaged in a coach
accident; there could be no question of departure for
many weeks and for some time he was confined to his
room with his leg on a chair and nothing to do—but
think of Clarinda. Letters began to fly like shuttles
between the Potter Row and Cruickshank's rooms in
St. James's Square; by the time Burns was able to get
about again, his objective had moved much nearer than
Mauchline; that desperate first quarter of 1788 was well
and truly launched. On to that road—downward, if you
like, but certainly walled and with no side turnings—
went Clarinda and Sylvander.

I have already said that, in order to understand and assess the Burns-Clarinda relationship, their Edinburgh correspondence must be read through as a whole; it is easy—as many have found—to tear from it this phrase or that in order to exhibit it as ludicrous or artificial or sham or silly or any other desired adjective. The effect and impress of the whole thing is very different. Much has also been made of the 'arcadian' folly of the nicknames— 'Sylvander' and 'Clarinda'—which they employed; but when have not lovers devised pet names for each other— and much more idiotic names than these? The idea was, as one would guess, Clarinda's, but her swain jumped at it— 'I like the idea of Arcadian names in a commerce of this kind.' A commerce of *what* kind? Of whimsy, perhaps, or semi-serious sentiment; that was Burns's programme, no doubt, on the 20th December, at the end of the first fortnight. His programme was to alter—and soon.

Formidable as the Burns-Clarinda correspondence is, it can be broken up readily into sections, whose close in each case marks a milestone on the tragic journey. Burns began it in earnest on December the 8th. (And here it must be remembered that the dates of these letters are very often *ad lib*; the originals were mutilated by Clarinda for some odd senseless secretive reason of her own; in any case, they were frequently undated and at times they came at the rate of two a day in either direction; considerable argument as to the day or even month of some of them is thus inevitable. But the opening gambits seem placed definitely enough.) Burns's lead was a skilful letter, not overplaying yet showing the keenest aroused interest; he 'never met anyone he more wished to meet again'. Clarinda concurred warmly; she 'had a presentiment that we should derive pleasure from the society of each other'. She enclosed some lines which Burns maintained 'are poetry, and good poetry'. (They were probably well enough.)[13] Pushing home the advantage, he told her that 'Friendship . . . had I been so blest as to have met with you *in time*, might have led me—the God of love only knows where.' This was quick work—too quick for Clarinda, who backed sharply; does he remember that he is addressing a married woman? Burns replied presently with disclaimers and subtle reassurance; and the next day played an adroit stroke—he has met the great Professor Gregory, who had opined that there was no young woman in Edinburgh capable of Clarinda's verses. (It is in this letter, in reply to a missing one of Clarinda's,[14] that the 'Arcadian' signatures first appear.) Clarinda took the Gregory bait beautifully and replied, by return, with a 'simile'—for Gregory to look at?—comparing Burns to the sun; she is a bigot in friendship and religion and—could perhaps be one in love, but for 'fixed principles'. 'PS.—Don't tell anyone on earth about our correspondence. . . . My situation is a delicate one.' Ten days later she would still like so much to meet Dr. Gregory; and presently she sends 'Talk not of Love! it gives me pain—For Love has been my foe.' Friendships are pure and lasting, but 'never talk of love'. PS.—Can he come round on Saturday? Burns was unable to come round on Saturday, but softened the refusal with that 'worthy of Sappho' compliment. On 5th January (1788) his leg has sufficiently recovered to allow him to visit Clarinda; these were 'marvellous hours', but he frightened her about 'my favourite hero' the Miltonic Satan and he had to devote part of his next letter to explaining that Lucifer was his hero *only* for his 'fortitude in disaster'. He had also shown her his Autobiographical Letter to Dr. Moore which—with sound taste—she admired 'in point of composition beyond all your productions'. During the next week there are some arch exchanges on the subject of a wife for Burns; she must be 'companion friend and mistress' (Clarinda); where can I find her? I can think of *One* possible (Sylvander); who *can* she be? (Clarinda). Incidentally she knew by this time all about Jean Armour—including presumably Jean's current condition of pregnancy for the second time. Burns—in the hope of jealousy?—dangled the 'divine' Peggy Chalmers; Clarinda parries neatly 'Why not add Miss Nimmo? You'll soon tire of *me*. PS.—Couldn't we go together in the Leith Fly with poor Willie? (her son.) What a pleasant

chat we might have.' Burns couldn't; had she then
offended him? Oh, *no*! The mere idea has given him such
a violent headache that he will be round at 8 p.m. in a
chair. These last three exchanges were on 12th January
and with the evening of 12th January we come to the
first milestone.

'I will not deny it, Sylvander,' wrote Clarinda the
next morning, 'last night was one of the most exquisite I
ever experienced.' The 'limits of virtue' had not been
overstepped; yet today she regrets. What would Lord
Craig say? To say nothing of God. And what did Sylvander
think of her 'unreservedness' when he saw Clarinda
'behind the scenes'? Sylvander replied satisfyingly that he
had seen only 'the noblest immortal soul creation ever
showed me'. As for God, he *must* approve Friendship and
Love. 'Oh, my angel! how soon must we part! and when
can we meet again?' What about Saturday? Clarinda was
captivated; Saturday certainly—tea if you like, but eight
would be less liable to intrusion. But come on foot—no
gossip-collecting chairs. 'Say my lover, poet and friend,
What day next month Eternity will end.' In reply Burns
drew a charming picture of Sylvander and Clarinda,
'hand in hand, or rather my arm about your lovely
waist'—had it been there already?—'making our remarks
on Sirius' or—making love on Venus. (The altered tempo
since 12th January will be noted.) And so to the next
milestone—the evening of 23rd January.

Their reactions to this next day were sharply contrasted.
Burns, writing in the midst of a convivial evening, could
remember only that 'I have drunk your health twice
tonight and that you are all that my soul holds dear in the
world'. Those with experience will recognise genuine
symptoms here—and not less in Clarinda's mood of
terrified remorse. 'My heart reproaches me for last night.
If you wish Clarinda to regain her peace, determine
against anything but what the strictest delicacy warrants.'
Burns's reply is a torrent; 'Clarinda, my life, you have
wounded my soul. I will pledge my honour'—and so on.
But the hour of Burns's departure from Edinburgh was

drawing inexorably nearer; the pace must quicken
further; the third milestone comes no more than three
days after the second—on 26th January. Clarinda wrote of
it next day—at very great length—'Another's wife. Oh
cruel Fate. . . . Last night we were happy beyond what
the bulk of mankind can conceive. Perhaps the "line"
you had marked was a little infringed—it was really; but
though I disapprove, I have not been unhappy about it.'
In fact, Clarinda is slipping, slipping. But the Reverend
Kemp has been at her with 'paternal advice'; if only
Sylvander knew him—'such worth and sensibility.' . . .
'Sylvander, I wish our kind feelings were more moderate
. . . try me merely as your friend (alas, all I ought to be).'
(So, then, what more *had* she been?) Sylvander, for his
part, had known 'happiness that the world cannot give'.
'I kindle at the recollection but it is a flame where
Innocence looks smiling on and Honour stands by.' . . .
and so on. 'You are an angel, Clarinda . . . to kiss your
hand, to live on your smile'—and so forth. Clarinda
thought this—as well she might—a 'dear letter', but
would like him to come and hear Mr. Kemp. (Burns
must have been damning Mr. Kemp pretty freely by
now.) Clarinda is going to Miers to have her silhouette
done; Sylvander wanted it 'for a breast-pin to wear next
my heart. I propose to keep sacred set times to wander in
the woods and wilds for meditation on you.' (Another
unmistakable symptom surely!) 'Then only your lovely
image shall be produced to the day with a reverence
akin to devotion. Tomorrow night (1st February) shall
not be the last.' It was not; but it was the fourth milestone.

A fortnight later Burns left Edinburgh, just two months
after his original intention; in the interval there were,
beyond doubt, many meetings. On the 13th Sylvander
wrote: 'I will be yours in the way you think most to your
happiness. . . . I love and will love you and will with
joyous confidence, approach the throne of the Almighty
Judge of men with your dear idea'—than which no man
can say much more. Yet the next day he *could* say more,
if to the same effect: 'I esteem, I love you as a friend; I

admire you, I love you as a woman, beyond any one in all
the circle of creation. I know I shall continue to esteem
you, to love you, to pray for you, nay, to pray for myself
for your sake.' (It may be argued that this was just what
he was afterwards to call it—'fustian rant': I think otherwise.) But there is a cloud; Clarinda's friends have been
down upon her: 'Clarinda, things are grown very serious
with us'; he will be with her next night at eight for the
last time till his return to Edinburgh, but 'don't tell your
jealous spying friends that I am *the* man'. Of what happened on that evening there is no record, but Burns rode
within twenty-four hours of it, so it makes milestone
number five.

It makes, in fact, the final milestone to the first, the
warmest, the best period of their association; they were to
meet again, but in circumstances sadly changed. Once
away from Edinburgh, Burns seems curiously cooled;
this, however, need not imply that he had previously been
but play-acting, for his was never a heart made fonder by
absence, and he had an extraordinary facility for living in
the immediate present and thrusting all else into limbo.
He wrote Clarinda a snatch from Glasgow, where he was
sitting down to a merry night with Richard Brown and
brother William; a longer letter from Kilmarnock, but all
about dull people in whom she had no earthly interest.
Clarinda was hurt and almost snappish, and for a time
they bandied and balanced statistics of letters written on
one side or the other. Meanwhile Burns reached Mauchline *en route* for the exploration of Ellisland and was
plunged once more into the miseries and vexations of the
second-time pregnant Jean. From Mossgiel, on 23rd
February, he wrote Clarinda a letter on this subject;
caddish as it is, there is no reason to disbelieve its sincerity.
He is disgusted with 'a certain woman': 'I cannot endure
her!' Jean is a farthing taper as compared to the cloudless
glory of the meridian sun he has left in Edinburgh. He
has exchanged polished good sense, heaven-born genius,
and the most precious, the most delicate, the most tender
passion, for tasteless insipidity, vulgarity of soul and mer-

cenary fawning. Once again, man could hardly say more, except to say—as he did say—'I have done with her, and she with me.' Clarinda accepted this calmly; she sent 'the little cherub' (the survivor from Jean's first pair of twins) fifty kisses, with some archness as to how they might be shared; she pities Jean and wishes 'a certain affair' happily over; clearly therefore she knew the whole story about Jean and regarded her as completely a non-competitor, revolving round the same sun, perhaps, but in an orbit with which her own could never become entangled. 'Oh, Sylvander, I am great in my own eyes when I think how I am in your esteem.'

She was to have a rude awakening. Burns was back in Edinburgh for a few days in the latter half of March; their final meeting there (if the dates are correctly calculated) was on the 22nd. On the 24th he returned to Ayrshire; presently Clarinda was orally informed *via* Ainslie that he had there committed the most extraordinary act of his life— he had married that 'certain woman' of whom he had written to her in such slighting terms some six weeks before.[15] The blow must have been murderous, and no possible excuse can be allowed to Burns for the cowardly way he dealt it; if, for reasons that are still obscure, his marriage to the 'farthing taper' had become inevitable, he might at least have faced the music in person. Even if he had not—as some suppose he had—pledged himself to marry Clarinda if and when a merciful Providence thought fit to remove McLehose, he might have had some thought for the woman who had written him, in Edinburgh a short month before: 'I am now convinced that, in the wide circle of the universe there are not two souls so completely formed for each other as ours. . . . I can now carry you with me to God's footstool and there feel sensations so delightful, so serene, as makes me almost hope that Heaven itself approves our union.' This is a passage in Burns over which his most idolatrous admirers can only bow their heads in shame.

Naturally the correspondence dropped; Burns's next letter is a year later in date, and may or may not be in reply to a missing one from Mrs. McLehose. He defends himself vigorously against 'the name of villain'; during the period of their love he was not under 'the smallest moral tie to Mrs. B——'; he was 'an honest man, struggling successfully with temptations . . . and preserving untainted honour in situations where the austerest virtue would have forgiven a fall.' That he struggled is true; how far successfully we shall never know; we must just take his word for it—and bear in mind that, whatever happened or did not happen, the temptation was sore. He wrote another explanatory letter two years later in which his sophistries would seem to be almost deliberately involved and meaningless; he was then brought to book by her communication about Jenny Clow which has already been quoted. He was obliged to see her in Edinburgh to repay her outlays in this matter; there was a reconciliation and another 'final' parting (which did, in fact, prove so this time) on the 6th December 1791. She was once again 'my ever-beloved my ever-sacred Clarinda'. Forty years later she was to write in her Journal, under 6th December 1831— 'this day I never can forget. Parted with Burns in the year 1791, never more to meet in this world—oh may we meet in Heaven!' Surely a long-lived and persistent 'flirtation'. In January of 1792 she wrote him a terribly goody-goody letter about her impending departure for Jamaica; her sense of humour seems to have deserted her with the passage of the years, and the letter—triumph of the Reverend Kemp?—is solidly religious; however, 'seek God's favour—keep His commandments—prepare for a happy eternity! There I trust we may meet in perfect and never-ending bliss.' This should have been the end of the story, but it was not; as we have seen, Clarinda returned from Jamaica post-haste. She did not tell Burns about it, but he heard and wrote to reproach her. There are a letter or two; Clarinda offering 'Friendship' and Sylvander damning it; his final letter—in 1793 or perhaps 1794—does read for once as if he were really as intoxicated as he pretended to be when he wrote it. And so exit Clarinda.

Scott, who was a man of 'sensibility', thought the

Burns-Clarinda correspondence 'the most extraordinary mixture of sense and nonsense, and of love human and divine, that was ever exposed to the eye of the world'. Professor Ferguson, on the other hand, who had seen more letters than Scott, read it as an 'ironic comedy—a full-length study of the mess into which two sentimentalists with a gift for words can get themselves'. Linklater, more recently—and more conventionally—speaks of it as a 'flirtation', 'unreality', a 'comedy' again. The reader must use his own judgment. I have set out the correspondence in as much detail as the space of this book will permit; if it does not of itself convince, I can do no more. Except to say that, far from comedy and unreality, the whole thing seems to me so tragic and true that my strongest feeling is a shrinking from the sight; it is indecent that one should be able to look and see so clearly betrayed the torments of two poor wretches who might, but for the grace of God, have been you and I.

The case of Mary Campbell—'Highland Mary' to the historians, though not to Burns himself[16]—is unique among Burns's women if only for one reason—that he held his tongue about her; she was the only personal topic on which he displayed any reticence whatsoever, and on Highland Mary he was a positive oyster. This may or may not be significant. We have seen his voluminous correspondence with Clarinda, and he mentioned her on occasion to his friends; he used poor Jean as a perfect butt for his shafts of literary wit—sometimes of the crudest kind. But of Highland Mary he said—at the critical period—not one word. Burns's own silence has been assisted by what would seem a league of circumstance—some of it indeed track-covering and clue-obliterating by interested persons known or unknown: his letters to Mary —which need not have been many or lengthy, as in all probability she could not read—have been 'destroyed by the Campbell family'; the Bible he gave her has had its inscriptions mutilated and defaced; important corroborative records are inconveniently 'missing'. With all this mystery, it is not to be wondered at if many began to doubt whether any such person as Highland Mary ever existed; or if the romantics, insatiably pursuing their own chimera, came to persuade themselves that Mary—if she had any corporeal being at all—was no more than a lay figure on which Burns draped some mystical ideal of pure chaste womanly perfection—a quality he had so disappointingly missed in real life. (He certainly never went out of his way to search for it; and just why he should have desired so earnestly to enshrine it has never been very satisfactorily explained.) Even the normally clear-sighted Angellier was captivated by this intriguing delusion; Mary was, he wrote, 'le plus pure, le plus durable et de beaucoup le plus élevé de ses amours. . . . La douce fille des Hautes Terres aux yeux azurés fut sa Béatrice et lui fit signe du bord du ciel.' To call a woman a Beatrice symbolising the borders of Heaven is as much as to say that she never, for practical purposes, existed. Were Burns's purposes, then, for once unpractical?

To attempt a documented, intelligible and authentic account of Highland Mary is one way of driving oneself mad; anything that looks like a reliable piece of evidence is immediately cancelled by another equally well—or ill—attested. But it seems as certain as anything can be that Mary Campbell, Burns's Highland Mary, did exist; and if the facts of the case are what they seem, she was anything to him except a pure and intangible ideal. The facts of the case are not what they seemed, less than twenty years ago, to Snyder and Mrs. Carswell, who optimistically believed that they had at last got at some semblance of the truth; but if they are facts at all, Beatrices and intangible ideals are balderdash. If 'Highland Mary'—who was no more 'Highland' really than the Cowal coast—did not exist as a flesh-and-blood figure, whence arose that tradition of her which was strong and flourishing by the time of Burns's death and before it? Far more was known about Highland Mary in the countryside of Ayrshire and the back streets of Greenock than appeared in any printed work, whether by Burns or anyone else. Currie, who was nearest in time and must have heard all this 'clash', could have done something to clarify it, but unfortunately he was attacked by yet another fit of delicacy which told him these were 'youthful passions . . . the history of which it would be improper to reveal, were it even in one's power'. (The 'passions' could not have been *very* youthful, as the Bible Burns gave to Mary was not even printed till 1782, when Burns was twenty-three and Mary nineteen.) The curtain of obscurity fell rapidly; by 1808 Cromek could only get as far as the name Mary Campbell and the story of the celebrated farewell on the banks of the Ayr; and no one has really got much farther to this day. Burns's relatives were, like everyone else, inclined to close up when questioned on this subject, or to prevaricate; but Gilbert said (untruthfully) that Mary was the heroine of *Sweet Afton*, Burns's sister Isabel said he met her at the time of Jean's 'desertion', and Burns's mother said he intended to marry her when freed from that entanglement. Some of these statements are unsustainable—and indeed their sponsors hedged over them freely, but they do establish that there was a corporeal and extant woman, Mary Campbell, in whom Burns was interested. That the Burns family knew more than they were ready to tell is also evident and one may draw from that such inferences as one thinks fit. Finally, Highland Mary is the *locus classicus* of Burns's moods; the few references he did make to her—in all cases long after the events—are so wildly variant as virtually to cancel one another out. But even if Mary *became* a lay figure on which he draped the emotions of the hour, that is no reason for supposing that she was, in her heyday, any such thing.

As if there were not already sufficient obscurity and difficulty in the matter, the trail is crossed by a second Mary Campbell, who was certainly in Ayrshire and within a few miles of Mauchline just about the time when Burns and 'Highland Mary' must have been *in flagrante delicto*. (The accepted date for the Burns-Mary affair is late 1785 to 14th May 1786, the date of their parting on the banks of the Ayr, as to which—on day and month, at least, 'the second Sunday of May'—Burns is categorical.) But *was* this a second Mary Campbell or were they one and the same? The question is of importance, because if the second part of it could be answered in the affirmative it would be, for reasons which will emerge, the death-blow to all Beatrices and all incorporeal ideals. It cannot, however, be definitely answered one way or the other; informed opinions have varied, and the point remains open to interminable argument. The facts are as follows.[17] On 25th April 1784 one Mary Campbell appeared before the Kirk Session of Dundonald (the parish on the north-west of Mauchline) and stated that she had brought forth a child *in the Parish of Mauchline* of which one Hay a farmer of Dundonald was the father. She brought the matter to the Dundonald Session, not Mauchline, because it was in Dundonald that the act of fornication took place. Hay denied the accusation, but Mary Campbell, re-appearing a fortnight later, repeated the charge, saying that Hay had given her money, but 'would not take with it publicly'. Despairing of the Kirk Session, the woman then seems to have gone to the civil courts with an action of paternity, and a long hiatus ensues; but on 26th July 1786 the Dundonald Kirk Session recorded that the Justices of the Peace had ordered Hay to pay four pounds a year for the child; they were uninterested in this, but passed on Mary Campbell to the Parish of Stair (next door again), 'where she now resides', for Church discipline. On 17th December 1787 the erring Hay at last appeared before the Session, confessed his guilt (in this and several other cases) and was ordered to appear before the Dundonald congregation for the usual penance and absolution—which, in due course, he no doubt rounded off the story by doing.

In the absence of any definite information as to Burns's Mary's movements prior to 1786, it is obvious that endless and intricate controversy may be spun out of these Dundonald records. True, if Burns's Mary was in Argyll-

shire in mid-1786, as the Burns story postulates, the
Hay's Mary then in Stair must have been somebody else;
but *was* there any Mary Campbell at that time in Stair?
The relevant Stair parish records have—needless to say—
been lost, and so have those of the civil action. What
became of the Hay child? Heaven knows. The trail and
all clues to it are gone. Just to complicate matters a little
further, there is a story (based on some discredited MSS. in
the Edinburgh Advocates' Library thought to be by Train
the antiquary) that Richmond, Burns's Ayrshire friend
and Edinburgh co-lodger, told a certain Mr. Grierson that
Burns's Mary was at one time the mistress of Captain
Montgomerie at Coilsfield and that this hideous fact
was 'demonstrated to Burns'; he was taken by Richmond
and others to see Montgomerie and Mary together at a
Mauchline public house (which Richmond, as recorded,
very suspiciously misnames), but his infatuation was so
great that he took no notice. Now, was this Burns's Mary
(who *was* said to have been employed for a time at Coilsfield) or was it the Dundonald Mary Campbell, or were
the two one and the same, or was it all only another lie of
Richmond's? It is a head-turning business, first and last.
The best argument in favour of the segregation of the
Mauchline and Dundonald Mary's is that Mauchline
gossip—which *must* have heard and tattled over that
civil-court case—never seems to have connected the
Mauchline or Burns Mary with any fornicator of the
name of Hay—or, indeed, with anybody other than
Burns himself. But—like everything else in this dreadful
tangle—the point is neither proved nor disproved, nor,
unless fresh evidence comes forward, can be. Were the
two Mary Campbells one and the same? Informed persons
have thought so; but that is no reason why we should.

Some conception must now be forming in the reader's
mind of what it means to start upon the trail of Highland
Mary; the jungle gets no thinner as one advances. All
that the most patient explorer can do is to attempt to
marshal, from this rout of incongruities and contradictions, such few items as can, without distortion of lan-

guage, be called facts. This has so far been best done by
Snyder[18] in a very careful, fair and patient analysis to
which the reader is referred; some attempt must, however,
be made to cover them within the compass of this book,
and here it is.

In the year 1762 one Archibald Campbell of Daling
married Agnes Campbell of Auchamore; of these, in the
following year—four years later than Burns—was born
a daughter Mary. A son, a daughter and another son
followed. This family resided first in the neighbourhood of
Dunoon, then at Campbelltown, and finally at Greenock,
where poor Mrs. Campbell ended up as a charge on
the parish rates. The younger daughter Anne married
a stonemason called Anderson, bore numerous issue, and
lived and died normally. The elder daughter Mary
gravitated, by some route and for some reason which are
unknown, to Ayrshire, where she would seem to have
been employed first as nursemaid in Gavin Hamilton's
house in Mauchline and latterly as dairymaid at Coilsfield (Burns's 'Castle o' Montgomery'). In view of the
Dundonald Mary, and for other reasons, it is extremely
desirable to fix the dates of her service in Ayrshire with
some exactitude; it is at least equally difficult. In 1784 the
Kirk Session of Mauchline began some rather absurd
proceedings against Gavin Hamilton for 'habitual neglect
of Church ordinances' in the course of which a list of his
'present' (in January 1785) servants was compiled; the
investigator might hope to corroborate by discovering
Mary Campbell's name in this list, but he would—as
usual—be disappointed; it does not appear. On the other
hand, Hamilton's married daughter, Mrs. Todd, remembered Highland Mary coming as nursemaid to her
brother Alexander, and a 'very pleasant and winning
girl' she was—though no beauty. Alexander Hamilton
was born on 13th July 1785. The testimony of Isabella
Burns and her mother—for what it is worth—was to the
effect that Burns took up in earnest with Mary Campbell,
whom he had known for some time, after he was 'deserted'
by Jean Armour. The erring and *enceinte* Jean was whipped

off to the Paisley friends early in March 1786. In that case the 'second Sunday in May', the date given by Burns for his solemn parting with Mary, would be May of 1786, and that 'pretty long tract of the most ardent reciprocal attachment' to which he referred in his notes to the song 'My Highland Lassie' would run from mid-1785 (at the latest—it might have started much earlier) to the aforesaid second Sunday. To sum this up, there was a Mary Campbell, reputed to have come recently from the Highlands and almost certainly *not* the Dundonald Mary Campbell, in and about Mauchline at the time when Burns's affair with Jean Armour was at its height and when he begat on Jean that first set of twins delivered on 3rd September 1786.

On that second Sunday in May 1786 Burns and Mary Campbell met to bid one another a solemn, if temporary, farewell. Leaving out all romantic details of the meeting —which are wholly imaginary—they certainly pledged themselves in binding vows of some kind or another, but most probably matrimonial. These they reinforced by the exchange of Bibles; such, at any rate, is the tradition and the presumption, though the Bible given by Mary to Burns, if indeed it existed, has not been seen by mortal eye from that day to this. The fine two-volume copy given by Burns to Mary is, however, extant and can be seen in the Ayr Monument; it is the sole Material Object which can be confidently exhibited in the case, and the story of its wanderings rivals that of Montrose's heart. The names inscribed on the fly-leaves of the two volumes —Mary's in volume one and Burns's in volume two—have been mutilated as if smudged out with a wet thumb or defaced by having a paper pasted over them for some time; but there remain a palpable 'M' and the first half of an 'a', a quite clear 'Robert' prefixed to a surname ending in 's', and a word which can only be 'Mossgaville' —an old spelling of 'Mossgiel'. There also remain, un-damaged, Burns's mason mark and two texts in his handwriting, unmistakable if a trifle shaky, one on the fly-leaf of each volume; the first is from Leviticus and the second from Matthew, and both deprecate vehemently false swearing and the non-performance of oaths. Who chose these texts—Burns or Mary? It would be interesting to know, but needless to say, one doesn't; I suspect Mary, who may have had more cause for anxiety about the keeping of oaths than her partner. It is interesting to observe that the Campbells, though they expunged Mary's name and destroyed Burns's letters to her, stuck to the valuable Bibles; as did their son-in-law the stonemason, who reckoned to get five pounds a volume to buy his two daughters a chest-of-drawers each.[19] The value of this long-sighted prudence to the historian has been inestimable; as it was to the Andersons, who eventually got a good deal more than five pounds each for the books.

Immediately after the farewell and exchange of the Bibles Mary Campbell left Mauchline and went back to her family. One may well ask—why? It was about the end of a term and she may have intended to leave her Ayrshire employers in any case, though there seems no reason why she should have done so—not while she was having so enjoyable a time with Burns. Burns himself, writing some time later, said it was 'to arrange matters among her friends for our projected change of life', which can only be supposed to mean that he intended her to share his Jamaican adventure, then theoretically imminent; this seems absured—how was he to raise her fare, let alone the suspicion that he had never any very serious intention of going to Jamaica at all? Why, then, did Mary Campbell leave Mauchline—unless there was a sinister reason which does not so far appear? As to the agreement, it was no doubt some form of Scots marriage; Burns had written, soon after the Armour defection, that he was looking for another wife. But it is worth remembering that all this time he was, by Scots law, married to Jean Armour; if he did not actually know this he quite probably suspected it, for he was extremely eager to procure, from the Church, his certificate as a bachelor.

All these arrangements, protestations and precautions, however, came to nothing; in October of 1786 Mary

Campbell died at Greenock, and was interred in the 'lairs' bought by a connection, Peter Macpherson, in the old Greenock West Churchyard. According to Burns, she contracted a 'malignant fever' and was dead ere he knew she was ill. Others, however, have suspected complications.

I suppose Burns's later references to Mary must come under the heading of 'facts', unhelpful as they are. As I have already said, they vary to a self-cancelling degree. In the passage from which I have been quoting above, his notes to the song 'My Highland Lassie',[20] she is that 'warm-hearted charming young creature as ever blessed a man with generous love', with whom he had that 'pretty long tract of the most ardent reciprocal attachment'. (Incidentally, with Burns 'the most ardent attachment' was rarely of a purely spiritual or Platonic kind.) But writing to Thomson in 1792, with 'Will ye Go to the Indies, my Mary,' he describes this as a 'farewell' he took of a 'dear girl'—nothing at all about 'our projected change of life', and a farewell, not an invitation. A few weeks later, submitting 'Highland Mary', 'the subject of the song is one of the most interesting passages of my early days'—as if the 'subject' were some negligible and forgotten inamorata not hitherto mentioned. Yet, between 1786 and 1792, he had written *Thou Lingering Star* and sent it to Mrs. Dunlop on 8th November 1789 with the famous outburst on 'another life' where he would 'with speechless agony of rapture again recognise my lost, my ever dear MARY! whose bosom was fraught with Truth, Honor [sic], Constancy and Love'. What is one to make of all this? Only that these Burnsian somersaults do not further us very much.

The remaining 'facts' of the story, such as they are, are to be found in and about that grave in the old West Churchyard of Greenock. In 1803 the Greenock Burns Club—who evidently thus early knew a good deal of the story of Highland Mary—resolved to request Peter Macpherson to allow them to add a tablet on his 'lairs' to the memory of the unfortunate young connection he had buried there seventeen years before. This permission was presumably granted; but nothing was done till some forty years later, when a new (and exceedingly ugly) monument was erected at the grave by public subscription. But the old Greenock West Churchyard was doomed; the quiet plot by the Clyde which Macpherson had chosen for his burial-place had been swallowed up in the hideous expansion of commercial Greenock; the vast shipbuilding yards of Caird and Company were encroaching upon it and desired to encroach still further; worse still, the surroundings had become an abominable slum which the Greenock Corporation regarded with justice as a blot upon its escutcheon. After an interminable period of argument and counter-argument, suits, injunctions and what not, it was resolved to remove the contents of the churchyard—including Highland Mary's grave, remains, monument and all—to the Greenock West Cemetery. On the 8th November 1920 the exhumation of Highland Mary was carried out in the presence of responsible officials and representatives of the Burns Federation. And *in* the grave was found—the bottom board of an infant's coffin. On this slice of woodwork, sodden with water but perfect and unmistakable in shape, the patient investigators of the Highland Mary mystery fell with a gasp of reverent delight; here at last was Material Object Number Two, and it explained everything. Mary Campbell had had an illegitimate child by Burns; she had died of it—plus or minus the 'malignant fever'; a hundred conundrums were resolved in an instant by this happy discovery.

Would God it had been as simple as they thought! The whole matter of this exhumation is so complicated and the questions arising out of it so important and so un-determined that I propose to reserve it for the section of this book devoted to 'Riddles'. [21] One can only say here that this unassuming piece of board was scarcely up to the weight of inference with which Snyder and Mrs. Carswell —to cite only two—proceeded to load it. Revelations— or at any rate assertions—were to be made later of which they knew nothing; but in any case, the coffin-board

would seem at best to lead only to a further string of
unanswerable questions. Was the child Mary Campbell's?
Probably. If so, was it Burns's? Probably again; if Mary
Campbell died in childbed in October 1786, then that
date would fit in with the corresponding period of her
intimacy with Burns at Mauchline. Next—and impossible
really to answer—did Burns know the child was upon the
way? From anything that ever appeared in his writings
one would say 'No'; but one cannot but feel that there is a
good deal to indicate that he did.

Indeed, the *a priori* reasoning provides a stronger case
than can now be based upon Material Object Two. If
Highland Mary, like Elizabeth Paton and Jean Armour,
had been put in the family way, a number of difficult
questions become soluble. *Imprimis* there is, of course, the
brutal but inevitable presumption that any woman with
whom Burns had a 'pretty long period of the most ardent
reciprocal attachment' was more than likely to find herself
in that condition sooner rather than later. *If* it were so, it
would explain Mary's sudden departure from Mauchline
at a time when she would most naturally have wished
to stay. It would explain all this pother over Bibles and the
performance of oaths—which could well be an attempt
on the poor girl's part to tie down her lover; Burns was
fresh from a somewhat disconcerting experience of the
value of binding documents which a pair of Armour
scissors could (as he thought) turn to wastepaper in five
minutes; he was hardly likely of his own volition to commit
himself quite so soon to a set of new ones. It would explain,
or strengthen, the lure of Jamaica and why he contemplated—if he did seriously contemplate—the necessity of
taking Mary out there with him; and more especially it
would explain why the entire Jamaican plan was dropped
like a coal after the news of Mary Campbell's death and
no more heard of. It would explain Burns's reticence over
what was a really terrible story; and still more so, the
remorse—not grief, *remorse*—with which in nostalgic
moments, he recalled her name. It would explain Currie's
delicatesse over matters 'improper to reveal', and the evasive

taciturnity of the Burns family. It would explain the
violent anti-Burns attitude of the Campbells, burning
letters and defacing Bibles,[22] which otherwise is really
rather difficult to account for, let Highland pride be what
it will; presumably they knew nothing of the Armour
complications, and even if they did, why should they be so
bitterly opposed to the courtship of their daughter by a
presentable young Ayrshire farmer? Sympathy, not fury,
should have been their normal reaction when that
daughter died—unless they believed the lover in some
way to blame for the disaster. And it would explain, or
help to explain, Burns's state of hysterical excitement and
anxiety during the summer and autumn of 1786; it would
explain that outburst to Aiken, on the 8th October of that
year—incidentally a fine specimen of his crescendos—that
even his gaiety was 'the madness of an intoxicated
criminal under the hands of the executioners'. The consequences of his follies 'may make it impractible' for him to
stay at home; the storm of mischief is thickening over his
folly-devoted head; 'inimical circumstances' may render
it beyond his power to reap the fruits of Aiken's friendly
efforts on his behalf. What follies; what circumstances;
what mischief; and why the 'mays'—unless there was
something still to be disclosed? That could not now apply
to the Armour affair; bad as it was, he had been through
the worst of that; Jean, when he wrote to Aiken, had
successfully borne her twins; the Armours were no more
implacable than they had been; they had taken out their
warrant and he had dodged it; they had destroyed his
paper of marriage long since and he had secured his
certificate of bachelorhood; bad as the Armour situation
was, there was nothing much more to come from that
particular airt. But if there was *another* secret marriage of
which nobody knew or must know; if the partner to that
transaction was also to give it away, and soon, by an
inevitable physical reaction; if despite all his single-man
certificates, there was more than a case in Scots law—
as his lawyer friends could have told him—for a charge of
bigamy against one Robert Burns; then indeed the

situation was pretty desperate. It matters little whether Mary was Angellier's Beatrice or Henley's 'light-skirts'; Burns's position was equally bad either way. Yes, taking it all in all, there would be a pretty strong case for supposing that Burns and Mary had gone to extremes even if no infant's coffin-board had ever been dug up out of the Clydeside gravel.

Well—*solvitur ambulando*. Mary Campbell died in Greenock—of a malignant fever, aggravated quite possibly by that premature child of which Mrs. Carswell was so certain; and Peter Macpherson buried her there, doubtless with no reflection on the text 'thy sin shall find thee out'. It is tragic to think that bitter as his grief must have been, galling the remorse for what must have seemed in the retrospect an abominable piece of conduct, the event must have carried for Burns a considerable element of relief. That letter with the news from Greenock—and by the way, who wrote it?—whose receipt so agonised him that October morning at Mossgiel, had good in it as well as bad. Whatever the mess had been, he was out of it. Burns was not one to dwell on past blunders—or learn from them; he recovered his spirits rapidly, forgot about Jamaica and rode off to Edinburgh. Highland Mary's memory was left to the traditions of Ayr and Greenock, to the 'Mariolaters', to W. E. Henley and the moods of Burns, which, as has been shown, were various.

When Robert Burns married—or remarried—Jean Armour with the blessing of the Kirk in 1788 he at least knew, much better than most men in his position, what he was getting. She had already borne him with startling rapidity two sets of twins, of which the second was conceived while she was still suckling the first; and though one child only out of the four—the original boy of Set One—now survived, this may be called a tolerably close pre-nuptial association and a reasonably adequate trial run. They had been off and on, in and out of irregular marriages, for the past two years or more. It could be said therefore that neither of them was taking on a pig in a poke. The times and seasons also seemed propitious; the Armour parents, at one time implacably obstructive, had been sycophantically reconciled to the returned Edinburgh lion, and were now furious with their daughter not —as they had been—because she wished to marry Burns, but because she continued to allow him the full freedom of her body while he showed no signs of wishing to marry *her*. Burns had indulged in what Linklater calls his 'Sabbatical year'; save for the dubious promise of Ellisland and the more solid hope of a post in the Excise, the Edinburgh adventure had fizzled out; at nine-and-twenty he might well settle down to domesticity—and what better companion could he find than one already so thoroughly tried and tested? On the face of it, therefore, the marriage seems a perfectly natural, happy-ever-after denouement to the story; yet taken in its context, it is one of the most extraordinary and perplexing things that even Burns ever did. It involves a *volte-face* so sudden and complete as to be, on the known facts, inexplicable.

Jean Armour was one of the eleven children of a master mason in Mauchline; her father, a solemn, churchy and respected citizen, did also some little business as a contractor—though he was hardly the 'architect' Burns made him when he desired to impress his patrons. Jean, who was to enjoy by far the longest run of all Burns's loves and alone among them was to have the opportunity—and the courage—to set up house with him, began the acquaintance early. The account of their first meeting, soon after Burns and Gilbert came to Mossgiel, and while Burns was still in that mood of emancipation and adventure that followed his father's death, is one of those Burns stories which have become incorporated in his Gospel because they are credible and because we would like to believe them. Burns had attended a dance where he was something of a wallflower; his collie dog suddenly appeared upon the scene and he was heard to remark that he wished he could find a lass who would love him as did his

JEAN ARMOUR
(Mrs. Burns)

dog. A day or two later he was crossing the village clothes-green when he was hailed by a sparkling brunette with a most enticing figure and asked whether he had yet found such a lass. It is a pleasant little story and may quite well be true—though Jean's own version of it was different. If truth it be, then Jean Armour, like Clarinda, made the first advance; like Clarinda's, it was eagerly taken up; soon Jean and Robert were coupled after the fashion of the village men and maidens. Pregnancy in any woman enjoying Burns's intimate acquaintance was only a matter of time; March of 1786 was not out when Jean's mother was horrified to learn of her daughter's condition and its author, being at the same time obliged to run for a cordial for her husband, who had fainted on hearing the distressing news. Mrs. Armour made some valiant attempt to lie the facts out of existence, but the redoubtable Holy Willie[23] was on the scent; it was no good—the cat would out. According to the Minutes of the Mauchline Kirk Session dated 18th June 1786, Jean Armour wrote that she was 'humbly sorry' to trouble them, but was obliged to acknowledge that 'I am with child and Robert Burns in Mossgiel is the father'; she was, with great respect, their most humble servant. (Those tyrannical Gestapo bodies; how did Scots ever put up with them!) This succinct announcement was presently confirmed by Burns, 'compearing' on 25th June. The interval between March and June is accounted for by the fact that Jean Armour had been shipped off to relations in Paisley—perhaps in the forlorn hope that a young gentleman of that city who had shown her some attentions in the past and to whom she had seemed not ill disposed might perhaps be induced to marry her and shoulder the coming brat as his own. If this was the hope, it failed; all that the Paisley treatment achieved was Burns's violent fury, because, as he regarded it, his Jean had 'deserted' him.

She had deserted him indeed, and deserted her written bond as well; for she and he had already got themselves into a very pretty legal entanglement. At some unknown time before or after she became pregnant Burns had given Jean a document which he was wont to refer to afterwards as 'the unlucky paper'. The document may or may not have been witnessed by his friend Smith and may or may not have been delivered at some sort of legal ceremony; it is immaterial. Precisely what it purported to convey we do not know, for it has long long since been lost or destroyed; but, to be any use, it must have been one of two things—either a promise of marriage or an acknowledgment that they regarded themselves as married already. The broad practical Scots law of the day, designed to cope with a nation of just such reckless hedonists as Burns and Armour, would have made no material distinction between these alternatives; nor would it, indeed, have cared a fig about the document itself, concentrating on the fact and admission of agreement without further proofs. Armour *père*, however, being an honest mason and contractor, had no knowledge of legal subtleties; he thought he was putting all to rights by extracting the document from his terrified and docile daughter and mutilating it by cutting out the names. In this he was aided and abetted by Aiken, Burns's lawyer friend, who had custody of the paper and may have thought—though he should have known his law better— that he was doing Burns a good turn. Burns himself took the Armour view—though he may have revised that later on; he thought everything was undone and cancelled, and a very grievously hurt and offended and angry man he was. He spoke of the 'damnable conduct' of his betrothed, but admitted that Aiken 'cut my very veins with the news'. For a time he oscillated in his correspondence between abuse of Jean and lamentations for his loss; but as to their future relations he was quite decided. 'Against two things,' he wrote to Smith at the end of July 1786, 'I am fixed as Fate; staying at home and owning her conjugally. The first by Heaven I will not do! the last, by Hell I will never do!' Well—'never', as the Scots proverb says, 'is a long word'. Meanwhile, as a counter-irritant, he turned more warmly to Highland Mary. Such at least is the version of his family—of his brother

Gilbert and of his grandnephew Robert Burns-Begg.[24] But if the suppositions we were considering some pages ago are correct, he must already have turned to Highland Mary in the warmest way possible to humanity. If Mary Campbell had a child, however premature, in October of 1786, and if Jean Armour had (as she certainly did have) twins in September of the same year, it is clear that for some overlapping period each of them must have carried a Burns embryo in her womb.

On the third of September 1786 Jean's first set of twins arrived—a boy and a girl; the latter was to succumb at fourteen months, an event which drew from Burns the paternal expression in a letter to Richmond: 'I hear I am a girl out of pocket . . . which has provoked and vexed me a good deal.' The boy Robert—perhaps because he was sent at once to Mossgiel, where they understood about children—put up a better fight and lived for seventy-one years. Burns is said to have been greatly moved by the sight of his offspring on Jean's maternal breast—though he wrote of it elegantly: 'Armour has brought me a fine boy and girl at one throw', and 'poor Armour has repaid my amorous mortgages double'. But his mind was elsewhere; he was just departing for Jamaica—or was it to be Edinburgh?—with or without Highland Mary—he didn't seem at all clear. No wonder he became, during this period, slightly hysterical. Many problems, however, were presently solved by Highland Mary's death; Burns went off to the literary deities of Edinburgh and away, one would have thought, for ever from his village goddess. But he hankered back; in the course of his Scottish tours in the early summer of 1787 he could not resist the temptation to show himself at Mauchline and to show himself to Jean; naturally the poor girl immediately became pregnant once more. It is possible that the Armours, whose new 'servility' he deplored, threw her at his head in hopes; if so they were hoist, for he rode away back to Edinburgh (and—if he had known it—to Clarinda) adhering to the resolution he had already expressed so vehemently to Smith. Burns's

brother Gilbert and his sister Isabel were later to suggest
that Jean had been habitually unfaithful to her lover
during his absence in Edinburgh—perhaps with the
Paisley weaver, perhaps with others; but after all, that
was a matter in which he was very much in a glass house
and could throw few stones. The Armours vented their
spleen upon their daughter; they refused to shelter her
during this second disgrace. Burns, on learning of this
about Christmas-time, was moved to do his best for her;
he arranged with his friend Muir to give her sanctuary at
Tarbolton Mill till his injured leg—and his Clarinda—
would allow him to leave Edinburgh for Mauchline.
Eventually he did leave Edinburgh for Mauchline, which
he reached, in leisurely fashion, on 23rd February 1788,
and he did arrange a room and a doctor and some comforts
for Jean. He also found time to write the letter to Clarinda
about farthing tapers, insipidity, vulgarity and the rest.

Jean's second set of twins made their punctual appearance at the beginning of March; both this time died
within a matter of days—an event for which Burns, on
his own showing, may have been partly responsible. On
the very day of Jean's confinement her 'husband' wrote a
letter about her to his friend Ainslie which Hecht—with
extraordinary forbearance and understatement—describes as 'downright elementary unsurpassable vulgarity';
it was much worse than that; it is—in all the circumstances
—one of the most caddish letters ever penned by mortal
man. He followed it up a few days later with a quasi-
facetious communication to his friend Richard Brown
which is in its own way nearly as tasteless.[25] He then
went back to Edinburgh for a few days, where he had
some pleasant walks and whatnot with Clarinda; and
then, returning to Mauchline, proceeded within the
month to marry the woman of whom he had just been
writing as he could hardly have written of a common
harlot or a tinker's slut! It is this *volte-face* which I have
called inexplicable on the known facts, and I should like
to return to it in some detail when we come to the section
of this book called 'Riddles'.[25] Meanwhile let us record

and pigeonhole the staggering fact. Burns went on to
announce to several of his friends, first that he was 'privately' and then that he was 'legally' married to Jean;
and on 5th August 1788 the Mauchline Kirk Session
recorded that the erring pair 'compeared', acknowledged
their irregular marriage in the past, expressed their
regrets and requested a solemn confirmation of wedlock.
The Session agreed that 'they be taken solemnly engaged
to adhere faithfully to one another as husband and wife all
the days of their life'. No scandal was to attach, and
Burns sealed the matter by the customary guinea to the
poor.

The happy couple had already spent some weeks
together in rooms in Mauchline, in the course of which
Burns wrote that odd letter to Mrs. Dunlop in which he
proclaimed himself an equal stranger to jealousy and
infidelity. He also devised a number of formulae in which
to explain his marriage further to his friends; even he
seems to have thought it required some explaining. He
sent out these apologia to a variety of correspondents—
Brice, Beugo, Andrew Dunlop and Geddes. He sat down,
too, to talking himself into a belief that he had done a very
good thing for himself; 'wedlock was what in a few seasons
I must have resolved on: in the present case it was un-
avoidably necessary. Humanity, Generosity etc, etc, all
joined to a rooted Attachment to urge the step. Nor have
I any reason on her part to rue it. I can fancy *how* but
have never seen *where*, I could have made it better.' And
he tells his friends how satisfied he is with Jean. But does
the ordinary happy and satisfied bridegroom sit down to
reason with himself on paper like this?

At Whitsun Burns entered Ellisland in earnest; there,
six months later, when a house had been built, his bride
followed him—though even then the house was not ready
and they had to live for some time at a place called the
Isle. Presently Young Robert was brought from Mossgiel,
and a little later he was joined by a newly arrived brother,
Francis Wallace Burns, who was, alas! to live for only
fourteen years. The more tenacious William Nicol Burns

and James Glencairn Burns, whose prowess in John Company's service was so to gladden their mother's widowed years, appeared in 1791 and 1794 respectively. When Burns moved to Dumfries, Jean—reluctantly, for she hated Dumfries and saw perhaps what was coming— moved with him, and stayed there with him till he died; and then alone for thirty-eight years more, when at last she was laid to rest beside the man she had rallied on Mauchline Green just fifty years earlier. She had suffered from high blood pressure and a series of strokes, the second last of which left her partly paralysed for some time before her death and to some extent dependent on the help of her favourite little granddaughter Sara. She had borne Burns in all nine children, of whom only three—the original twin Robert, William Nicol and James Glencairn—survived to maturity. None of her four girls would stay the course to carry on the title and traditions of Bonnie Jean.

It would be interesting to present a picture of this remarkable woman whose hold on Burns was so strong that, despite all his explicit contempt and abuse of her, he took her under his roof for life. No portrait of her exists or is known till she had become a grandmother, when there are two—one by Mackenzie, complete with well-grown grandchild Sara, the other by Gilfillan; needless to say, as in all Burns portraits, the two contradict one another. The Mackenzie shows a strong, careworn, tragic-heroine's face with heavily chiselled, almost gypsy features: the Gilfillan (which, in fact, depicts a Jean seven years younger) a much chubbier, doucer body—and incidentally a more credible version of a woman who was, of all things, comfortable and submissive; one can hardly see the Mackenzie Jean taking in Anna Park's bastard with the resigned remark that Robbie should hae had twa wives. The only points on which the two portraits agree are the ringletty black hair, the brilliant black eyes and the pursed, rather disapproving—and no wonder!— mouth. There is also a silhouette by W. Seville, practically contemporaneous with the Mackenzie picture, but supporting rather the Gilfillan; the profile is flattish with a wide space between mouth and nose, which last is ever so slightly retroussé; there is no sign of the uncompromising beak down and over which the Mackenzie lady stares so broodingly. The artists having failed us, we must fall back upon the pen-portraits of those who met her; these are pleasantly laudatory, slightly patronising and but feebly illuminating. Mrs. Dunlop found her 'in rosy bloom' and was delighted with the 'cheerful openness of her countenance, the intelligence of her eyes, and her easy modest unaffected manners'. Ramsay of Ochtertyre, dropping in at Ellisland and keeping up the current Horatian ideal, was 'pleased with [Burns's] uxor Sabina qualis'; Mrs. Grant of Laggan thought her, at fifty-five, 'a very comely woman with plain sound sense and very good manners'; her house was 'a model of neatness and good taste'. She was neat, too, in her person and at times dressy—in the Ellisland days she went to church in black silk stockings, a lace collar, kid gloves and a brooch of pebbles set in gold; the allegation that she became slovenly rests mainly on some statements made by Jessy Lewars to Chambers; a certain untidiness in such a household as hers would surely have been excusable. McDiarmid, who conversed with her so tirelessly in her widowhood, lamented that he came upon the scene too late to see her dance, but testified that her 'wood-note wild', to which her husband so frequently alluded, could live up to his claims for it; it was a 'brilliant treble' and 'rose without effort as high as B natural'.

It has become conventional to call Jean Armour the great love of Burns's life, and he himself frequently asserted that she was. One can only remark that if this were so he had an odd way of showing it. Indeed, it is difficult to accept the statement in any exalted sense—even in any understood sense—of the word 'love'. In his letters she is— or was right up to the marriage—too often alluded to in terms contemptuous or worse; she is 'poor Armour', 'poor unfortunate Armour'; he doubts if he shall ever meet with 'so delicious an armful' again; and 'my Rib begs her compliments to you' seems hardly quite the way to refer to one's wife when sending an order to a Glasgow grocer.

These, if hardly the language of love, are harmless enough; but there is worse than that. At the time when his 'love' for her was supposedly at its purest he wrote a long letter to Arnot of Dalquhatswood of which he thought so well that he transcribed it six years later for the Glenriddell collection—and indeed it is a very good and amusing if rather a showing-off letter. Although the damned star has long kept his zenith—and so forth —he has for some time been looking for a wife. There follows a string of quite good *double entendres*—which would be well enough if the person referred to was not quite obviously Miss Armour—all about stones, holes, 'a practicable breach behind the curtin in the gorge of the very principal bastion', about escaping with only 'bare bayonet and cartridge pouch' and so on. Worse still was to come; the letter in which he sent his Mauchline news in March of 1788 to Ainslie was, as I have already said, simply unspeakable. I am quoting it—reluctantly, because I like Burns—on p. 222 below; read it and tell me if it could conceivably have been written by a man who had any 'love' or even respect for its subject. It is possible to say that the earlier items in this list were mere pique at Jean's supposed desertion of him or mere bravado designed to impress his correspondent for the time being along the lines most likely to succeed; even so, the taste would still be execrable, and in any case how could pique or bravado so overcome and shout down a 'love' such as Burns is credited with feeling for Jean? It is true that once the marriage was a *fait accompli*, he devised more tender formulae in which to refer to her; but formulae they are— or at any rate sound; they come off with the ring of a lesson learned by heart. That Burns once loved Jean Armour—after his fashion of loving—is certain enough; but it is hard to believe that by the spring of 1788, when they 'compeared' before the Session to have their irregular marriage recognised, he had not long outgrown that love in everything but a purely physical sense. One is left asking vainly: 'Why did he marry her? And *why*, of all times, just then?'[25]

Exalted conjugal sentiments should not perhaps be
expected from a man who, at five-and-twenty, could write
to John Tennant of Glenconner that a certain lady's
'portion' was three hundred pounds; 'and then to have a
woman to lye with when one pleases without running any
risk of the cursed expence [*sic*] of bastards and all the
concomitants of that species of smuggling'.[26] And in any
case, it will be urged, the marriage was none the less
and in fact a success. So it was in the sense that any
marriage must be moderately successful—in an un-
ambitious way—where one partner completely dominates.
Whether or not Burns remained in love with Jean,
Jean must have remained besottedly in love with him.
He could do no wrong; he went unquestioned and
accepted, whatever excesses he thought fit to commit.
Within these limits the marriage was no doubt successful;
but they *are* limits of a very circumscribing sort; a man
such as Burns might have looked for a very different kind
of partnership from this animal sharing of a den. He
married at the crisis of his life, when he required of all
things a stimulant; he obtained an opiate instead—an
opiate he no doubt enjoyed and which his partner was
well equipped to supply, but an opiate none the less. It
has been said that the physical delights of Jean wore out
his mind and his faculties; that they certainly did not do—
for these were never worn out—but perhaps they helped
to kill his poetry. As he wrote to Sillar after a year or so of
wedlock, 'I know not whether the Nine Gipsys are jealous
of my Lucky, but they are a good deal shier since I could
boast the important relation of a husband.' A month or
two later he had the curious fit of nostalgia which produced the poem commonly called (though never by
Burns himself) 'To Mary in Heaven'. There comes on a
curious little series of anti-marriage poems—henpecked
husbands, termagant cuckolding or ugly wives—of insignificant merit, but perhaps significant in content. In
plain fact—despite his occasional protests to the contrary
—the marriage, like most marriages, was no more
successful than one might have hoped it would be; and
in this case that is not saying very much.

A number of people, perhaps wishfully thinking, have attempted to depict Jean as the ideal companion for Burns; 'She and she alone', says Robert Burns-Begg for instance, 'was capable of acting the part of Burns's *alter ego*.' What on earth *was* or could have been Burns's '*alter ego*'? One's imagination soars—soars—crashes—in trying to picture the woman who could have filled that ambitious role. Burns never met her—that much is certain. And in any case, how could Jean Armour have been to him the ideal counterpart and companion—except in that purely physical sense of which he never seemed to tire? (He could, on his own admission, attack her when she was eight months gone with child, and she bore him his last infant on the day of his funeral.) In one of his longest apologia for his marriage—that which he wrote to Peggy Chalmers—he depicts himself as having won not polite tattle, modish manners, fashionable dress, 'the multiform curse of boarding-school affectation', but the handsomest figure, sweetest temper, soundest constitution and kindest heart in the country. That is well said; but even so, these qualities were not enough to make an *alter ego* for Robert Burns, and it ill became his grandnephew to say that they were.

That Jean had and was all these things nobody is going to deny; the handsome figure is traditional—and she preserved it, God knows how; the constitution must have been sound indeed; she survived by means of a temper that nothing could sour, ruffle or dismay; and to the heart let one tribute suffice—and that from the source best qualified to utter it, the Anna Park 'Betty Burns': 'There was something good and charitable about her surpassing all women I ever yet met with.' Jean had all these things, and she had no doubt the shrewd sense and practical judgment of her class. But her intellectual attainments must have remained relatively negligible. 'She scarcely ever in her life', wrote Burns to Peggy Chalmers, 'except the Scriptures of the Old and New Testament and the Psalms of David in metre, spent five minutes together on either prose or verse.' No doubt her accomplishments have been over-decried; she was not illiterate, she could do much more than 'just sign her name', as Mrs. Carswell would have it—though it might *per contra* be suggested that she could not do even this, for her signature in the Mauchline Kirk Session Book on 5th August 1788 looks suspiciously like the hand of her husband. Mme Perochon, *née* Agnes Dunlop, would not have dined Sunday after Sunday, after St. Michael's service, with an ignoramus. On the other side, the letters to Thomson in her hand— or in some hand which did not change over a period of years—display an elegance of style and diction which is stretching our credulity too far;[27] someone—Gilbert? Mme Perochon? McDiarmid?—must surely have helped her here. However much, as her grandnephew says, she 'insensibly acquired' during her long widowhood 'by frequent intercourse with families of the first respectability', it could hardly have amounted to these dignified, woman-of-the-world, almost aristocratic letters. One letter of Burns's to her (that one beginning 'My dear love') seems to suggest that she was capable of taking an interest in his Excise intrigues and in his contributions to Thomson's collection of songs; but it is idle to pretend that she could ever have been his intellectual companion, much less his inspiration. Burns was fortunate in a good honourable sweet-tempered wife who kept him within his means when he was alive and stood up for his good name after he was dead; who interpreted literally 'love, honour and obey'; who put up with him with a noble patience—and enjoyed it. But for Robert Louis Stevenson's view of the marriage—that it had no root in nature—there seems much to be said.

[1] *p. 105.* For further discussion of the delicate subject of Burns and Mary Campbell see *infra*, pp. 141-153 and 242-252.

[2] *p. 111.* It was at one time supposed that Elizabeth Paton's child was born in 1784, but the agreement drawn up between Burns and Paton makes it clear that the day of birth was 22nd May 1785. William Burness died in February 1784. Once again, as with Anna Park, the child is the redeeming feature of the story. Dear-bought Bess was brought up at Mossgiel at Burns's expense and drew her £200 from the Fund at her majority. She then married one Bishop the grieve at Polkemmet and had several children, one of whom was able to attend the Glasgow festival in 1859, three-quarters of a century after his grandmother's lapse.

[3] *p. 113.* See her article 'Jessie Lewars, Last of Burns's Heroines', *Burns Chron.*, 1940. The authoress also calls Jessie the 'most satisfactory of Burns's women', which is surely going a little too far; Jessie, at the time when Burns knew her, was not a woman at all—still less a Burns woman.

[4] *p. 113.* Currie spelt this name 'Ellison'. The name appears only as an initial in the drafts of Burns's letters to her quoted—and lost or destroyed—by Currie; in the only surviving MS. the initial is 'A', not 'E'. The discrepancy is immaterial; if her name was Alison, it would be pronounced in Scots either 'All——' or 'Ell——', or with some indefinite Scots vowel between the two. She would have made a suitable enough wife for Burns—supposing, that is, that he ever really sought her; she was a farmer's daughter, though she worked on another farm in a capacity that could be grandly called 'housekeeper'. Burns credited her with 'an education much beyond anything I ever met in any woman I ever dared to approach', and it was said that she could actually read—even handwriting. The evidence connecting her with 'Mary Morison' is negligible. According to the Centenary Edition (Henley and Henderson, 1896) there *was* a girl called Mary Morison in Mauchline at the time.

[5] *p. 115.* See J. de Lancey Ferguson, *The Letters of Robert Burns* (1931).

[6] *p. 118.* See *Robert Burns and Mrs. Dunlop*, the correspondence edited by Wm. Wallace (1898)—the only complete version, so far as I know.

[7] *p. 122.* A good specimen of Mrs. Dunlop's critical acumen combined with humour is in her objection to the line in *The Twa Dogs*, 'They set them down upon their arse'—where the Boeotian word could certainly have been avoided with very little effort. Mrs. Dunlop wrote: '. . . where you describe a dog sitting in the only way a dog could sit, or rather two dogs sitting as they could not possibly sit, both on one tail.' This gem is unfortunately tucked away in a letter of such length and verbosity that Burns may never have reached it.

[8] *p. 123.* For much detail about Maria, relevant and irrelevant to Burns, see an excellent article by the late Sir Hugh Gladstone, *Maria Riddell the Friend of Burns; Trans. Dumfries and Galloway Natural History and Antiquarian Society*, 3rd Series, Vol. 3 (1914-15).

[9] *p. 125.* See infra, p. 231.

[10] *p. 128.* After Walter Riddell's death Maria lived at Hampton Court—probably with Lady Lavington, who had been given rooms there; she was in the running for the post of looking after Prinny's daughter Princess Charlotte, and moved in the 'highest circles'.

[11] *p. 129.* See *The Correspondence of Burns and Clarinda*, W. C. McLehose (1843), to which I am indebted for the details of Clarinda's life story.

[12] *p. 130.* McLehose did not actually start till 1784, when his family finally tired of supporting him and paying his debts. His mother advanced him his fare—and was never repaid.

[13] *p. 134.* Only eleven of Clarinda's poems have survived or were known to her grandson.. They are all in simple rhyming couplets and unpretentiously imitative—'To a Blackbird Singing in a Tree', 'On the Death of Mrs. Ridley's Linnet' and so forth. 'Talk Not of Love' is as good as any of them; none are really bad, except where she essays a theme beyond her compass—as in 'On the Loss of my Child (1788).' Burns's

praise of them need not have been deliberately false; to his generous nature all his geese were swans, and the blindness of love is proverbial.

[14] *p. 135.* The letter of Clarinda's, to which Burns's is obviously a reply, is missing in the correspondence; but in a curious collection of sixteen doctored and 'improved' letters mysteriously published about 1800 there is an item which is evidently a transcript from it. This purports to bear the date 20th December 1787 and runs—'I have proposed to myself a more pastoral name for you . . . although it be not much in keeping with the shrillness of the Ettrick Pipe. What say you to *Sylvander*? I feel somewhat less restraint when I subscribe myself—Clarinda.' Clarinda may have got the name from a love-story published in Edinburgh some twenty years before. (cf. J. C. Ewing, *Burns Chron.* 1934, p. 74).

[15] *p. 139.* The precise date of Ainslie's disclosure is not known, but it would seem that it must have been somewhere between 8th and 28th April 1788. For more on Burns's astonishing marriage, see *infra*, pp. 215-230.

[16] *p. 141.* Burns used the expression for the first and only time in the title of a song he sent to Thomson on 14th November 1792.

[17] *p. 144.* See D. McNaught, *The Truth About Burns* (1921), App. C., and his article 'Highland Mary Chronology' *Burns Chron.*, Vol. XXIV (cf. Chambers, *Life and Works of Robert Burns*, edited Wm. Wallace (1896), Vol. I, App VIII).

[18] *p. 146.* See F. B. Snyder, *The Life of Robert Burns* (1932), pp. 129 *et sqq.* See also D. McNaught, 'Highland Mary, a Summation', *Burns Chron.*, Vol XIX, and 'Highland Mary Chronology', *Burns Chron.*, Vol. XXIV.

[19] *p. 148.* See Allan Bayne, 'The West Highland Tour and Highland Mary', *Burns Chron.*, Vol. XV, from which my data re the Campbell family are also taken.

[20] *p. 149.* I follow what seems to be the best authority in taking these suspect notes on the song 'My Highland Lassie' as genuine. *Will ye go to the Indies* was a substitution for a song

Thomson disliked; it was written 'in my very early years when I was *thinking of going* to the West Indies'; it was 'quite trifling' (Burns), and Thomson rejected it as a 'very poor song', as indeed it is. Four months before *Thou Lingering Star*, Burns sent Mrs. Dunlop the mournful and *à propos* 'Elegy on Stella', which (*pace* Scott Douglas and others) he probably did *not* write.

[21] *p. 150.* See *infra*, pp. 242-252.

[22] *p. 152.* Someone indubitably did deface the Bible. Campbell's burning of letters and refusal to hear Burns's name mentioned rest naturally on less substantial evidence. They were stated, however—and without subsequent contradiction—by John Kerr in the *Scots Times* as long ago as 1827, when there must have been many persons in the West of Scotland from whom the author could have got his facts, and many who could have come forward to the contrary had his statements been palpably wrong.

[23] *p. 155.* Burns's own prose description of Holy Willie (William Fisher) is too good to omit; 'A rather oldish bachelor elder in the parish of Mauchline, and much and justly famed for that polemical chattering which ends in tippling orthodoxy, and for that spiritualised bawdry which refines to liquorish devotion.'

[24] *p. 157.* See his article 'Bonnie Jean', *Burns Chron.*, Vol. I.

[25] *p. 158.* For a further discussion of Burns's marriage with extracts from these letters, see *infra*, pp. 215-230.

[26] *p. 163.* The refrain in his own *Broom Besoms*—'I maun hae a wife, whatsoe'er she be; An she be woman, that's eneugh for me'—has a curiously personal application!

[27] *p. 165.* For a summary of these letters see 'Some Addenda to the Thomson Correspondence', *Burns Chron.*, Vol. VIII, p. 46.

PART FOUR

BURNS THE WRITER

I

PROSE

BURNS always believed that he could write a play; the Autobiographical Letter to Moore is proof that he could have written a novel; when he had shed some of his more ponderous models he would have given us many pleasant if not very profound essays; as a critic he would have been, if partial, refreshingly outspoken. Of all these might-have-beens not one has materialised. Burns's prose works as we know them consist of the Journals of his Scottish tours, his two Commonplace Books (so-called) and seven hundred and odd Letters which fortune—or the foresight of their owners—has preserved and industrious scholarship has edited. Buried and scattered among these last is the finest and best-informed critique of Scottish song-writing ever put on paper; but its exponent never seems to have thought of extracting and assembling and amplifying the disjointed fragments. The play and the essays—which he *did* think of—remain for ever unwritten.

Of the prose works that survive, the Journals and the Commonplace Books are of minor interest; the former are merely a series of jottings or notes, sometimes in ink sometimes in pencil, often bearing witness in their shaky handwriting to the jolting of the carriage in which they were scribbled down. They would seem to have been memoranda for an extended account of these expeditions which Burns never sat down to write;[1] they begin ambitiously, but degenerate rapidly into an itinerary: 'Came through mist and darkness to Dulsie to lie. . . . Came on to Castle Cawdor. . . . Saw the bed in which King Duncan was stabbed. . . . Elgin to breakfast, meet with Mr. ——, a pleasant sort of man. . . . Came to Kinross to lie. . . . Reflections in a fit of the Colic.' Here and there a woman catches more than a passing word, like the young lady at Carlisle who, 'seeing me a little cut with the bottle', suggested a move to Gretna Green; she was given, however, 'a brush of caressing and a bottle of cyder', found herself '*un peu trompée*' in her man and 'sheered off'. Of the Harviestoun expedition in pursuit of Miss Chalmers there is no journal at all—though rumour has a pleasant story of Adair posing on the cutty stool in Dunfermline Abbey while Burns thunders at him from the pulpit. Burns carried out these pilgrimages to the 'sights' of the country to which he was so devoted ostensibly and explicitly in search of inspiration, yet curiously enough he was inspired by them to nothing of any value. He seems indeed to have been altogether a home bird; transplanted from his 'ancient Baileries of Carrick, Kyle and Cunningham', he did not thrive and drew no stimulus at all. It is perhaps therefore as well that he refused that tempting offer to go to London; if Edinburgh so reduced his flow, the great wen might have withered him altogether.

Of his first Commonplace Book something has already been said. The second of the two—or such of it as has survived—is of meagre interest; its life was short and it consists almost entirely of a few sketches of notables he met in Edinburgh, and his Ellisland attempt to talk himself into a contented husband. (It must be remembered, however, that much of the manuscript is lost and we are left only with selections.) Even the first book is attractive not so much for the sentiments he set down in it, which are often pompous and trite, as for the naïve and charming young man who shines through them and the indications they give of what was to come. The thought 'it might be possible for a Scotch Poet, with a nice, judicious ear to set compositions to many of our most favourite airs' was indeed to bear remarkable fruit. And there is much self-revelation in 'I never had the least thought or inclination of turning Poet till I got me heartily in Love, and then Rhyme and Song were, in a manner, the spontaneous language of my heart'. If the Books were to be—as he says in the second of them—his 'confident' [*sic*], they are curiously cannily written; one feels there was at least a hope that some of their more sententious 'Observations and Hints'—as, for instance, the dissertation on love in Number One—would be seen by other eyes: 'Notwithstanding all that has been said against Love . . . still I think it, in a great measure, deserves the highest encomiums that have been passed upon it.' But beyond some useful sidelights on Burns's character, the student will get little from either the Journals or the Commonplace Books. We are left with the seven hundred Letters—which are quite a different story.[2]

Many of Burns's admirers and critics pride themselves on their extreme modernity when they declare that his prose writings are at least comparable—if not superior— to his verse. This is often said as if it were a new and daring discovery; it is, of course, nothing of the kind. That alert young woman Maria Riddell, always quickly off the mark, wrote within a fortnight of his death: 'Poetry is not actually his *forte*'; and she added in her Diary four years later: 'His letters are the finest things of the kind, in their own peculiar strong enthusiastic way, that have been given to the public for a long while. Some persons have preferred his prose to his poetry; I think the greater part of both excellent.' Among those 'persons' was as well-qualified a judge as Principal Robertson of Edinburgh University, who rated Burns's output in this order—talk, prose, poetry. There is nothing new in the discovery that Burns could write good prose. And it would be strange if Burns's letters were not well written, for he took immense pains with them; he drafted and copied them and the final fair-copy often shows many emendations; and if this were done partly as a literary exercise, there was perhaps one eye on posterity as well.

Burns's idea of a letter was *always* a literary exercise. 'Surely,' he wrote to brother William, 'writing a handsome letter is an accomplishment worth courting'? He courted the accomplishment himself assiduously—though he was less eager to pursue that virtue of taciturnity which he enjoined on William in the same letter. 'Answer a letter?'

he wrote to Ainslie. 'I never could answer a letter in my life!—I have written many a letter in return for letters I have received; but then—they were original matter—spurt—away! Zig here; zag there; as if the Devil that my grannie . . . often told me, rode on Will-o'-Wisp, or, in her more classic phrase, SPUNKIE, were looking over my elbow.' This, besides being an excellent example of Burns's letter-writing at its best, is in part truth; no doubt, few of his carefully prepared letters were really written on 'Will-o'-Wisp' principles, but he spoke truly when he said he never wrote them as replies. He never regarded a letter as a personal, practical communication of everyday necessities; when he felt the need to expound his current feelings or opinions, or to announce—with objects and reasons—a cardinal development in his affairs, he chose a selected correspondent—often a very odd one—and let fly. With the exception of Mrs. Dunlop there was no one to whom he wrote regularly over a period of years; and even she persisted only because she could be depended upon to remain static and because she was, he found, a stimulating personality to whom he wrote his best. Letter-exchanging as a method of 'keeping in touch' was an idea altogether strange to his mind; and this at times gave pain to his friends—as when poor Clarinda, neglected after his departure from Edinburgh, wrote 'a word would have done' and deplored the necessity he felt of 'doing justice' to his letters. But justice to them he would do—or he would not write them at all; he would not sit down to a letter unless he had the time and the inclination to make a real literary job of it. Often and often he made far too literary a job of it altogether; his best letters—which are all too few—are those dashed off in a moment of gaiety or tantrums. Would that he had written more of them.

Everybody knows the story of how Burns's Uncle Robert—feckless old fellow—was sent from Lochlie to Ayr to buy a copy of *The Complete Letter-Writer* and how he came back bearing instead a *Collection of Letters of the Wits of Queen Anne's Reign*—which may or may not have been by Pope. *Faute de mieux*, the Wits had to serve young Burns as a model; although—as he could not know—their beautifully balanced antitheses were already outmoded. As Professor Ferguson has pointed out, *Masson's Collection of English Prose and Verse*—a book which played an inestimable part in Burns's literary development—contained specimen letters by the ladylike and sanctimonious Mrs. Rowe; we find, therefore, Mrs. Rowe blending, at times somewhat incongruously, with the Wits. Of the copy-book productions which resulted Jeffrey could say with fairness that they were 'composed as exercises or for display'. Fortunately, however, there are moments when both models are forgotten and the natural Burns gives us a chance to see what he could do.

Burns was a methodical correspondent; Currie found among those 'sweepings of his desk' a holograph list of letters addressed to him, some three hundred in number; Currie diligently catalogued these with a précis of their contents which has unfortunately been destroyed by the ravages of time and damp. It was possibly from his own original list that Burns selected the target for any particular bulletin he had in view; the choice seems sometimes arbitrary. (Why, for instance, so many and so candid details of the Jean affair in 1786 to David Brice? Why elaborate apologia for his marriage to Andrew Dunlop or the Rev. Mr. Geddes?) There necessarily follows from this a quality in Burns's letters which has been noted by everyone who has read them—his acute consciousness of the audience he was for the moment addressing. This at times led him into serious error; as, for instance, in the letters he wrote to Ainslie and Brown about Jean in March of 1788 and the earlier 'showing-off' letter to Arnot of Dalquhatswood, all of which have already been cited. His most fervent admirers have been forced to admit that in his letters he 'accommodated his words to expectations'.[3] The fault is not a serious one—it is a thing we all of us do to some extent; but it imposes a caveat on taking the self-expression of his letters at face value; one must always look first at the address on the outside. Between an outward eye on the addressee and an inward eye on his own mood for the time being, Burns—so often hailed as the 'natural man'—too often made himself incapable of being natural at all.

Quite apart, of course, from this audience-consciousness are those letters—fortunately not very many—which he wrote for the express purpose of cajoling, entreating or—let us put it frankly—toadying. From occasional manifestations of these his boasted 'independence' did not save him; and the resultant letters are among his worst. After the best Scriptural example, he brought forth butter in a lordly dish, and it would be difficult to say which is the more repellant, the dish or the butter. He could write the most dreadful bombast to John Kennedy on the 'little Angels to whom he (Kennedy) has given existence'; had the Earl of Eglinton sent him a thousand guineas instead of ten, he could hardly have merited the raptures with which the poet received his donation; while McMurdo of Drumlanrig (who had merely asked for a copy of some verses) was belauded as if for an act of life-saving generosity. The bread-and-butter letter he wrote to Josiah Walker after his visit to Athol is almost painful to read; one shudders at the 'little angel band' . . . 'the amiable, the truly noble Dutchess [sic] with her smiling little seraphs in her lap'—those little seraphs who were the 'future hope of Caledonia'. Even Willie Dunbar's nieces are raised to the rank of 'seraphs and angels'—unlikely qualities if the children took at all after their uncle. To Glencairn and Fintry—to whom he was really indebted for genuine kindness and help—he could be positively grovelling. A man who could carry his creed of independence to the point of boorishness should have been above these contortions of humility or the fawning archness which sometimes took their place.

A curious consequence of all his drafting and revising and fair-copying was the formulae—one can only call them that—which appear time after time in his letters. In his careful composition he every now and then struck out some phrase which particularly pleased him and on which he thought he could not improve; he then broad-

cast it to any of his correspondents to whom he happened
to be writing on a kindred topic. These phrases reappear
with such exactitude over considerable intervals of time
that one is tempted to believe that he kept a list of them;
or perhaps he only looked up previous drafts; they were
not involuntary or unconscious, for he told Mrs. Dunlop:
'Indeed, when I write from the heart, I am apt to be
guilty of these repetitions.' The truth was rather the
reverse. An outstanding example of this was the formula
he devised in which to communicate the bombshell news
of his sudden and belated marriage; its original and
grandiose form appears in a letter to Johnson on 25th
May 1788, which runs: 'I found I had a long and much-
loved fellow creature's happiness and misery among my
hands; and though Pride and seeming Justice were
murderous King's Advocates on the one side, yet Humanity, Generosity and Forgiveness were such perfect such
irresistible Counsel on the other side, that a Jury of old
Endearments and new attachments brought in a un-
animous verdict—Not Guilty!' In one form or another,
this did duty successively for Andrew Dunlop, Cunningham, Peggy Chalmers, Geddes and James Burness, the
interval between the first use of it and the last being nearly
nine months. Again, the damned squinting star that held
his zenith was first devised for Arnot of Dalquhatswood
in 1785 or 1786; it reappears almost verbatim three years
later. Those of his correspondents whom he was approaching for a favour must have become accustomed to hearing
that he asked in faith nothing wavering. He more than
once announced his return from Edinburgh to his
'shades' (or 'rural shades') with the rider that his Edinburgh friendships were of so tender a construction that
they would not bear carriage. Her 'woodnote wild' is an
essential element in almost any description of his wife
from 1789 onwards. And there are other instances. There
is no harm in it; Burns would doubtless argue: 'Having
said a thing well once, why say it worse the second time?'
True; but stock phrases and sincerity do not go very well
together.

M   177

And, of course, if someone else has said a thing as well as it can be said, why not use that? Burns had a positive mania for quotations; he almost *must* have kept a note-book of these on his desk, for he told Clarinda, in a letter containing four of them: 'I like to have quotations ready for every occasion; they give one's ideas so pat and save one the trouble of finding expression adequate to one's feelings.' Five days later he sent Clarinda a letter which is almost solid quotation and is one of the most artificial things he ever wrote in his life. To Mrs. Dunlop he wrote that he treasured quotations as 'ready armour, offensive and defensive'; and again later: 'My favourite quotation now, for I always have one. . . .' A very interesting sidelight on Burns's life might be thrown by tracing the series of 'favourite quotations' that creep into his letters from time to time. We have seen the irruption of the Miltonic Satan with his 'Hail, horrors! Hail, infernal world!'—a rather uncomplimentary reference to Mauchline, whence, in mid-1787, this was first issued. The Fallen Angel, that unquestionable product of Edinburgh, was to reappear at frequent intervals. Job, wishing his adversary might write a book, was a godsend on several occasions—as he has been to every writer since his day. For a time Burns was very fond of Blair's line 'dark as chaos ere the infant sun'. When he was writing to a superior, Kent 'gave his ideas pat' when he told Lear there was 'that in his face he could like to call master'; if Clarinda was not 'dear as the ruddy drops that warm my heart', she was 'dear as the light that visits those sad eyes'; and when he sought—unnecessarily and dis-ingenuously—to excuse himself for accepting a post in the Excise, he found the long quotation from Thomson's *Edward and Eleonora* beginning 'The valiant in himself, what can he suffer' most helpful and an excellent opening for some relevant pathos about his 'train of helpless little folks'. But towards the end all these 'favourite quotations' crystallised into two: 'On Reason build Resolve, that column of true majesty in man', and 'What proves the hero truly great Is never, never to despair'—and it cannot

be said that he failed to live up to them. If he sometimes
took Resolve for accomplishment, Despair was a word he
did not countenance.

One reason for liberal quoting is the very sound one
that Burns gave; another, of course, is to show one's
erudition. Burns was not without his little bits of pretentiousness—like those cheap French tags[4] with which he
interlarded his letters to Peggy Chalmers and for which
she so meanly requited him. He employed them on other
occasions when he sought to impress—on three successive
pages of the Autobiographical Letter he has 'l'adorable
moitié du genre humain', a 'charming fillette' and 'a
belle-fille whom I adored'; it seems as if he simply could
not bring himself to write the word 'girl'. Big heavy-
weight English words would do nearly as well, as when he
told young Niven (in the Lochlie days, in the course of
what was to be a very highbrow literary correspondence,
but died an early death) that his mind was 'hebetated',
and described himself as a 'Physiognomist'; or in those
wonderful Pope-encrusted letters to Alison Begbie (if they
were to Begbie) and young Orr. These conceits died out as
he grew older; and, of course, quite apart from these
bogus bits of learning, he had a real erudition which is at
times positively startling. In that same celebrated letter to
Arnot of Dalquhatswood, where he escaped with bare
bayonet and cartridge pouch, he likens his defeat to those
of Pharaoh, Darius, Pompey, Edward at Bannockburn,
Charles at Pultaway and Burgoyne at Saratoga; he was
'left staring like Lot's wife besaltified in the plains of
Gomorha [*sic*]'. Reason, in the same letter, was screaming
in the vortex of the Moskoeström and Religion a beaver
carried struggling over Niagara. He could employ to
Aiken 'a Gentoo phrase, the *hallachores* of the human race'.
He knew that Sirius was the nearest of the fixed stars; if
this was an error, he shared it with many astronomers of
his day. He knew that Potosi was a place of fabulous
wealth and that dragons guarded the 'Hesperian fruit'.
If all or any of this was showing-off, there was solid
backing behind it; how many contemporary Ayrshire

farmers (we will say nothing of 'unlettered ploughmen') could have put pen to paper if confronted by a list of words culled from the above and the formula 'State what you know'?

These are the less successful aspects of Burns's letters. Yet it is possible—and delightful—when all this dross has been cleared away, to come upon a rich vein of really wonderful ore that shows us what a brilliant and living writer he could be when he cast off his second-hand Anglicisms and spoke out as himself. I do not mean that he must necessarily write in Scots; in all his prose works there is only one item of consequence written in the broad Doric—the very good letter to William Nicol on the first of June 1787. Yet throughout his letters one is constantly rejoiced by encountering phrases which are the equivalent of the crashing crescendos of *Scotch Drink* or the *Address to the Toothache*, though they are innocent of any single word not as English as Addison.

He had, for one thing, a remarkable gift for hitting off a description: of Grose, the antiquary—'a cheerful-looking grig of an old fat fellow . . . wheeling about your avenue in his own carriage with a pencil and paper in his hand': of 'an obscure, tippling but extraordinary body of the name of Tytler' with his 'sky-lighted hat' and contrasting knee-buckles 'as unlike as George-by-the-Grace-of-God and Solomon-the-son-of-David'. 'Mrs. S—— is a huge, bony, masculine, cowp-carl, horse-godmother, he-termagant of a six-feet figure, who might have been bride to Og King of Bashan.' What a wealth of insult resides in 'thou Englishman, who never went south the Tweed'. How well he hits off that feeling from which we have all suffered—'Here I sit, altogether Novemberish, a damned melange of Fretfulness and Melancholy.' And what better description of toothache was ever written than 'fifty troops of infernal spirits are riding post from ear to ear along my jawbones'. And one is constantly coming across little memorable jewel phrases; the 'Holy beagles' are on his track; Peggy Chalmers, looking kindly to another, gives him 'a draught of damnation'; he condemns his own 'enthusiastic idiot piety' and the 'mean servile compliance' of the Armours; Francis Wallace Burns is 'a fine chopping boy' and his brother William Nicol (in the Doric for once) is that 'ill-deedie, damned, wee, rumble-gaivie hurchin of mine'. Counterpart in music is but 'melodious din'; in flattering a poor performer he 'went agonising, over the belly of my conscience'; in song-writing 'to talk of money, wages, fee, hire, etc. would be downright Sodomy of Soul'. Such phrases have the quality shared by burrs and good writing; they stick.

There are, too—especially in the earlier letters—some magnificent set-pieces which show how Richardson, Fielding, Smollett, Sterne must have looked to their laurels had Burns ever embarked upon fiction. Witness the lively account of the hasty departure of the Buchanites from Irvine: 'one left a washing on the green, another a cow bellowing at the crib without meat.' Or the great roup at the Ellisland crop sale, when a free fight raged outside while within were 'folks lying drunk on the floor, and decanting until both my dogs got so drunk by attending them that they could not stand. You will easily guess how I enjoyed the scene; as I was no farther out than you used to see me.' This may be disgusting—it is; but it is also vivid writing. In the lodging-house where Burns shared a room with Richmond the floor immediately above was occupied by a pair of professional harlots; I defy anyone not to be amused by Burns's most diverting— if somewhat indelicate—picture of this *ménage*. The ladies could be heard 'when they are eating, when they are drinking, when they are singing, when they are &c'; the landlady, Mrs. Carfrae, a 'sculdudery-abhoring [*sic*] widow' consoled herself for the apparent prosperity of these 'daughters of Belial . . . who, in her own words, lie up gandy goin with their filthy fellows, drinking the best of wines and singing abominable songs' with the thought that they should 'one day lie in hell, weeping and wailing

and gnashing their teeth over a cup of God's wrath'. The
prize of all these set-pieces, however, it has always seemed
to me, is carried off by the description of Burns's riding
accident on Loch Lomond side. After a heavy night,
which had been carried well into the following day, Burns
and his party were making their way along the lochside
road when they were overtaken and passed by a solitary
Highlander mounted on a steed 'which had never known
the ornaments of iron or leather'. Burns was not in the
mood to stand this sort of thing; he gave chase and was
catching up the Highlandman when the quarry swerved;
whereupon 'down came his horse and threw his rider's
breekless a—e in a clipt hedge'. (The bowdlerising
dashes are Burns's own, not mine.) As a phrase this is
simply unbeatable, it is writing of the very best; and it is
not merely the rough word 'a—e' which makes the effect;
'breekless' and 'clipt' do just as much of the work. Only a
man with a natural ear for words could have struck all
these hammers at once.

These may be highlights—perhaps conscious high-
lights. But there is a great deal of good straight English in
the letters as well. Such quite simple and uncalculated
writing, I mean, as the letter about the drain-diggers at
Ellisland: 'They very well deserve 14 or 15d. per day, as
they wrought both hard and dirty and kept no stated
hours, but from sun to sun almost.' Or in the letter to
Mrs. Dunlop from Annan Waterfoot (with a baddish
ballad on Lesley Bailie)—'So ends this heterogeneous
letter, written at this wild place of the world, in the
intervals of my labour of discharging a vessel of rum from
Antigua.' Little Francis Wallace Burns is 'the finest boy I
have of a long time seen.—He is now seventeen months
old, has the small-pox and measles over, has cut several
teeth and never yet had a grain of Doctor's drugs in his
bowels.' New-laid eggs for Mrs. Findlater are "all of
them couch, not thirty hours out'. 'From my late hours
last night and the dripping fogs and damned east-wind of
this stupid day, I have left me as little soul as an oyster.'
There is no conscious effort in any of these; but the words

run. A man who could open a letter *in medias res* with
'That d-mned mare of yours is dead' had little to learn
from Horace; he could close another with an equally
artless sincerity—'You knew Henderson—I have not
flattered his memory.' Rather more self-conscious are, 'if
horning and caption be absolutely necessary grip him by
the neck and welcome' or 'the cares and passions that
render human life one continued up-hill gallop from the
cradle to the grave'; more self-conscious still (being to
Clarinda)—to add 'a little of the tender witchcraft of
Love' to 'the generous, the honourable sentiments of
manly Friendship' is 'like adding cream to strawberries—
it not only gives the fruit a more elegant richness, but has
a peculiar deliciousness of its own'. And how fast-moving
is this, on receiving pleasant news from Dunlop House—
'I seized my wangee rod and stride—stride—quick and
quicker—out skipt I among the broomy banks of Nith.'
Strange that a man who could write all these could almost
in the same breath 'pay court to the Tuneful Sisters'!

Burns had a quite individual genius for phrases which
skated on the verge of mock-heroics and yet skated
successfully away from them. The celebrated peroration
to the letter he wrote to the papers after hearing certain
ill-natured animadversions against the House of Stewart
comes near to a burlesque on the antithetical style; comes
near it, but never quite reaches it. What are we to say of
such polished—all too polished—sentences as 'Good God,
sir! to such a shield, humor is the peck of a sparrow and
satire the pop-gun of a school-boy'; or those married
lovers the Riddells who contrasted so agreeably with 'the
Yawn of Satiety or the malignant Squint of Disgust'; or
the story of William Wallace which 'poured a Scotish
[*sic*] prejudice in my veins which will boil along there till
the flood-gates of life shut in eternal rest'. They approach
perilously near to the edge of the abyss; yet it seems to me
they have a sturdiness that keeps them on their feet on the
right side of it. It must be admitted that when Burns
really tried to write English he tried a great deal too hard.
Yet on the other hand he could write, when occasion

demanded it, the plainest and soberest sense. The letter he sent to Lady Elizabeth Cunningham in his second winter at Ellisland is a good example; no shrewder summing-up has been made of the dilemma which besets all writers sooner or later; shall I continue to produce the same old stuff and be told—*ex hypothesi*—that I am falling off, or shall I strike out into a new line altogether and be told that I should have stuck to my last? In contrasting moods he could write to the Rev. John Skinner in genuine delight over *Tullochgorum*; or to Moore in sorrow for Glencairn's death sanely and sensibly expressed—a contrast indeed to the flamboyant poem he wrote for the occasion. When Wilson (ex Hornbook of Tarbolton) wrote asking his help towards a clerical post in Edinburgh he received a straightforward and honest reply;[5] and its author could be equally practical and helpful to the Rev. Mr. Carfrae of Morham, who sought his advice on publishing the poems of the deceased Lothian farmer Mr. Mylne. If it were not for these few examples one might be tempted to say that Burns never wrote a letter which was not a thought-out and deliberate literary composition; these show that when his natural kindness moved him he could be naturally kind with the best of us.

The truth about Burns's prose is that it succeeds where —and as—his verse succeeds, for the same reason and from the same gift—his particular knack of assembling groups of strong pungent hard-hitting quick-scoring words. In his verse he normally sought no very high poetical concepts and in his prose he achieved no great depth of thought; in both therefore he depended on technique and expression. Where it was possible for these qualities to carry him to success—and where, in his mania for copy-book examples, he gave them any chance to do so—he succeeded. For either first-class technique or first-class expression, a mastery of words is a condition precedent; and it was here that Burns drew steadily and easily away from his competitors. According to Reid's Concordance of his verse, he had a vocabulary of 11,400 different words (excluding the unprintables); and Snyder estimates that his prose should bring this up to 13,000—the same muster as Milton's and more than half of Shakespeare's. This in itself must have placed him beyond the reach of most of those who could claim to compete at his level; his quick facility for combining these words into new patterns set him further forward still. In the last resort any writer is dependent on his words; Burns had words to beat his fellows, and he could use them. To that extent, therefore, he excelled.

II

VERSE

THE first business of a writer of verse is to achieve technical efficiency; the second is to strike a note human, widely intelligible and of general appeal. Burns could do both. What he could not do—and what he unfortunately longed to do and tried incessantly to do—was to write 'poetry' according to the accepted precepts and models of his day. He could make a very good imitation of it—so good sometimes as to be almost a parody; but that was as near as his own natural genius, seeking its own robust and lively expression, would let him go. It was not a question of language, of Scots versus English; the only Scots word in *Ae Fond Kiss* is 'ilka' and there is no Scots *word* at all in either *Scots Wha Ha'e* or *My Luve is like a Red Red Rose*; yet these three poems are essentially Burns, while the *Address to Edinburgh* or *Sensibility* or the *Lament for Glencairn* as essentially are not. If only Burns could have realised that he possessed a greater genius than most of the models he venerated, and—along his own lines of work—a greater technical skill than *any* of them, he would have saved himself trouble and his readers disappointment. Like all of us, he valued what he lacked and discounted what he had.

The boundary line between what is called 'verse' and what is called 'poetry' was as ill defined in Burns's day as it is in ours; if I refer here to Burns's metrical writings as 'verse', it is not with any intention of implying a lower form or standard of art; but simply because the word seems more applicable to the particular sort of writing in which he excelled. Burns had the qualities of a poet—the passion for nature and natural beauty, the power to immerse himself wholly in a scene or an object or a person or an animal, and to draw out the universal from the particular. But to talk of *Tam o' Shanter* or *The Twa Dogs* or *Scotch Drink* as 'poetry' seems to strain a little the accepted meanings of words. And there is no earthly reason why a writer of 'verse' should not be a genius.

It is obviously impossible, within the limits of a book of this sort, to embark upon any general survey of Burns's verse, its merits and qualities; indeed, 'this is so exhausted a subject'—and one so well traversed by the highest authority—that even a new light on it is hard to come by. I shall be concerned, therefore, in this necessarily brief discussion, less with matter than with methods, less with *what* he wrote than how and why and on what lines he came to write it. I should like to keep myself on the level of technical criticism; to note how his verse arose out of the character and adventures we have just been studying, to consider the tricks of his trade, and to enquire why he sometimes gloriously succeeded and sometimes quite ingloriously failed.

Burns's metrical writings, then, can be classified under four heads; verse commentaries on current events, personal and domestic or public and political, and on current social, religious and political ideas; songs, collected and generally rewritten or re-shuffled; derivative exercises; and the two unexploited veins of *The Jolly Beggars* and *Tam*—a 'cantata' and a tale. Almost from his earliest days he had a compelling need to express himself, along all these lines, in verse—which indeed came to him far more naturally than prose; hence the 'Epistles', a device of his predecessors which he readily adopted, and such *jeux d'esprit* as *The Inventory*—a list of his staff and belongings compiled for the tax collector—or the lines to Gavin Hamilton 'Recommending a Boy'. Yet two conditions were precedent to his success. In the first place, his subject had to come from his heart and to force itself upon him; he could not set himself a topic and write about it, nor when time and circumstance set him a topic, could he do any better; he could not write to order or for occasion. In the second place, his subject had to be intimate and domestic; though he lived within a few miles of the western ocean and within sight of its splendours, he scarcely mentions the sea—except during the somewhat bogus excitements of the Jamaica period; the historic battlefields of Scotland, the Highland mountains and lochs and glens, gave him no inspiration whatever. Parish-pump politics, on the other hand, local religious skirmishes, the clods and creatures of his own field and the immediate inmates of his own social circle could fire him to the most remarkable effect. What he himself saw, read, heard, felt at close quarters must come out in metre; expressed again, just as in his prose, by those telling combinations of vital, exact, hard-hitting, quick-scoring words. To the words he added a technical skill in handling metre and rhyme, and that indefinable quality essential to first-class verse—and especially to the class of verse practised by Burns—which we may perhaps call 'punch'.

If our Portrait of the Artist by Himself was a true one, we should expect to find Burns's verse very largely autobiographical; it is so to an extent found perhaps in no other writer. One has only to turn over the pages of any edition of his poems, and Burns—Burns—Burns—Burns comes springing from the pages. In a sense his poetical works are merely an expanded Autobiographical Letter. *My Father was a Farmer*—an essay on resignation written

THERE WAS A LAD

at the advanced age of twenty-three—sets out very clearly
his view of his own life and perhaps all life—a struggle in
which misfortune comes from without rather than from
within, the product of damned squinting stars rather than
remediable defects of character. In the first *Epistle to Davie*
there follows that rudimentary 'philosophy' of honest
independence and continued poverty on which he never
very greatly advanced, and in the first *Epistle to J.
Lapraik* he is able to formulate, once and for all and with
considerable insight, his theory of poetry—

> Gie me ae spark o' nature's fire,
> That's a' the learning I desire;
> Then tho' I drudge thro' dub and mire
> At pleugh or cart,
> My muse, though hamely in attire,
> May touch the heart.

And the genuine, he says in the second *Epistle*, will always
win—in life as in writing—

> For thus the Royal mandate ran,
> When first the human race began;
> The social, friendly, honest man,
> Whate'er he be—
> 'Tis he fulfils great Nature's plan,
> And none but he'.

From these early—but more or less final—pronounce-
ments we follow Burns through his life, seeing what we
saw in the Self-Portrait. His aim is success as a writer—
'But tell him, he was learn'd and clark, Ye roos'd him
then!'; he is disgusted with the ministers of the Church—
'Their three-mile prayers an' half-mile graces'; he is
attracted to women—'But for how lang the flie may stang,
Let inclination law that'; he is a naughty young man, but
he will dodge the Devil whom he does not at all fear—
'He'll turn a corner jinkin', An' cheat you yet'; 'I rhyme
for fun'; 'Leeze me on drink! it gies us mair Than either
school or college'—and he is soon boasting of being 'as
fou as Bartie' when he was probably as sober as most
judges of his day; he is piqued and 'insulted' at Inverary

188

and pities any visitor 'Unless he come to wait upon The
lord *their* God, "His Grace" '; he sits lonely and nostalgic
by the ingle-cheek and backward muses on wasted time;
marriage has its disappointments and wives are trouble-
some creatures; in Dumfries he is ill and hard up, so—
'farewell folly hide and hair o't, For ance and ay!' The
man's whole life unrolls before us like a film. And, of
course, like stars marching across the night sky, the
women come on in procession—Jean, Clarinda, Mary
Campbell (late but brilliant), Maria, Lorimer, Lewars.
Yet even they advance mainly against the counter-rota-
tion of his own moods—amorous, recriminative, tragic.
Of all his intimate and domestic subjects, none was so
attractive as Robert Burns.

He had also, of course, an acute and partisan interest in
current affairs; if *When Guildford Good*, that informed
summary of the American War, is now unintelligible
without footnotes, it remains a remarkable effort for a
young Ayrshire farmer of twenty-five; if the *Sketch in Verse*
of C. J. Fox tries to be too clever and ends therefore in
some confusion, it has shrewd sense and insight; the *Lines
to a Gentleman* returning his newspaper afford not only a
bird's-eye view of its front page, but yet another glimpse
of Burns's characteristic and reckless daring; he asks, 'If
that daft buckie Geordie Wales, Was threshin' still at
hizzie's tails; Or if he was grown oughtlins douser, And
no' a perfect kintra cooser' (*anglice*, country stallion). And
every now and then we come on an outbreak of that
odd whimsy I have called his 'Stewarting'—particularly,
as one would have expected, after his Highland tour and
in the Dumfries period. The name of Stewart (or as he
spelt it Stuart) led him into such appropriate but doubtful
rhymes as 'true heart', as well as into several downright
horrors such as the celebrated 'Tho' something of moisture
conglobes in my eye' in the indifferent poem he addressed
to Tytler of Woodhouselee. It also led him into sentiments
as dangerous as those born of the Gentleman's newspaper;
the famous 'idiot race to honour lost' verses on the window-pane in Stirling are scarcely more injudicious than

the *Birthday Ode for* 31*st December* 1787, where 'Perdition, baleful child of night,' is adjured to lead on the unmuzzled hounds of hell upon the base usurping crew, the tools of faction and the nation's curse. Burns's interest in current affairs is significant as showing the lines along which he might have developed; his 'Stewarting' as illustrating his gift for self-persuasion. He could write with beautiful— and quite genuine—emotion: 'My fathers that name have rever'd on a throne; My fathers have died to right it'—a statement for which, as we have seen, there is no foundation whatsoever.

Arrayed, too, in sequence in his verse, we meet his rather trite 'philosophies'—

> The honest heart that's free frae a'
> Intended fraud or guile,
> However Fortune kick the ba',
> Has ay some cause to smile.
>
> And certes, in fair virtue's heavenly road,
> The cottage leaves the palace far behind;
> What is a lordling's pomp? A cumbrous load,
> Disguising oft the wretch of human kind . . .
>
> But why o' death begin a tale?
> Just now we're living sound and hale;
> Then top and maintop crowd the sail,
> Heave Care o'er-side!
> And large, before Enjoyment's gale,
> Let's tak' the tide.

These may be well expressed, but are certainly what oft was thought—if they were worth thinking at all. They are as stereotyped and tedious in theme as that procession of 'laddies awa' ' and 'hopeless loves' with which his later pages are uncomfortably crowded. Yet Burns was often capable of sustained and cogent argument—as, for instance, on the *Ars Poetica* in the first *Epistle to J. Lapraik* and in the debate between *The Twa Dogs* on the old theme —riches versus poverty—and in the admonitory *Epistle to a Young Friend*, all of which hold well together. (The last is

not by any means so sanctimonious as is commonly made
out.) Yet here again, the more pretentious the less successful; the *Earnest Cry and Prayer*, for all its splendid lines, is far
from clearly argued as a counter-blast to the Excise laws,
The Vision—intended as a heart's outburst of patriotism—
wanders and stumbles, missing one target after another,
and *The Brigs of Ayr*, starting excellently as a wrangle
between old and young, degenerates into a dreadful
Thomsonian procession of Personifications. Perhaps these
particular poems have suffered because—as they pro-
claim—they were written in stages, a method which
succeeded no better with Burns than with many others.
His was the hit-or-miss method; take up pen and paper,
start boldly—'spurt—away! Zig here; Zag there'—and
hope for the best. It is a method which, if it pays at all,
pays very handsomely; it often paid very handsomely
with Burns.

Burns's technique, then, if it could be brilliant, was by
no means flawless; he certainly worked it hard. He was
bold and daring to a degree; he enjoyed metrical and
rhyming difficulties and set himself to overcome them; he
went out of his way, indeed, to search for them. The six-
line *rime couée* 'Epistle' stanza, which he took from Sempill
via Ramsay and Ferguson and in which so much of his
best work was done, is not very difficult—though ingenuity is required to keep the rhymes going through a
poem of any length without repetition; but the ten-line
Cherry and the Slae stanza with its four-line double-rhyming
"bobwheel" is a terror. Well handled, it produces a good
and cumulative effect, but to sustain the five repeating
rhymes of its main portion and to contrive double two-
syllable rhymes within the cramped confines of its 'bobwheel' requires the greatest skill; yet Burns, almost at the
outset of his career, tackles it in the *Epistle to Davie* and
brings it off exceedingly well. Later, there was practically
no metre he did not or would not attempt; he even
(*Bannocks o' Barley Meal*) essayed that of the Pibroch of
Donal Dhu—than which no man can do more.

Of his rhymes he was not always the complete master,

and rhyming necessities often led him into weaknesses which should have been mended or cut; the Rev. Peebles had the word of a 'gentleman who read the whole with a pencil in his hand' that 'as to carelessness, the faulty rhimes [*sic*] or corresponding endings of lines were very numerous'. This would depend on what the gentleman with the pencil was looking for; if he, or we, are to insist on *exact* rhymes we shall not find very many; for Burns depended very largely on his half rhymes and they form a great part of the charm of his work. They would be more in the mode today than they were in the time of the Rev. Peebles. It must be remembered, too, that the indeterminate Scots vowels gave them a licence inadmissible in the precision of pure English; this applies noticeably to the series quoted by Snyder—'fornicator; matter; clatter; better'—which could actually, in Scots, be quite perfect. 'Howl' and 'soul', in *Winter*, will not do perhaps even under this criterion; but there is a good example in *The Twa Herds*—which incidentally is worth quoting for itself—

> The thummart, willcat, brock, an' tod,
> Weel kend his voice thro' a' the wood,
> He smell'd their ilka hole an' road,
> Baith out an' in;
> An' well he lik'd to shed their bluid
> An' sell their skin.

Tod—wood—road—bluid may not look very like rhyming in English print but they come near it in Scots speech.

There is also much clever rhyming of a deliberately *outré* kind—sometimes perhaps too clever altogether; 'gab like *Boswell*—Tie some *hose well*', '*Sackville*'—*pack vile*', 'that hour o' night's black arch the *keystane*'—'Tam mounts his *beast in*'—these will pass; 'this may do—maun do, sir, wi' *them wha* Maun please the great-folk for a *wamefou*', and 'in gore a *shoe-thick*—A towmond's *toothache*' are brilliant; but 'Anna—volcano' is too Scots altogether, 'Wycombe—like 'em' is too little Scots, while of '*respectueuse* [*sic*]—sister Susie' the less said the better! The trick

of the accomplished practitioner in dealing with *outré* or
perverted rhymes is to get in the awkward ones first and
finish with the master word which pulls all together—a
trick which Burns knew and worked time after time; two
stanzas, good again in themselves, will illustrate this; the
first the opening of *Scotch Drink*—

> Let other poets raise a fracas
> 'Bout vines and wines an' drucken Bacchus,
> An' crabbet names an' stories wrack us,
> An' grate our lug;
> I sing the juice Scotch bere can mak us
> In glass or jug.

And the second from *The Vision*—

> Had I to guid advice but harket,
> I might, by this, hae led a market,
> Or strutted in a bank and clarket
> My cash-account;
> While here, half-mad, half-fed, half-sarket,
> Is a' th' amount.

Note how the weaker 'wrack us' and 'led a market' are
tucked away in the middle, and the consequent crashing
effect of 'mak us' and 'half-sarket'; the man who wrote
these knew everything about verse.

I have been thinking so far, of course, of incidental
rhymes occurring *passim*; but Burns wrote several pieces
which were simply rhyming exercises and nothing—or
little—more. They begin, almost among the *juvenilia*, in
1780, with *The Ronalds of the Bennals* and the comparatively
simple key-rhyme 'an' a', man'; the result was not very
successful, but young Burns must have been pleased with
it, for he followed it up almost at once with the 'roguish
e'en' repeater of *The Lass of Cessnock Banks*. A more
ambitious attempt a few years later produced a good
tour de force on 'naething'; 'Chalmers' led to some gallant
tries and one conspicuous failure—'*a*-mours'. (If this was
a sample of Burns's French pronunciation, it would go
far to explain the difficulties of that French lady in

conversing with him.) He became more and more ambitious; 'Isabella' defeated him, as did the almost impossible 'Fête Champêtre', but he scored with 'hoggie' and was moderately successful with 'Killiecrankie' and 'Davies'. 'Stewart', on the other hand, attacked more than once, simply would not come to heel. These ephemerae are not, of course, to be taken seriously; I dwell on them here because I have met people who had not realised that they were a sort of game, and were in consequence bitterly critical; and also because it is pleasant to think of Burns, who had so much sorrow and unease, sitting down for an hour or two to this light-hearted and harmless diversion.

In the same manner those with indifferent ears—or at any rate with ears a great deal worse than Burns's—have fallen foul of his errors in prosody. One would not expect many of these in a man who could fit appropriate and running words to almost any tune; and indeed, if he is read with intelligence, rough or non-scanning lines are very few indeed. It is necessary to warn the southern reader that every 'r' and every 'l' combined with another consonant becomes a syllable; thus 'girl' is 'gir-ril', 'bairns' are 'bair-rins', 'helm' is 'hel-lim', 'tumbler' 'tum-bil-ler' and so on; similarly 'fire' is 'fi-yer' and 'mire' 'mi-yer' and 'Ochtertyre' 'Ochterti-yer'. If once this is grasped some ninety per cent of Burns's apparently rough lines smooth out. There remain some genuine errors of pronunciation—mostly in foreign words; 'aqua' is apparently 'a-*koo*-a', 'gravissimo' is 'graviss-*eemo*' and 'anathema' (with a mistaken pedantry) 'ana-*thee*-ma'. But if it is remembered that 'real' is almost always a dissyllable, 'en*vy*' and 'dis*trict*' are accented on the last, and 'rhe*toric*' on the penultimate, there are not half a dozen nonscanning lines in the whole of Burns's works—and two of these are obvious printer's errors which with a little intelligence need not have been perpetuated so long.

The variety and scope of Burns's experiments in metre would require a book to themselves. He fails on his 'Sonnets', which are not sonnets in the classical sense at all; but his Spenserian stanza (employed only in *The Cottar's Saturday Night*) is correct—which is more than can be said for Fergusson's. We have seen his battles with the *Cherry and Slae* eight-rhymer which never terrified him; indeed, he seemed to prefer it to the easier *Christis Kirk o' the Green* jingle of *Hallowe'en* and *The Holy Fair*, with its fewer rhymes and short single-line 'bobwheel'.⁶ His blank verse, let it be admitted, is mediocre; but once he got his rhymes running he could do almost anything with them— as witness the pace and swing of 'O leave nov*els*, ye Mauchline belles', and the stately tramp-tramp of 'Orthodox, Orthodox!' There was scarcely any of the established song or dance rhythms he would refuse to tackle, from Donal Dhu and Bab at the Bowster to Samuel Hall ('Ye Jacobites by name'). Any reader who still doubts Burns's courage and ability in handling difficult metres should sit down and try a verse—on any subject that occurs to him— in the metre of *Sherramuir*; following this by a stanza or two to the tune of *Robin Adair*.⁷ If he fails, he will have the consolation that they both almost—if not quite—defeated Burns himself.

It was Burns's first-class sense of the beat that helped him so much with his purely derivative exercises; at times these are so faithful in imitation as almost to fall within the category of parodies; at others (as is also the case with his songs) they are barely more than patchworks or transcripts. In the ballad school, '*Indeed will I*', *quo Findlay* and *John Barleycorn* follow their originals almost too closely, but *The Five Carlins* is a fine take-off of the folk-story in verse. The little conceit for Maria—*On Mrs. Riddell's Birthday*, where 'Old Winter with his frosty beard' craves, as consolation for his cheerless suns and dreary nights, 'Maria's natal day', is worthy of an older school; as are the series of Prologues to be spoken on the stage which he wrote for Woods, Sutherland and Louisa Fontenelle, which—just because they are a throw-back to old models —read oddly modern. (The best of them is probably Miss Fontenelle's on *The Rights of Woman*—into which he managed to squeeze the great words '*Ça ira*'.) If the words

'Smellie' and 'Crochallan' were removed from the context, few would recognise Burns in—

> The old cocked hat, the gray surtout, the same;
> His bristling beard just rising in its might,
> Twas four long nights and days to shaving night.

And who, unknowing, would set down this to Burns—

> The order'd system fair before her stood,
> Nature, well pleas'd, pronounced it very good;
> But ere she gave creating labour o'er,
> Half-jest, she tried one curious labour more.
> Some spumy, fiery, *ignis fatuus* matter.
> Such as the slightest breath of air might scatter;
> With arch-alacrity and conscious glee,
> (Nature may have her whim as well as we,
> Her Hogarth-art perhaps she meant to show it),
> She forms the thing and christens it—a Poet:
> Creature, tho' oft the prey of care and sorrow,
> When blest today, unmindful of tomorrow;
> A being formed t' amuse his graver friends,
> Admir'd and prais'd—and there the homage ends;
> A mortal quite unfit for Fortune's strife,
> Yet oft the sport of all the ills of life;
> Prone to enjoy each pleasure riches give,
> Yet haply wanting wherewithal to live;
> Longing to wipe each tear, to heal each groan.,
> Yet frequent all unheeded in his own.

Yet Robert Burns it is—in the *Epistle to Graham of Fintry*; it is derivative, as he said himself, 'just to try the strength of my Muse's pinions'; but did not the pinions bear him up well?

It is always difficult to identify the methods, the tricks of his trade, by which any author achieves his effect; one can indicate, without necessarily getting much forrader, some of those employed by Burns. He developed a number of little mannerisms which are of no great importance; the occasional alexandrine or third rhyme among couplets, to

serve as a punctuating colon; a participial contraction—
'When past the shower' for 'when the shower has passed';
jargon overfalls like the one he took (with a good many
other things) from the Herd manuscript—'Igo and ago
. . . Iram, coram, dago'; emphatic repetitions—'O let me
in this ae night, This ae, ae, ae night' or 'O wert thou,
Love, but near me! But near, near, near me!' But far
more important than these minutiae is his great gift for
using, quite naturally and effectively, the phrases of local
speech or common thought. This is first seen in the very
earliest of all his poems, that inspired by Nelly Kilpatrick,
'And then there's something in her gait Gars ony dress
look weel'; that might have been said—probably was—by
Mrs. Burness or Agnes or Isabel in the Lochlie kitchen.
Upon a Lammas night 'I held awa' to Annie'; the old
mare Maggie and her master 'Hae turn'd sax rood beside
our han' For days thegither'; 'Now haud you there'—to
the Louse in the Lady's Bonnet; 'But aye fu-han't is
fechtin' best' in *The Country Lass*; the auld Guidman
'maist like to rive' in the *Haggis*; and of course in *The
Cottar* passim and *Last May a Braw Wooer* par excellence.
He is adroit, too, with his place names and has a good
ear for them—as in *The Silver Tassie*, where they ring like
bugles; or such musical chimes as 'Knockhaspie' or
'Linkumdoddie'. And this leads us, of course, to a more
important item still—his use and command of excellent
words generally; the 'heartless day', the 'day-detesting
owl', 'gulravage', 'hoodock', 'fodgel', 'reaming swats'.
Wallace's heroes were 'red-wat-shod'; the Cottar's children, running to meet him, made a 'flichterin' noise';
warlocks and witches renew their leagues 'owre howket
dead'; the old mare Maggie going up the brae just
'snoov't awa' '; the Rantin' Dog the Daddie o't would
make his mistress 'fidgin' fain'; the poet meeting Lord
Daer went 'goavin', as if led wi' branks'. Strange that the
master of all these wonderful expressions should allow
himself to sink to such imitative abominations as 'conglobe', the 'tenebrific scene', and the 'unweeting groan';
should refer to the gentle and quite inextensive Loch

Turit as 'these savage liquid plains'; should believe persistently that hearts can be 'trepanned'; should take such repeated pleasure in an unhappy conjunction like 'the dear idea' which—*so* like Cicero's '*o fortunatam natam*'—is among the ugliest phrases ever penned.

Burns's mastery of words is not merely a trick of his trade, it is a facet of his genius; and so is his gift—when he would deign to use it—for a perfectly compelling simplicity. 'Of a' the airts' is a good example of this, but it reaches its apotheosis in 'John Anderson'; I find at this moment that I cannot read the song—for, I suppose, the two hundredth time—without the start of a tear. 'If this be not art,' says Snyder, 'I do not know what art may be' —and there is no more to be said. The best lines of *Ae Fond Kiss* partake of the same quality—as if they flowed in one burst from the fountain, expressing once for all an emotion which could be expressed no otherwise; so also in *The Lea-Rig* where the honest Scots words draw double value. Sad it is again to think that the author of this purest gold could content himself with such tinsel as the description of Bredalbane written 'over the chimneypiece at Kenmore'; the sickly falsity of the *Bruar Water*, where showers are 'prone-descending' and where the shepherd— the Perthshire shepherd!—sits 'to weave his crown of flowers'; and the endless wearisome catalogues of his later poems—lambs and laverocks, primrose and hawthorn, violet and woodbine, Cynthias and zephyrs, all wimpling and warbling and languishing and anguishing to despair.

But the trick of his trade or the facet of his genius which has made Burns is that to which I have already referred —for want of a better name—as his 'punch'. It was essential to him and to his style of verse; he seems always to need a chorus or a summing-up and culminating line; he succeeds in triumph when he can find one and he succeeds in less measure when he cannot. At its best his punch is like the kick of a horse; it makes one sit up in one's chair; one can with difficulty restrain a round of applause; one feels one should 'lose one's wits and leap

BURNS'S COTTAGE

sky-high', as Christopher North said Josiah Walker should have done when Burns read him the 'Ode to Liberty'. There is something grand, something heart-lifting about these magnificent crescendos. One could fill many pages with examples and extracts; it is better to refer the reader to the entire poems *Scotch Drink* and the *Address to the Toothache*; if he can read through these without the sensations I have just indicated, he had better desist from reading Burns. And, of course, the Rankine *Epistle*, the *Love-Begotten Daughter* and *Holy Willie* are full of this Burns quality of 'punch'; as are the *Burlesque Lament for Creech*, with its terrific closing rhymes which so impressed Snyder, and *On the Late Captain Grose*—though here he spoilt a glorious finish by trying one verse too many. It is as if Burns himself knew and recognised this 'punch' as his crowning gift; he searched for a metre that would carry it, and when he found one—the Sempill six-liner—he stuck to it through thick and thin. Its cadences had power to revive him when he was far gone; see how the *Verses to Collector Mitchell* and the *Epistle to Colonel de Peyster* shine through the dark days in which they were written and the second-rate pages that surround them. All the very best of Burns that is not a song and that is not in rhymed couplets—such as *Tam* and *The Twa Dogs*—is in this metre; so much has he made it his own that in any other metre he seems a little non-Burns and artificial, while others employing it seem but his ineffective imitators.

It is strange that a man who carried this wonderful weapon—lethal or life-giving—should have failed in just that line of verse-writing where he should most brilliantly have succeeded. But the fact must be faced—Burns's 'Epigrams' and 'Epitaphs' and 'Versicles' rarely come off. Perhaps it is because his effect was, as I have said, one of crescendo and he needed space to develop it; perhaps his weapon was a claymore, not a dirk; be that as it may, he could not swing it in a little space. His best 'Epigram'— because the simplest and least assuming—is that in the Kirk of Lamington—

As cauld a wind as ever blew,
A caulder kirk, and in't but few;
A caulder Preacher never spak—
Ye'se a' be het or I come back.

And among his pure personalities that *On Commissary Goldie's Brains* has always seemed to me the prize-winner—

Lord, to account who dares Thee call,
Or e'er dispute Thy pleasure?
Else why, within so thick a wall,
Enclose so poor a treasure?

But *Cardoness* has merits and so in a cruder way has *Andrew Turner*. But however much tastes and opinions may differ in selection, I think it will hardly be denied that Burns never gave us those four lines of murderous or canonising magic which we might have expected of him.

That Burns was over-influenced by his models is a point which has surely been already established; as also that their influence over him was almost invariably bad. The exercises in refinement into which they lured him contrast horribly with his natural 'punch' on the one hand and his natural John-Anderson simplicity on the other; these genuine perfections make his strayings among Bards and Night Thoughts all the more glaringly incongruous. He handicapped himself throughout by a passion for the second person singular which in turn derived from his imitative delight in apostrophe; 'thous' and 'wasts' and 'didsts' and 'lovedsts' are simply unmanageable on any large scale, and are in any case quite definitely non-Scots. A great deal of what can be called really bad in his writings is chargeable to the false gods he so distressingly worshipped; witness the incongruous ode embedded in *A Winter Night* from which he comes back to himself at last like a man rousing from nightmare; or that fearsome 'fairy train' (including 'rustic Agriculture') in which those stout Scots citizens the

Brigs of Ayr are finally engulfed; or the lurid glooms of *The Lament* and *Despondency* and that dismal old man who presided over the passing of Glencairn, who could sing 'the reliques o' the vernal quire' and wonder naïvely and originally why 'worth should have so short a date While villains ripened gray with time'. It is simply dreadful that Burns, of all people on earth, should begin a quite serious poem *To a Kiss* with the line 'Humid seal of soft affections'.[8] Much indeed has Masson's *Collection* to answer for.

There are other and intrinsic causes for his failures. One was his excess in flattery or fury; none of his admirers can read with any great satisfaction either the *Verses Intended to be Written Below a Noble Earl's Picture* (Glencairn), or the quite ridiculous violence of 'Dweller in yon dungeon dark' in which poor Mrs. Oswald of Auchencruive, a 'wither'd beldam', 'laden with unhonoured years', rheumy of eye and keeper of Mammon's iron chest, descends, poor old soul, to torturing fiends and realms where rest is not. Another was his inability to write for an occasion and his unfortunate determination to write for all possible occasions. He *would* write of what he did not feel, proclaiming meanwhile willy-nilly his own insincerity as ruthlessly as the microphone proclaims the insincerity of a broadcast speaker; Edina, Scotia's darling seat, rings false and counterfeit, and when he declares 'My heart's in the Highlands' it quite clearly is not—how could it be? And I cannot but feel—though this may be personal prejudice—that the same applies to all those Highland-Mary or quasi Highland-Mary verses about the West Indies, in which he never really believed; if a man is writing from the heart in circumstances of intense emotion, his 'crimson currents' do not 'flow', nor does his sweetheart's bosom 'burn with honour's glow', nor does he produce such banalities as the two contemporary *Farewells* (Eliza and Jean). (Even here, however, his old metre almost saves him when, inadvertently, *On a Scotch Bard Gone to the West Indies*, he strays into it.) If Burns thought he could hide his heart or write successfully with his tongue in his cheek, he was mistaken.

Failing health, pressure of official duties, a too prolific

output and a congenital laziness of mind led Burns to pass a good deal of work which he should have held back or even thrown in the fire as hopeless; no man can enhance his reputation by putting his name to such lines as—

> The winter it is past and the summer comes at last,
> And the small birds they sing on every tree;
> Now everything is glad, while I am very sad,
> Since my true love is parted from me.

Some of these causes are readily pardonable; others less so. He was always lazy—long before he took to the pernicious practice of filling a page by repeating half his lines: even in his best days many of his most promising openings peter out for lack of just that finish and pulling together which an extra ounce of effort could have supplied. *The Twa Herds*, the *Reply to a Tailor* and the *Elegy on Willie Nicol's Mare* are cases in point; and there is really no reason why *There Was a Lad* should not go on, as it is going on, for ever—at all events it never ends. Many good choruses are left with poor or makeshift verses—for example, *The Birks of Aberfeldy* and *M'Pherson's Farewell*. On the other hand, there were times when he went over a poem again and again, never apparently able to select a finally approved version; the *Verses in Friar's Carse Hermitage*, *Craigieburn Wood*, *Behold the Hour*, *Wandering Willie*, *Meg o' the Mill*, *Ca' the Yowes*, *The Last Time I cam o'er the Moor* and *As I stood by yon Roofless Tower*—all appear in two versions; *Ye Banks and Braes* has actually three. It cannot be said that the second thoughts are much better or much worse than the first, though it is instructive to note just what he altered and what he left standing. At one time—1786 to 1788—he was undoubtedly writing too much and too fast; a hundred and ninety poems in three years is more than human power can produce at any high level; no wonder some of them were slipshod. 'My poetry', he wrote to Mrs. Dunlop, 'is the result of easy composition but of laborious correction'; the former is often more in evidence than the latter.

Burns's inability to write to order has already been

noted; time and again he positively fell to the occasion. Nothing could be good that did not come from his heart or chime with the inclination of the moment; the Tuneful Sisters, as he so terribly called them, must solicit the Bard and not the other way round. His particular anxiety to excel in these occasional tributes or censures made things worse; instead of trusting, as he so well might have done, to his own genius to carry him through, he fell back upon the more ambitious of his models. As a result, all his poems of occasion reek of a dictionary of quotations. Even in instances where one might have expected something straight from the heart—the death of Glencairn, the death of Robert Riddell, the birth of Mrs. Dunlop's fatherless grandchild—one is put off with pretentiousness and cold affectation. Burns's funeral poems for John McLeod and Sir James Hunter Blair are among his worst, while that on the death of Dundas—which in all the circumstances he would more wisely have left alone—is a bombastic string of personifications and pomposo. The Shade of Thomson receives very much what Collins had already given it. Fergusson is poorly served indeed; even the elegy on Monboddo's Miss Burnet—whom Burns really liked—is the merest 'exercise'. And yet he could have done this sort of thing very well; the last verse of the Lament for Glencairn, where the poem comes suddenly out of its trance, like a train out of a tunnel, is worth the whole of the rest several times over—

> The bridegroom may forget the bride
> Was made his wedded wife yestreen;
> The monarch may forget the crown
> That on his head an hour has been;
> The mother may forget the child
> That smiles sae sweetly on her knee;
> But I'll remember thee, Glencairn,
> And a' that thou hast done for me!

No one in his sober senses would attempt to set down in print a prize-list of Burns's poems and I have no intention of doing anything so foolish here. Personally I think overrated: *Hallowe'en*, which is so terribly Ayrshire in dialect that it requires, in Scott Douglas's edition, a glossary of sixty-five terms and eighteen separate notes: *The Vision*, which begins brilliantly but descends, when the Vision opens her mouth, into a sequence of clichés, bromides and heroics: *The Holy Fair*, which, while excellent as a descriptive piece, is surely too crude for successful satire: and *Sweet Afton*, which is sugar-and-water—and perhaps borrowed at that.[9] *Per contra*, these never seem to me to receive their due: the *Rantin' Dog*; the *Epistle to a Young Friend* (sounder and more human than Polonius's more celebrated homily); the *Dedication to Gavin Hamilton*, which has self-revelation, some clever rhyming and first-class 'punch'; *Lord Daer*; the *Lament for Creech*; the *Epistle to Blacklock*; *Grose*; and a number of 'guid-gaun' if not wholly original trifles such as *Hey ca' thro'*, *Robin Shure in Hairst*, *A Waukrife Minnie*, *Sic a Wife as Willie Had* (surely a masterpiece of invective!), *Gude Ale Keeps the Heart Aboon*, *Steer Her up*, and *Rattlin' Roarin' Willie*—the last verse of which has remained solidly in my head since first I read it. Whatever may be said for or against these candidates, they are all at least the genuine Burns; not one of them could conceivably have been written by Thomson, Gray, Pope, Young or the Rev. Dr. Blacklock.

Nor is there any need here to catalogue Burns's great and unforgettable lines—such tremendous sayings as 'man's inhumanity to man', 'the best laid schemes o' mice an' men Gang aft agley' or 'Wha does the utmost that he can, Will whyles do mair.' Oddly enough many of his 'household word' phrases are from poems not themselves in the front rank; 'man's inhumanity', for instance, comes from *Man was made to Mourn*, the rest of which is pretentious and poor; 'O wad some Power' is from the *Louse on the Lady's Bonnet*; 'dear-bought Bess' is part of *The Inventory*; and 'facts are chiels that winna ding' from the political broadside called *A Dream*. But the Burns ore was always full of nuggets—if not the size of a whole line, then at least a shining and remunerative word.

When Burns could forget his tuneful songsters warbling

by verdant bower and wimpling rill, he could execute
those descriptive passages which only genius can compass;
indeed, there is perhaps no aspect of his work in which he
so excels. The dog Luath—

> He was a gash an' faithfu' tyke,
> As ever lap a sheugh or dyke.
> His honest, sonsie, bawsn't face
> Ay gat him friends in ilka place . . .
> His gawsie tail, wi' upward curl,
> Hung owre his hurdies wi' a swirl . . .

The fireside before the Vision arrived—

> There, lanely by the ingle-cheek,
> I sat and ey'd the spewing reek,
> That filled, wi' hoast-provoking smeek,
> The auld clay biggin';
> An' heard the restless rattons squeak
> About the riggin'.

The falling New Brig of Ayr—

> Then down ye'll hurl (deil nor ye never rise!)
> And dash the gumlie jaups up to the pouring skies!

Grose's collection of antiquarian junk—

> He has a fouth o' auld nick-nackets:
> Rusty airn caps and jinglin' jackets,
> Wad haud the Lothians three in tackets,
> A towmont gude;
> And parritch-pats and auld saut-backets,
> Before the Flood.

The too-old husband—

> He's always compleenin' frae mornin' to eenin',
> He hoasts and he hirples the weary day lang;
> He's doylt and he's dozin', his blude it is frozen—
> O dreary's the night wi' a crazy auld man.

And—to make an end of a list that might go on for long
enough—the too-ugly wife—

She's bow-hough'd, she's hem-shin'd,
Ae limpin' leg a hand-breed shorter;
She's twisted right, she's twisted left,
To balance fair in ilka quarter:
She has a lump upon her breast,
The twin o' that upon her shouther;
Sic a wife as Willie had,
I wad na gie a button for her.

Burns' *gradus ad Parnassum* is not very difficult to trace; he ascends by two parallel ladders—the 'punch' poems to which so many references have already been made, and the Songs. If one turns over in sequence the pages of any edition of his poems arranged chronologically, one at first encounters but little to encourage any very lively hope— though the shining second verse of *Mary Morison* (surely it was touched up in maturity of genius?) flashes a very definite promise. Then suddenly the young poet, who has so far been tottering between rather amateurish lyrics and abysmal religious gloom, lights on the six-line Sempill metre—and the scene is instantly changed. No one, reading steadily forward, is likely to miss or overlook *Poor Mailie's Elegy.* The new metre sets Burns on his feet and jerks him to attention; he delivers himself of the two fine songs—*Corn Rigs* and *Green Grow the Rashes*; then he comes back to it, more successfully still, in the *Epistle to John Rankine.* The songs are not to come in again until *There Was a Lad*; meantime the poet has consolidated himself unassailably in the six-liner with the *Love-Begotten Daughter, The Twa Herds, Holy Willie's Prayer, Hornbook* and the first two *Epistles to Lapraik.* He has found his metre now and nothing will ever throw him off it; it has become his accepted medium for his standard Class A work; presently he puts it to new use in the *Mouse* and the *Mountain Daisy.* He tries, all with success, the *Cherry-and-Slae* fourteen-liner, the Spenserian Stanza and *Christis Kirk o' the Green,* but it is to the Sempill six-liner that he comes back and back, for there he is really at home. He is on Parnassus now and plants his standard high on its slopes with *Scotch Drink,* the *Address to the Deil,* and the *Auld Mare*

Maggie. There will be nothing more now but ups and downs, troughs and crests, till the new start and the new blaze of *Tam o' Shanter.*

Two charges have been preferred against Burns's poetry by two separate schools of his detractors—indecency and plagiarism. The former of these may be readily dismissed; there is some indecency in the *Reply to a Tailor,* there are implications of it in such songs as *The Deuk's Dang O'er my Daddie* and *O Can ye Labour Lea?*—and it certainly raises its head in the late poems *The Lass that Made the Bed to Me* and *Had I the Wyte?* which seem to be the sort of erotic self-stimulus he normally reserved for the Crochallans. On the other hand, there were times when he conspicuously avoided it; what tempting opportunities for lasciviousness, for instance, are presented by the louse crawling on the lady's bonnet in church? But they are resisted; the louse goes upwards on the lady's 'Lunardi', not downwards. With the exception of the items cited— and if allowance be made for a few rough words and a realistic attitude towards human habits—the remainder of Burns's published poems, some six hundred and fifty in number, are not only free from bawdry, but are uncomfortably crowded with the noblest and most improving sentiments. His claim to Mrs. Dunlop that he regarded bawdry as a pastime to be reserved for the male sex and the tavern is justified.

The charge of plagiarism requires a little more attention. In approaching it two preliminaries must be considered; in the first place, Burns's own limited and self-acquired education. It cannot be too repeatedly stressed that he depended *entirely* on what he had read for himself at Lochlie and Mossgiel, and that what he read there was not what a professor of English would have prescribed for him, but what happened to come his way. The few books that he possessed—and, rightly or wrongly, revered—he conned over and over again with the closest attention, memorising and annotating; it would have been impossible that they should not leave a deep sediment in his mind from which particles every now and then came floating to the surface. And secondly it must be remembered that borrowing was the practice of the age; Allan Ramsay thought nothing of borrowing from Montgomery, who had thought nothing of borrowing from Maitland; Fergusson went back to Sempill, who had gone back in turn to Alexander Scott. To an extraordinary extent all the Scots 'makars' rewrote one another. If Burns therefore took a version of Fergusson's and 'improved' upon it, he probably regarded himself as free of offence; he was merely doing what everybody else had done. And it is common sense to add that unconscious plagiarism—however much its examples may horrify him when he is confronted with them—is a thing no author can escape; and further, that the citing of parallels can be carried to a preposterous extent—as the curious may discover from the *Quellenstudien zu Robert Burns* of the Teutonically industrious Dr. Ritter.

Whether the word 'plagiarism' can be applied to Burns at all will depend on how much one accepts or denies a copyright in ideas. As far as the deliberate lifting of phrases and passages goes, Burns must be held practically blameless; when he consciously quoted he acknowledged it—and if he generally *mis*quoted, that was just his laziness. He was, on the whole, ready to admit his indebtedness to others—as in the Preface to the Kilmarnock Edition, where the examples of Ramsay and Fergusson are 'often in his eye', 'though rather with a view to kindle at their flame than for servile imitation'. He was himself the first to point out—though he was not always so frank—the resemblance between the concluding stanza of *Scots Wha Ha'e* and Blind Harry's *Wallace*. Robert Anderson wrote to Currie, 'in company he would not suffer his pretensions to pure inspiration to be challenged', though in private he would admit his 'obligation to previous writers'; and Josiah Walker found him ready enough, in a quiet moment, to acknowledge that *Poor Mailie* had some resemblances to

The Ewie wi' the Crooked Horn. The most industrious search
will not reveal many instances of word-plagiarism in
Burns, and such as there are may well have been unconscious; Nannie, in *Tam*, the 'winsome wench and walie', is
from Ramsay; 'A fig for' is Ramsay; Shenstone appears
(without acknowledgment) twice in *Man was made to
Mourn* and Blair in *Bruar Water*; 'Never, never to despair'
is allowed no quotation marks in the *Regency Bill* ode;
everybody has noticed Amiens' winter wind and man's
unkindness reborn in *A Winter's Night*. 'Man's inhumanity
to man' is fundamentally Young—but how immeasurably
improved in expression! Young also contributes the
dreadful words 'tenebrific' and 'conglobe'—the sad thing
here being that Burns must have admired or he would not
have repeated them. (Young and his *Night Thoughts* and
his gloom and his pedantries have had considerable
influence throughout.) There are distinct 'echoes' of *The
Seasons*, the *Dunciad* and *The Rape of the Lock*. These, then,
would seem to be Burns's plagiarisms—not a very
formidable collection compared with his output as a
whole.[10]

That Burns borrowed metres is, of course, undeniable;
so did and does everybody else, since the number of
possible metres is limited; he also, however, devised them.
And if he went on to borrow ideas, it must be remembered
that some of these were already in the nature of conven-
tions. You wrote serio-comic 'Elegies' on serio-comic
people (as Sempill had done for Habbie Simson the
Piper of Kilbarchan); you made animals talk on their
death-beds (as Hamilton of Gilbertfield had done for
Bonnie Heck, the greyhound of Fife). Dunbar (whom
Burns had probably never read) had pilloried an earlier
and tougher Hornbook, as all wits have invariably
pilloried all charlatans. All these were established lines on
which any poet might think himself entitled to proceed.
It is only when one comes to Fergusson (to whom, however, Burns frequently acknowledged a general debt)[11]
that his unacknowledged borrowings in ideas and setting
grow significant. The parallels—the prototypes—are too

numerous to overlook; *The Farmer's Ingle* against the *Cottar*, *Caller Oysters* for the *Haggis*, *Caller Water* for *Scotch Drink*, *Leith Races* for *The Holy Fair*, *Plainstanes and Causey* for the *Brigs of Ayr*, *Hallowfair* for *Hallowe'en*, *Bee* and *Gowdspink* for *Mouse* and *Daisy*. It is impossible to enter here into the minutiae of all these; the reader who desires to see how far the parallelism can go may compare the opening stanzas of *Leith Races* and *The Holy Fair*; Fergusson strolls out 'In July month ae bonny morn When Nature's rokelay green Was spread owre ilka rig o' corn', while Burns 'Upon a simmer Sunday morn, When nature's face is fair, I walked forth to view the corn'. Fergusson 'Glow'-rin about I saw a quean' who turns out to be Mirth on her way to the Races; Burns also 'glow'red abroad lightsomely' and met 'three hizzies' who turn out to be Fun, Super-stition and Hypocrisy on their way to Mauchline Holy Fair; the conversations of Fergusson with his quean and . Burns with the spokeswoman of his hizzies run on very similar lines. With the best will in the world it cannot be denied that Burns's imitation here is barefaced enough to merit a more damaging word.

Yet, after all, Henley's view is the right one; if Burns was only 'the last of a school to which he contributed nothing but himself', he was also 'a final expression of sovranty'. If he wrote more Anglicised rubbish than he need have done—or than we would have wished, the Scots he did write was good enough and strong enough to pull his country's Muse out of the doldrums where Blair, Beattie, Blacklock, Alves, Colvill, Cuthbertson *et hoc genus* were enchaining her. He may have required, to be at his best, someone else's draft to work on and re-write, but his re-writings were almost invariably better writings, they were the ultimate fair-copy. Even in the most glaring instance —that opening of *The Holy Fair*—Burns is better than Fergusson; he is more alive, more interesting and readable, he grips where Fergusson does not. And where Fergusson, too, fell into the snare of English imitation, he was defin-itely worse than Burns—difficult as that may sometimes seem. It all comes back to Burns's mastery in speech;

every now and then he could whistle up a word that left Fergusson pointless and Ramsay gaping at a standstill in the rear. If there ever arises a new vernacular poet who is to Burns as Burns was to Fergusson, Scottish verse will be fortunate indeed.

And if Burns borrowed and imitated he was punished for it by those who borrowed in turn from him—by that 'shoal of ill-spawned monsters' who made Scots vernacular poetry a drug in the market. It is astonishing how many people in Scotland in those days wrote 'poetry'—Mrs. Dunlop, Maria Riddell, Clarinda, almost all young ladies, a tribe of farmers, weavers, blacksmiths, dairymaids, tailors, butchers, bakers and candlestick-makers. How have our accomplishments declined! But few of these could say—as Burns could say almost always—that they improved upon their model.

FOOTNOTES TO PART FOUR

[1] *p, 171*. The 'vision' seen at Bannockburn, and other extensions, are now generally supposed to be the inventions of Cunningham.

[2] *p. 173*. In all matters relating to the text of Burns's Letters I follow Professor de Lancey Ferguson's scholarly edition (1931).

[3] *p. 175*. D. McNaught, *The Truth about Burns* (1921).

[4] *p. 179*. Evidently French and Peggy Chalmers were connected in some way in Burns's mind—though just how or why is not clear. Burns's French is usually said to have been the product of a fortnight's study with Murdoch at Ayr, but this is manifestly nonsense; he must have gone much further with it than that. His French is school-book French, but he avoids grammatical errors and makes no serious mistake— though '*belle-fille*' does not mean what he thought it did. He is said to have studied the language in Edinburgh during his first winter there. Dugald Stewart had a poor opinion of Burns's French; he thought it no better than a smattering and an affectation and doubted if Burns could read French authors 'with any facility'.

[5] *p. 184*. It is plesant to be able to record that Hornbook Wilson profited by Burns's good advice. He took his talents to Glasgow instead of Edinburgh and there obtained a lucrative appointment as session-clerk of the Gorbals, which he held for thirty years. See *Burns Chron.*, 1941, p. 32.

[6] *p. 195*. Burns got the *Christis Kirk o' the Green* metre through Ramsay and Fergusson, but used it in its pure and original form only in *The Ordination*, which has the classic two rhymes (in *Hallowe'en* and *The Holy Fair* he gives it four). The original form differed also in the 'bob', which is double, with a very short line and a long—

> 'Though all her kin had sworn her deid
> She would have but sweet Willie
> Alane,
> At Christ's Kirk o' the Green that day.'

For an interesting article (to which I am indebted) on Burns's Scots exemplars, see Frank Beaumont, 'Fergusson and Burns', *Burns Chron.*, Vol XXII.

[7] *p. 195.* Burns tried to set words to 'Robin Adair'—not very successfully—in *Dumourier, Phyllis the Fair* and *Had I a Cave.* He called it a 'crinkum-crankum tune' and wrote to Thomson (13th August 1793) that it was 'such a d-mned, cramp, out-of-the-way measure, that I despair of doing anything better to it'.

[8] *p. 201.* To do him justice, he may *not* have written this horrible poem, though it appears in almost all editions of his works. See Henley and Henderson, *Poetry of Robert Burns*, IV, 107.

[9] *p. 204.* Incidentally, Sweet Afton seems to have nothing to do with Highland Mary; Gilbert Burns first said it had, but then recanted. The Afton is a tributary of the upper Nith and is sundered from Highland Mary as much by space as by time. There *is*, however, an A*l*ton burn which runs into the Fail just above its confluence with the Ayr, the traditional scene of Burns and Highland Mary's farewell. Is Afton Alton? *Another* complication!

[10] *p. 209.* I am to be understood, of course, as referring here to the work which Burns put forward as his own original composition: it would be absurd to say that the innumerable songs he produced for the Johnson and Thomson collections were other than adaptations—often almost transcriptions—of earlier work; but as he never pretended that they were anything else, the question of plagiarism does not arise. He thought little of his songs and treated them cavalierly: 'I think it is better to have *mediocre* verses to a favourite air than none at all. On this principle I have all along proceeded.' Many of his verses are certainly 'mediocre', but then many of them are not his.

[11] *p. 209.* As in the Autobiographical Letter: 'Rhyme, except some religious pieces . . . I had given up; but meeting with Fergusson's *Scotch Poems*, I strung anew my wildly-sounding, rustic lyre with emulating vigour.' For Burns's debt to Fergusson, see again Frank Beaumont, 'Fergusson and Burns', *Burns Chron.*, Vol. XXII. The 'debt' can be overstated; apart from the generic similarities in the titles there are resemblances in structure and sequence, metre and thought and arrangement; one can say that if Fergusson had never written his verses, Burns might never have written *his*. On the other hand, a parallel reading of any of the several pairs shows up Fergusson fearfully.

PART FIVE

RIDDLES

THIS section may be taken as corresponding to that chapter in the old-fashioned primers of arithmetic which was headed 'for more advanced students'. I have designed it—at the cost of some repetition—as a receptacle for a closer examination of one or two questions bearing on Burns, an examination involving so much detail that it would have interrupted the straight narrative of the earlier sections—and quite possibly wearied the less earnest followers. Let none read further except those who find puzzles diverting and who take pleasure in the unravelling of highly complicated knots. Not that much unravelling can be done; there is no answer to these riddles—or none that I have been able to discover; yet they are worth study- ing they have all the allure of the true mystery story. I propose here to consider three of them—Burns's marriage to Jean Armour, his quarrel with the Riddell family, and the fate of Highland Mary Campbell. I do not pretend for a moment that this is an exhaustive list of the unsolved problems relating to Robert Burns; but these three are certainly among the most important, and they have arisen in the course of this essay, so let us be content with them meantime.

I. Burns's Marriage

Two problems confront us here—(i) how far was Burns bindingly married to Jean Armour from 1786 onwards? and (ii) if he supposed, as he certainly seems to have supposed, that these obligations had been rendered null, why did he marry—or re-marry—Jean Armour in 1788, an act which involved the recantation of everything he had been saying and doing for the past two years? The former of these is more easily answered than the latter.

In Burns's day two sorts of marriage were recognised in Scotland;[1] the regular bell-book-and-candle affair solemnised by a Minister of God; and a variety of other irregular forms solemnised by nobody. The Church and the Law alike had to adapt themselves to the fact that Scots public opinion laid no great weight on rituals and ceremonies and was prepared to waive them, concentrating on the admissions and statements of the two persons most closely concerned. Public opinion argued, quite sensibly, that in the economic conditions of the day no man would promise or aver marriage unless he meant it; or alternatively, if he did not mean it, he should have meant it and should be held to his undertaking. If the parties had said, with bona fide intent to be taken seriously— preferably but not necessarily in the presence of witnesses—that they were or were about to be married, then it was so. The practice of ante-nuptial coitus on the understanding that at the first sign of pregnancy marriage would be acknowledged was also generally approved; it holds good in many parts of Scotland to this day. (There is a good deal to be said for it; it makes the marriage ceremony less of a licence to possess —with all the false emotional values arising from the 'bridal bed' aspect—and more of a cool-headed ratification of an already established partnership.) Against these irregular forms of marriage the Church naturally strove, but without unanimity in procedure; one Session or Presbytery adopted one set of criteria which it was prepared to 'recognise', another another. Practically any form of agreement could in popular usage constitute a binding marriage, but—this is the important point—the mere fact of the agreement *was* binding and unalterable; it could not be annulled by the destruction of evidence any more (as Chambers was told by the counsel he consulted in this matter) than the destruction of bloodstained clothing by a murderer can annul the fact of the murder.

Early in 1786 Burns gave to Jean Armour some sort of written declaration, which must have been either an acknowledgment or a promise of marriage. (More probably the former, as he wrote to Arnot in April 1786, 'I have lost a *wife*', and described himself as a 'widower' wiping his eyes to look for another.) Jean Armour was born on 25th February 1765; in 1786 she was twenty-one years of age and competent to enter into such a contract.[2] The agreement was therefore binding on the parties, and the document, maliciously mutilated by old Armour with the connivance of the lawyer Aiken, was no more than corroborative evidence. Whether or not this document was then or later fortified by some sort of proceedings before a magistrate and in the presence of witnesses is not clear; though there is some reason to suppose it was at least witnessed—by James Smith. Local tradition in Mauchline insisted that the 'marriage' took place in Gavin Hamilton's house in the presence of a Justice of the Peace who imposed a fine for breach of the 'regulations'. (But *what* 'regulations'?) This story seems almost incredible in the light of future events; it would have been well nigh impossible in a small village to keep an affair of this sort dark—and especially from the Parish Minister; yet within a matter of months Burns was applying for a 'single-man' certificate, and Dr. Auld and his Kirk Session were granting one. Dr. Auld was quite incorruptible; if he granted, as he did grant, such a certificate, he must have been in ignorance of the marriage, and Burns must have been able to deceive him or at least withhold information about it; the marriage must therefore have been a much more hole-and-corner affair than a J.P. transaction *chez* Gavin Hamilton. That there was something fishy and secretive about the whole business is suggested by the tone of Burns's letter to Smith in June of 1788, when the truth had to come out: Burns wrote that he had told Dr. Auld he had been fined for an irregular marriage by a Justice of the Peace and Auld had asked for the attestation of two witnesses; so—'as soon as this comes to hand please write me in the way of familiar Epistle that, "such things are".' If the facts were as Burns had represented them to Auld, Smith's 'familiar Epistle' would surely not be the best evidence. The tangle is a tiresome one, but not really material, for in any case any legal or quasi-legal proceedings would not have made much difference to the fact that by agreement with Jean,

217

supplemented by the document he gave her, Burns had committed himself to marriage.

The degree of Burns's duplicity in this matter depends on the extent to which he himself realised this cardinal fact. As regards the 'single-man' certificate it is not necessary to accuse him of deliberate trickery; he may have believed—or induced himself to believe—that his 'marriage' being annulled by the mutilation of the Unlucky Paper, he and Jean were left in the position of common fornicators. In that case they could, jointly or singly, take advantage of the system under which the partners in an act of fornication could 'do penance' publicly in church, whereupon the male participant was cleared and could claim and be given a certificate that he was a single man. At all events, whatever his conscience told him, Burns made haste to procure this certificate and said nothing about the 'marriage' at all. On 9th July 1786 he wrote to Richmond that the certificate would be given him 'if I comply with the rules of the Church which for that very reason I intend to do'; the letter continues, 'Sunday morn: I am just going to put on Sackcloth and ashes this day.' Eventually, in August, after the prescribed appearances in church, the certificate was issued. Burns might well draw a breath of relief at sight of it; for, three months previously, he had again compromised himself matrimonially with Mary Campbell. The precise extent of this new obligation is unknown and will remain so, but again it must have been some sort of promise or acknowledgment of marriage and may or may not have been confirmed by pre-nuptial intercourse. Thus Burns, being irrevocably married to Jean Armour by his uncancelled undertaking to her, was not only not a 'single man', but was perilously near to being a bigamist; the suspicion of this, combined with other rubs and uncertainties, may partly account, as I have already suggested, for the curiously hysterical state of mind in which he passed that summer and autumn, and for the appallingly doleful series of poems—*To Ruin, The Lament, Despondency*—in which he expressed himself.

If he did entertain such a suspicion, it was, however,

easily suppressed; during his Edinburgh adventure and the Clarinda affair, he had evidently convinced himself that he was free of Jean Armour. On the 30th of July 1786 he had written to Smith that one of the two things he would never do was owning Jean Armour conjugally; and this resolve was not shaken by the Armours' 'mean servile compliance' of which he wrote to the same correspondent a year later. When, much later still—on 9th March 1789— he wrote defending himself against the outraged Clarinda's accusations of villainy and duplicity, he could say with honesty: 'I have already told you, and I again aver it, that, at the period of time alluded to [i.e. during the Burns-Clarinda affair] 'I was not under the smallest moral tie to Mrs. B. . . .' It has been hinted—though the evidence one way or the other is negligible—that Jean at this same time or all the time had another lover whom she actually preferred to Burns—and to whom it is to be supposed she granted equal favours; if this was true, and if Burns was aware of it, as he probably would be, it must have strengthened his decision to cut free. The boy component of Jean's first pair of twins, born on 3rd September 1786, was whisked off to Mossgiel as soon as possible—as had been done with the child of Elizabeth Paton; this also suggests that a final cleavage was intended. If there is any meaning in language or any sequence in human actions, one would say that, from the Spring of 1786 onwards, Burns was thoroughly disgusted with Jean and the whole Armour connection, and had no intention whatsoever of renewing it.

Unfortunately, however, this did not prevent him from renewing intimacy with Jean at the first physical opportunity—his conquering-hero visit to Mauchline in June of 1787. How far Jean was thrown in his way by the now converted Armours—or by herself—is unknown, and immaterial. The fact remains—and perhaps it is one of the best arguments against the charge of her infidelity— that she immediately conceived; the unpleasing news of her pregnancy presently reached Burns in Edinburgh. This disconcerting bulletin was followed by one still worse:

the Armour parents, not unjustifiably annoyed with their daughter—if he was so taken up with her as all that, could she not have lured the man into wedlock before falling into his arms again?—had come to an end of their patience and told her to find other quarters for her confinement. Burns received this information very late in 1787 or very early in 1788; it was at the time when his injured leg had disabled him from action, for he could misrepresent this as the reason for Jean's eviction which otherwise, he said, he would have prevented. He was also at the time disabled from action by Clarinda—who detained him longer than his leg. There is no obvious reason to suppose that he regarded Jean's predicament as more than an infernal nuisance; the story of it, which he must have got from herself, was not too credible. The Armours could not in cold reality have seen their daughter—as Burns was later to describe her to Andrew Dunlop in one of his apologia for his marriage—'literally and truly cast out to the mercy of the naked elements'; even if old Armour would have contemplated this drastic treatment, his wife—who had twice his courage and humanity —would never have allowed it. One suspects that Jean, pretty uncomfortable under the parental roof and perhaps dreading a second Paisley, made the most of it—indeed, there is nothing to disprove the suggestion that she walked out herself in a huff. However that may be, Burns did do his best for his unseasonably fruitful sweetheart; he secured a temporary refuge for her at Tarbolton Mill, the home of his friend Muir, and he went to Mauchline in mid-February of 1788, on his way to look at Ellisland, for no obvious reason except to make more elaborate and detailed arrangements for her comfort. Jean must be got— and was got—into quarters of her own; a doctor must be bespoke; and so on. If he thought at all of the future of the coming child, he probably contemplated one more addition to the growing household at Mossgiel; the arrangement had served well with young Robert and might serve again. That he had any intention of allowing it to blackmail him into marriage seems incredible.

It is rendered incredible—as is the whole notion that he was at this time 'in love' with Jean—by his own actions and by his own words. He did not hurry to Mauchline on the news of this fresh pregnancy, and the steps he did tardily accomplish were not so much those of an anxious and devoted lover as of a man whose mistress has in her folly made *the* unpardonable mistake. Let us give Burns credit for what he did, but let us at the same time admit that it was in the nature of a minimum. Having settled Jean in some sort of comfort, he went off to inspect Ellisland; he was back in Mauchline when the twins were born—on 3rd March 1788—but did not trouble to remain there till they died and were buried— the one on 10th March and the other on 22nd; before the latter date, at least, he was back in Edinburgh with Clarinda. In short, he did what decency demanded of a man in his position—he saw the girl through—but he did no more. He made no mention of the death of the twins in his correspondence, and apparently was moved by it as much or as little as he was by the thought of Jean's maternal feelings. He certainly said no word about marriage. But, as was, of course, his nature, he could not keep altogether quiet about his own doings and emotions; and during those tedious visits to Mauchline he wrote three most illuminating letters. One was to Clarinda, one to Ainslie and the third to Richard Brown—in continuance, no doubt, of their conversation on that merry evening in Glasgow three weeks before.

The letter to Clarinda has been cited already, but is worth quoting here in full; it is dated from Mossgiel, 23rd February 1788, and begins with the announcement that he has delivered her kind present—it was a pair of shirts—to 'my sweet little Bobbie'. It proceeds ingratiatingly: 'Now for a little news that will please you. I, this morning as I came home, called for a certain woman— I am disgusted with her; I cannot endure her! I, while my heart smote me for the prophanity, tried to compare her with my Clarinda; 'twas setting the expiring glimmer of a farthing taper beside the cloudless glory of the meridian sun. Here was tasteless insipidity, vulgarity of soul, and mercenary fawning; there polished good sense, heaven-born genius, and the most generous, the most delicate, the most tender Passion.—I have done with her and she with me.'

This was fairly outspoken, but the letter to Ainslie, a week or so later, is more explicit still.[3] It is dated 3rd March 1788—the day Jean was in labour with his twins; it is a long letter, dealing at first with Tennant's report on Ellisland, but the passages relevant to the present discussion run as follows: 'I have been through sore tribulation and under much buffetting of the Wicked One, since I came to this Country. Jean I found banished like a martyr—forlorn, destitute and friendless; all for the good old cause: I have reconciled her to her fate: I have reconciled her to her mother: I have taken her a room: I have taken her to my arms: I have given her a mahogany bed: I have given her a guinea; and I have f . . . d her till she rejoiced with joy unspeakable and full of glory. But— as I always am on every occasion—I have been provident and cautious to an astounding degree; I swore her, privately and solemnly, never to attempt any claim on me as a husband, even though anybody should persuade her she had such a claim, which she has not, neither during my life, nor after my death. She did all this like a good girl, and I took the opportunity of some dry horselitter, and gave her such a thundering scalade that electrified the very marrow of her bones. O, what a peacemaker is a guid weel-willy p . . . le! It is the mediator, the guarantee, the umpire, the bond of union, the solemn league and covenant, the plenipotentiary, the Aaron's rod, the Jacob's staff, the prophet Elisha's pot of oil, the Ahasuerus's sceptre, the sword of mercy, the philosopher's stone, the horn of plenty, and Tree of Life between Man and Woman.'

The letter to sea-Captain Richard Brown is dated four days later, on March 7th. 'I found Jean—with her cargo very well laid in; but unfortunately moor'd, almost at the mercy of wind and tide: I have towed her into convenient harbour where she may lie snug till she unload; and have taken the command myself—not ostensibly, but for a time, in secret—I am gratified by your kind enquiries after her; as after all, I may say with Othello—"Excellent wretch! Perdition catch my soul, but I do love thee!" '

It being impossible to doubt the genuineness of these three letters, the apologists have insisted that the first was a picee of pure blague written to please and pacify Clarinda: the second was false and youthful bravado and had no basis in fact; and the third was merely an example of Burns's habit of suiting his letters to his audience. The only one of these claims which is really sustainable is the third; the Brown letter is in questionable taste, but nothing worse—though one would like to know what Burns had, thus early, in his mind when he wrote of taking 'command—not ostensibly, but for a time, in secret'. Probably no more than that he assumed responsibility for Jean till her confinement was over; it does not, at any rate, sound like marriage. But there seems to me no ground but pure perversity for taking the Clarinda letter at other than face value. Burns was in love with Clarinda, and though distance did not, with him, lend enchantment, his reaction to the squalors and shabbiness of the outcast Jean after the urbane comfort of the Potterrow is precisely what one would expect in any natural being. No doubt he piles it on—but he always did; that does not prevent the letter from being a basically accurate representation of his current feelings towards Jean Armour. As to the quite dreadful letter to Ainslie—not even a very close or solid friend—one can only wish it not only a lie but a forgery, for it throws the most unbearable light on Burns. If he could really commit the act he says he did, in a stable, on a woman over eight months gone with child and showing all the attractions of that physical state, he must have been plain brute. And how much harm did he do his unfortunate twins who were to appear in three weeks and die in four? But leaving out all the unpleasant implications of the letter, and allowing it to have been written from any ulterior motive open to man, could any human being have written such a letter about a woman he 'loved'? It is all very well to say, as did Henley,[4] that the letter was a 'Crochallanism' as from one Fencible to another; but even Crochallans do not write thus about women with whom they are seriously contemplating marriage. Nor does any other man in his senses.

So far this episode in Burns's story, though far from creditable, is credible; but its progress now becomes wholly fantastic. Burns left Jean and the doomed twins as soon as he decently could and went back to Edinburgh; there he saw Clarinda and he saw also important personages in the Excise. By the end of March he was in Mauchline again, and from there, on 7th April, he wrote a letter to Peggy Chalmers in which he has 'lately made some sacrifices for which you would applaud me'—an ambiguous phrase which might apply to Clarinda or Jean or the Edinburgh surrender or something else altogether. It may, on the other hand, be the first note in the new and extraordinary developments. From 7th to 28th April he was silent: he then wrote in series the following letters—(i) to James Smith dated 28th April 1788 (after a nervously 'clever' opening about a 'twenty-four gun battery' and men with '1.25-1.5-1.75' ideas in their minds) 'to let you a little into the secrets of my pericranium, there is, you must know, a certain clean-limbed, handsome, bewitching young hussy of your acquaintance, to whom I have lately and privately given a matrimonial title to my corpus . . . I have irrevocably called her mine . . . Mrs. Burns ('tis only her private designation) begs her best compliments to you.' (ii) To his uncle Samuel Brown at Kirkoswald, 4th May 1788—'I engaged in the *smuggling trade* and God knows if ever any poor man experienced better returns—two for one!—but as freight and delivery has turned out so dear, I am thinking of taking out a licence and beginning in fair trade.' (iii) To James Johnson, 25th May 1788—'I am so enamoured with a certain girl's prolific twin-bearing merit, that I have given her a *legal* title to the best blood in my body; and so farewell Rakery!' (iv) To Ainslie (the recipient of that letter of 3rd March, in which, *inter alia*, Jean had been 'reconciled to her fate' and successfully sworn to attempt no claim on Burns, dead or alive!) dated 26th May 1788—'I have been extremely fortunate in all my buyings and bargainings hitherto; Mrs. Burns not excepted, which title I now avow to the World—I am truly pleased with this last affair; it has indeed added to my anxieties for Futurity, but it has given a stability to my mind and resolutions, unknown before.' These communications, which must have somewhat staggered their recipients, were followed up by appropriate action; Burns set matters in train for a reconciliation with the Church and the whole geometrical progression of incredibles culminated in that Minute of the Mauchline Kirk Session already quoted in which on 5th August 1788 that body recognised Mr. and Mrs. Burns as man and wife. The happy couple had meantime spent some weeks in Mauchline before Burns's final departure for Ellisland; a period which he—like his grandnephew after him—was to describe, somewhat quaintly, as a 'honeymoon'.

If the seven letters I have just quoted be read in series, from the Clarinda to the second Ainslie, they present a *volte-face* which on the known facts is simply unacceptable. Burns could not possibly have contemplated marriage with or cared twopence for the woman of whom he wrote that letter to Ainslie on 3rd March; to suppose otherwise is to posit in him a degree—and a type—of caddishness or duplicity which are literally unthinkable. Yet in the Johnson letter, two and a half months later, she has a *legal* title to the best blood in his body. He has hedged over this word 'legal', boggled at it; in the Smith letter, a month earlier, Jean's title and designation are still 'private'; in the Samuel Brown letter he is still 'thinking' of taking out a licence. But this evidently would not do; he was forced out into the open. Is not the inference compelling that between the extremes of these dates—or to narrow it down, between his return to Edinburgh in mid-March and the letter to Smith on the 28th April—some fresh occurrence took place or some new consideration intruded itself which cardinally altered Burns's whole attitude to Jean Armour? And with that we are at last able to state this present riddle—what *was* that occurrence, or what *was* that consideration?

And having thus stated it, there alas! we end. As to a fresh occurrence, no event is known which could possibly have produced so cataclysmal an effect. Between 19th March and the Chalmers letter of 7th April, Burns wrote to Richard Brown, Cleghorn, Creech, Stewart, Blair and Mrs. Dunlop: these letters, which are preoccupied with the Ellisland adventure, contain no word of Jean or of marriage and it is difficult to believe that he had any marriage in mind when he wrote them. As regards a new consideration, there are several—unsatisfactory—suggestions. There is first of all that which Burns himself took pains, during that 'honeymoon' in Mauchline, to promulgate among his correspondents; we have already seen the variant formulae in which he expressed it. The gist of them was that, on return to Mauchline, he had found there a 'long and much loved fellow creature' faced with almost total destitution; moreover, the happiness or misery of this fellow creature were in his sole control—'and who could trifle with such a deposit?' He therefore married her—and had no regrets. I have no doubt that by the time he had written this once or twice he thoroughly believed it; and indeed in a heart so warm and so ready for compassion as Burns's these sentiments were perfectly natural. But the calculated solemnity with which this formula was hatched and then broadcast in almost identical terms over a period of months makes it a little suspect from the first; and besides, its premises are unsound. Jean's happiness or misery were no more in Burns's hands or out of them than they had been for the past two years—during which time he had regarded them with indifference. And as to destitution, common sense scouts the idea that the Armours, who were respectable folk dependent like all tradesmen on local public opinion, would really have flung their daughter into the ditch, however exasperating might be her penchant for the role of unmarried mother. Till the storm at home blew over, or if it never blew over, she could turn to her married brothers and sisters, or to the relations in Paisley; she might have been faced by unpalatable alternatives, but she could not have been destitute..Ah, but then there were the children to provide for? But there were no children—or no *new* children; little Robert, the survivor of the 1786 twins, had been living at Mossgiel almost ever since his birth, and might apparently go on living there till he died; and Providence had seen fit to remove the new twins before they could even be baptised; though this, under the quaint religious ideas of the day, condemned the poor mites to everlasting Hell, it at least cancelled them out as encumbrances upon Jean. Jean's situation, though bad enough, was not desperate; one would hazard the guess that if Burns had done nothing, she would have been back under the parental roof within six months at most.

If Burns's own explanation does not wholly convince, let us see what his apologists have done for him. They have not really done much more than pick up two alternative lines of explanation which he tried out for himself. One is outlined in the long letter he sent to Mrs. Dunlop on 10th August 1788, supplementing his more curt announcement of 13th June—'I am indeed a Husband.' This contains a tolerably honest account of his relations with Jean and then goes on to argue that while bachelor life would have given him more friends 'conscious Peace in the enjoyment of my own mind, and unmistrusting Confidence in approaching my God' would not have been among them. He was therefore faced with marriage, and 'circumstanced as I am, I could never have got a female Partner for life who could have entered into my favourite studies, relished my favourite Authors, etc., without entailing on me, at the same time, expensive living, fantastic caprice, apish affectation with all the other blessed Boarding-school acquirements, which (pardonnez moi, Madame!) are sometimes to be found among females of the upper ranks, but almost universally pervade the

Misses of the Would-be-gentry'. This is extremely sensible and sound, but it does not explain either why *immediate* marriage was essential or why he should have chosen as his 'female Partner for life' a woman whom he held so lightly as he did the heroine of that letter to Ainslie. It has been urged that Burns was now moving to Ellisland; he must have a working woman there; as he could not afford to hire, he must marry. But there was no hurry about Ellisland; he could not take a wife to a place where there was not even a house, and in point of fact Jean did not see Ellisland for six months after her 'marriage'. He might have looked round a little. . . .

The other line of explanation follows his own letters to the Rev. Mr. Geddes (3rd February 1789) and Dr. Blacklock (November 1788); to the former he wrote 'the alternative was, being at eternal warfare with myself, on account of habitual follies'; and to the latter, 'Virtue's ways are ways of pleasantness and all her paths are peace.' The theory based on the Geddes letter is that he had gone perilously near the abyss with Clarinda and had got a severe fright; like many another man, he married in the hope of avoiding the everlasting nuisance and distraction —to say nothing of the danger and expense—of repeated 'affairs'. Again this is a perfectly sound theory, but it again fails to explain why he should have rushed into wedlock with a woman who had so ineffably disgusted him so short a while back. And it has this in common with all his other explanations—that it sounds like a conclusion he had thought and reasoned himself into. Why all these justifications? Why all these apologia for the institution of marriage? . . . As to the pleasantness of Virtue's ways and the universal peace of her paths, this was not a consideration that normally carried much weight with Robert Burns, nor was the conscious enjoyment of Virtue for Virtue's sake likely to afford him much real or lasting solace. On 30th June 1787 he had written to Smith that, as a 'younger son of Parnassus', he might 'intrigue if I choose to run risks, but may not marry'; and certainly he was not what is called a marrying man—and never less so than when white-hot from Clarinda. Why, then, did he marry so suddenly and why Jean Armour?

I may be making mountains out of molehills; Burns's own explanation may be the true one and may be acceptable at face value, as it has been accepted by so many of his admirers down the years. If so, his action in tying himself for life to a woman of whom he thought and from whom he could expect so little, was Quixotic to the verge of lunacy. I am not going to say that such an action was impossible in Burns; only that it accords ill with his habitual shrewdness and caution. And I cannot rid myself of the conviction that, if we knew all, we should find that *something* happened, between mid-March and mid-April of 1788, which made marriage with Jean unavoidable; and that, complying with fate, he turned his coat and married her and thereafter made the best of it—which was, of course, the only thing to do. In that letter of 9th March 1789 in which he defended himself to Clarinda, and which has the air of a perfectly honest and sincere document, he wrote—besides what has already been quoted—'nor did I, nor could I then' (i.e. during their friendship) 'know, all the powerful circumstances that omnipotent necessity was busy laying in wait for me'. Now what 'circumstances' were these? Not that Jean was pregnant; not that her parents were in a fury; both these were known, and what is more, discussed freely with Clarinda herself. And again, in his letter to Clarinda in the spring of 1791; 'I cannot, will not, enter into extenuating circumstances; else I could show you how my precipitate, headlong, unthinking conduct leagued, with a conjuncture of unlucky events, to thrust me out of a possibility of keeping the path of rectitude; to curse me, by an irreconcilable war between my duty and my nearest wishes, and to damn me with a choice only of a different species of error and misconduct.' This is no doubt obscure and meaningless—deliberately so, one would suppose; but again, what *was* that 'conjuncture of unlucky events'? Something must have happened to bring about the *volte-face*. What was it?

I can make only one suggestion. It has not, I think, been put forward before, and I venture it now with the utmost diffidence. On that visit to Edinburgh in mid-March of 1788—between the scurrilous Ainslie letter and the 'private title' letter to Smith, Burns achieved one of his ends; he was put on the list of persons selected as suitable for posts in the Excise. On 17th March he wrote to Clarinda that the Excise affair was 'just concluded and I have got my order for instructions'—that is, an order to place himself under an Excise office for tuition in his new duties; he was to dine and sup with the 'principals of the Excise' and one of the Commissioners. (Actually the order for instructions of which he was so certain was *not* issued till the 31st.) Twenty-four hours later he is 'just hurrying away to wait on the Great Man'. Is it not possible that Burns was told confidentially at these interviews, or shortly thereafter, that if he desired an Excise appointment—or the chance of one—he must first regularise his position with Jean Armour? The Board of Excise were exceedingly particular as to the good name of their officers; they would not countenance the slightest indebtedness; flagrant immorality could hardly pass, either. Burns had already Paton's illegitimate daughter growing and flourishing at Mossgiel and nothing very much could be done about her; but the young Robert who lived there with her, the renewed scandal about Jean Armour, with the 'clash' of which all Ayrshire must have been ringing—could not and should not something be done about these? Faced with the alternative—Jean and the Excise or lose the Excise for ever and fall back only on the hazards of Ellisland, Burns would really have little choice. I fly this balloon in the expectation that it will promptly be shot down by scholars much more learned than myself; but let it be shot down fifty times, I shall remain convinced that *something* happened. Otherwise this part of the Burns story simply does not make sense.

II. The Riddell Quarrel[5]

The problem this time can at least be posed simply and straightforwardly at the outset—what was the event which caused the split between Burns and the two 'county' families of Riddell with whom he had been so friendly; and where, if anywhere, did that event take place?

To recapitulate for a moment; it will be remembered that soon after Burns moved to Dumfrieshire he was taken up by a local landowner, Robert Riddell of Friar's Carse, an amateur musician and a dabbler in various 'ologies. Riddell was intelligent enough to be keenly interested in Burns, who became a frequent and favoured visitor to his house. Robert Riddell had a wife, *nee* Elizabeth Kennedy, whose qualities—if she had any recordable qualities at all—tended towards primness, propriety and a readiness to feel insulted; he had also a brother Walter, who had just bought himself (or at least put down a deposit on) an adjoining estate which he had renamed Woodley Park. He gave it this name in honour of his wife Maria, *née* Woodley, who came from gubernatorial circles in the Leeward Islands and who was not prim or proper to any noticeable degree. Burns, who had been able to make nothing at all of Mrs. Robert Riddell—though he wrote conventionally that she was sweet and lovely, with sense, wit and taste—became very friendly indeed with Mrs. Walter. Their relationship has already been described and no more need be said about it here.

The disaster occurred somewhere in the very last days of 1793 or in the first days of 1794; until recently it was believed to have occurred at Woodley Park, but on this point there will be more to say presently. All details are lost and the whole affair is wrapped in obscurity; all that can with any certainty be said is that Burns apparently drank too much at a dinner-party and misconducted himself in such a way as to give serious offence to his hostess. In dealing with the episode, the authorities fall back oracularly on 'traditions'—mostly, it appears, a re-hash of Chambers; but—beyond the general consideration that as there is no smoke without fire, so any 'tradi-tion' has usually something behind it—the evidence in support of them is quite negligible. For what they are worth, these 'traditions' say that at a large mixed dinner-party at Woodley Park the gentlemen sat long over their port—a habit of gentlemen in those days, though not, if Mrs. Montagu is to be believed, of Burns. Some bright spirit then suggested that it would be a grand idea to stage a Sabine Rape on the ladies patiently waiting in the drawing-room; let each gentleman seize the lady of his choice, but let Burns have the hostess. It is further sugges-ted by some writers that the whole plan was what would in these days be called a 'frame-up'; Burns, egged on to make an exhibition of himself, was to be—and in the event actually was—deserted and then accused and thrown out. Doubtless there were those present who would have grasped delightedly at such a proposal; Burns, during 1793, had been giving out a good deal of class-hate and anti-gentry stuff, and his remarks about 'lobster-coated puppies' and the like had probably got round. But the evidence for a 'frame-up' is even worse than the rest; for the only document which can in any sense at all be said to give an account of the incident categorically states that others behaved as badly as Burns. Setting aside the 'frame-up' theory, then, the tradition is that a concerted rush was made to the drawing-room, where some lively embracing took place. Either Burns's conception of a 'Sabine Rape' was more vigorous and his presentation more realistic than that of his fellow Romans or else his presumption, as a mere gauger, in joining in the Rape at all was held to be unforgiveable; at all events he was requested to leave the house and not come back. The solid fact does emerge that, whatever may have happened, Burns's connection with both Friar's Carse and Woodley Park did abruptly terminate as did, for a time, his friendly relations with Maria Riddell. With this lady he eventually achieved a reconciliation, but there was no reconciliation with the Friar's Carse branch of the family. Death carried off the good-hearted Robert Riddell in the middle of 1794, while relations were still hostile; and there is no evidence that his lady ever forgave the affront she had apparently received.

There was, then, some kind of a row—and a bad one— between Burns and the Riddells; one might, however, be inclined to write off the whole Sabine Rape story as a *canard* or a magnification by some of the many persons in Dumfries whom Burns had succeeded in annoying—but for the single document referred to above. This is Burns's letter of apology written on the morning after. It is not in itself a very satisfactory document, for it is undated, and it bears no name or address; on the other hand, it seems unmistakably genuine. Currie, playing safe, listed it as 'To Mrs. R——'; but then, there were *two* 'Mrs. R——s'. The letter is worth quoting in some detail. It begins briskly: 'Madam, I daresay that this is the first epistle you ever received from this nether world. I write you from the regions of Hell, amid the horrors of the damned.' Burns has been tried and sentenced to endure 'the purgatorial tortures of this infernal confine for the space of ninety-nine years, eleven months and twenty-nine days, and all on account of the impropriety of my conduct yesternight under your roof.' His torments are described with enthusiasm; a 'bed of pityless furze', a 'pillow of ever piercing thorn', the 'tormentor *Recollection* with a whip of scorpions'. These agonies would be alleviated if the sufferer could be 'reinstated in the good opinion of the fair circle whom my conduct last night so much injured'. His apology, however, is directed entirely to the ladies; he makes none to the men: 'Your husband, who insisted on my drinking more than I chose, has no right to blame me; and the other gentlemen were partakers of my guilt.' He apologises especially to Miss I—— and Mrs. G——, who 'did me the honour to be prejudiced in my favour'. 'To be rude to a woman, when in my senses, was impossible with me.' And then the celebrated peroration— 'Regret! Remorse! Shame! Ye three hellhounds that ever dog my steps and bay at my heels, spare me! spare me!'

The connoisseur of Burns's letters will at once recognise here one of his self-flagellations working itself up to a crescendo of hysteria; he will also recognise it, however, as something else—one of his literary exercises. Persons who have, in a moment of alcoholic exuberance, bitterly offended a hostess they like and respect, and who see their whole social position and a number of valuable friendships standing in deadly jeopardy, do not write letters like this. The grossly overdone penitence, the serio-comic account of his torments, all suggest that the letter was written in a mood quite other than that it purported to represent; a mood either of defiance or of mock-seriousness. There would have been no possible point in defiance; the letter, therefore—or so it seems to me—is the half-in-jest apology of a man fairly confident of ready forgiveness. As usual, poor Burns had blissfully underestimated the degree of offence he had given and was happily persuaded that he could carry it all off.

When he found he was mistaken—when no reply was vouchsafed at all to his elaborate excuses and there was no withdrawal of the embargo on his visits to the house, he flew into one of his sullen uncomprehending hatreds. The chief target of his abuse was the unfortunate Maria, who received in succession the *Monody on a Lady Framed for her Caprice*, the verses *Pinned to Mrs. Walter Riddell's Carriage*, and—though it is possible to doubt whether Burns wrote this—the bitter *Epistle from Esopus to Maria*. The *Monody*, which is—as it was meant to be—like a shower of vitriol, closes with the lines—

> Here lies, now a prey to insulting neglect,
> What once was a butterfly, gay in life's beam;
> Want only of wisdom denied her respect,
> Want only of goodness denied her esteem.

And the *Carriage* verses run—

> If you rattle along like your Mistress's tongue,
> Your speed will outrival the dart;
> But a fly for your load, you'll break down on the road,
> If your stuff be as rotten's her heart.

MARIA RIDDELL

Neither of these were very agreable compliments for a Squire's wife to hear bandied about the county town; and like Miss Ballochmyle's brothers, her husband came in for it, too; this was the *Epitaph for Mr. Walter Riddell*—

> Sic a reptile was Wat, sic a miscreant slave,
> That the worms even d . . . d him when laid in his grave:
> 'In his flesh there's a famine,' a starved reptile cries,
> 'And his heart is rank poison!' another replies.

Crude stuff, no doubt, harming author more than victim, but scarcely calculated to ameliorate the situation.

The fact that these pleasantries were fired at the Woodley Park branch of the Riddells, Maria and Walter, not at Robert and Elizabeth at Friar's Carse, was always taken as corroborative evidence to the traditional story that the fracas took place at Woodley Park, the outraged hostess being, therefore, Maria. But here the mystery begins to thicken. Burns's letter of apology quite categorically states that the 'husband' of the addressee was present and made him drink too much; now it seems perfectly clear that at the time the occurrence must have happened Walter Riddell was—and had been for some time—in the West Indies. In the first place, Burns, in a letter to Thomson in July of 1793, mentions that 'Mr. Walter Riddell of Woodley Park' is a subscriber for the whole work (i.e. Thomson's *Collection*), but he is 'at present out of the country'. Next, on 17th November 1793, Maria, writing to Smellie, the publisher-printer in Edinburgh, with whom she kept up quite a correspondence, says that her husband had been 'recalled' to the West Indies in June or July of that year; his departure had been immediate and his absence was to have been short. But on 12th January 1794 Maria tells Smellie, 'my lord and master does not talk of returning till after the equinox is past'. (Presumably she meant the spring equinox in March.) On 3rd March Smellie writes to her, 'my friend and your husband whom I hope you will soon have the pleasure of seeing'; and two months later, 'What! Of your husband not one word!'—and Smellie hopes they are now happy together at Woodley Park. If any reliance is to be placed on these entirely fortuitous and disinterested letters (and it is hard to see how they can be ignored), then Walter Riddell was not in Dumfriesshire between July of 1793 and at least March 1794; *ergo* he could not have been the 'husband' of Burns's letter and Maria could not have been the offended hostess; *ergo* the husband (as he was certainly a Riddell) must have been Robert and the hostess Mrs. Robert; and because Burns says 'under your roof', the scene must have been not Woodley Park, but Friar's Carse.

What are we to make of all this? In a way, the substitution of Elizabeth for Maria seems at first helpful; Maria was a broad-minded little body and unlikely, perhaps, to raise the roof if gentlemen were a trifle boisterous in their cups—provided, of course, they did not go *too* far; certainly she was unlikely to hold it as a permanent and unforgiveable offence against an old and valued friend. A woman who could sympathise sufficiently with a tortured spirit to forgive the *Monody* and the *Carriage*—as Maria did eventually forgive them—would hardly be implacably upset by a little after-dinner horse-play. The prim and pettish Elizabeth was much more likely to be outraged beyond repair. But then why are all the attacks directed against Maria? The only traceable communication launched by Burns at Friar's Carse after the 'regions of Hell' letter was a civil request for the return of 'all my trifles in verse' which had been given to Robert Riddell; this was addressed, not to Mrs. Riddell, but either to her sister, Miss Kennedy, or, as Ferguson supposes, to her unmarried sister-in-law, Elinor Riddell. The letter is dated 7th May 1794, and meanwhile Maria was catching it hot. There are possible reasons for the concentration of fire upon Maria—quite apart from that which one does *not* like to suggest, that she was a grass widow with her husband and his whip safely away in the West Indies. Burns was genuinely fond of Robert Riddell, as well he might be; perhaps he loved him so well that he would in no circumstances attack him. He had never been able to get any forrader with Mrs. Robert, who had already disgusted him by making a scene with that 'fine fat fodgel wight', Captain Grose, and he was by this time probably indifferent to her opinion of him one way or another; in any case, he probably regarded her as quite implacable and impervious to argument or abuse. (His writing to her sister or sister-in-law for the return of his 'trifles' instead of to herself would support this idea.) But that Maria—his friend who had met him on such unequivocal terms, who had exchanged verses with him and shared with him a very pretty flirtation, of whom perhaps he had still hopes of something more—that *she* should join forces with her clan and cut him was an intolerable affront that drove him to fury. And down came the fruits of that fury on Maria's head—and vicariously on Walter's.

It is, of course, supposable that Maria was a guest at the party (a most likely thing indeed) and that *she* was the recipient of Burns's amorous assault in the drawing-room (she would have been a much more probable and enticing target for him than Mrs. Robert). But this idea will not do very well; it was hardly likely that Maria would have raised such a pother if Burns had snatched a kiss in public—and really the 'outrage' can hardly have amounted to anything worse than that—and if the insult to Robert and his wife was thus only vicarious, the punishment they inflicted was incredibly severe. It seems better therefore to stick to Mrs. Robert as the point of attack and the *casus belli*.

That Maria's part was that of a spectator or a collateral driven for a time into taking the family's side against this presumptuous gauger is suggested by the progress of the subsequent reconciliation between herself and Burns, in which—all honour to her—she met him at least half-way. In January of 1794 (the date is from Maria's own docketing) he wrote: 'I have sent you Werter: truly happy to have any, the smallest opportunity of obliging you'; and went on to say that her reception, on the sole occasion when he had recently seen her, 'froze the very life-blood of my heart'. On 12th January he returned her Commonplace Book, 'as it seems the Critic has forfeited your

THERE WAS A LAD

esteem': but while 'De-haut-en-bas rigour may depress an unoffending' (so Maria had not been directly insulted?) 'wretch to the ground', it at the same time rouses 'something in his bosom' which is at heart an 'opiate'. Incidentally these two letters seem incredible as an almost immediate follow-up to the 'regions of Hell' which can hardly, in view of them, have been written to Maria. During the rest of 1794 Maria was 'out', but some time towards the end of it—perhaps inspired by that spirit of Christmas love which means so much to the English—she must have made some sort of overture, for in January of 1795 Burns wrote her a very dignified third-person letter—'Mr. Burns's compliments to Mrs. Riddell—is much obliged to her for her polite attention in sending him the book.' Perhaps it was the Commonplace Book back again or the Metrical Miscellany, for he will 'pay that attention to Mrs. R——'s beautiful song "To thee, lov'd Nith", which it deserves', ('Being at present acting Supervisor of Excise, a department that occupies his every hour of the day, he has not the time to spare which is necessary for any belle-lettre pursuit.') When the enemies to each other get the length of calling their respective poetic efforts beautiful, reconciliation is not far distant; so it was with Burns and Maria, for in a couple of months or so he was writing to her chattily about the miniature portrait he was having made by Reid, and not long after that she was pestering him to get one of her protégés a post in the Customs. The feud was over. But there was no further communication with Friar's Carse, whose lord was now irrevocably dead and buried.

We seem, therefore, to have got thus far; that the scene of the fracas, whatever it was, was Friar's Carse, not Woodley Park; that the outraged lady who never forgave or forgot was Mrs. Robert Riddell; that Robert Riddell, taking his wife's side perhaps somewhat half-heartedly, died before he could effect a reconciliation; that Maria was a spectator only—if even as much—but was dragged into the family feud and cut her friend Burns from *noblesse oblige*; that Burns turned upon *her* because it was

238

her defection that he really felt and, rightly or wrongly, regarded as unjust; and that, being a large-minded lady, she overlooked his lampoons and patched things up after a decent interval, because she was sorry for him and could not really get along very well without him. This certainly hangs together and makes a credible and satisfactory picture. But alas! we are not yet out of the wood; there are complications which cannot be ignored and must now be taken up.

If our theory is correct, the 'regions of Hell' letter must have been written to Mrs. Robert Riddell; yet it would seem that somehow it was Maria who had possession of it. After Burns's death, Maria had a considerable correspondence with Currie—and naturally, for she knew more about Burns than anyone living. And after the appearance of Currie's *magnum opus*, she wrote to him in July of 1800 'that letter of his from the other world . . . I am puzzled to guess how you came by. I had somehow mislaid it and it certainly was not among those I delivered for your perusal.' In any case, went on Maria, it was a pity that Currie published it; 'the stile [*sic*] is not fanciful enough for the *intention* of the composition and it is not altogether a creditable one to Burns'. If Currie informed the puzzled Maria where he got hold of the letter (it may have been a draft among Burns's papers) his reply has not survived; but the important point is that Maria at one time had it. Now, Mrs. Robert Riddell did not die till 1801, and in 1800 the letter, if it survived at all, should still have been in her keeping; yet Maria writes rather as if *she* had had it for some time and indeed as if she had been its natural custodian all along. That simple phrase 'I had mislaid it' is most difficult to get round or explain—except on the supposition that she was, after all, the original recipient of the letter. As to what she meant by the other odd phrase in her letter—'the stile is not fanciful enough for the *intention* of the composition'—I do not pretend to know; unless she had reason to believe that—as I have suggested above—it was not quite seriously written. Otherwise, why on earth should a letter of

repentance be, of all things, 'fanciful'? If that was indeed
what she meant, then she was right; for it is a mixture of
the genuine and the fantastic, and between these stools it
falls to the ground.

One would be inclined to guess that Currie's reply to
Maria—if he replied to her at all—would be evasive. For
he had already been warned off the 'regions of Hell' letter
as long ago as 1798 and he had not listened to the advice
he received. Feeling, and with justification, some doubts
about it, he had mentioned it to Miss Kennedy, Mrs.
Robert Riddell's sister in Edinburgh. Miss Kennedy
answered in a four-page reply dated 20th January 1798;
her view was that the letter 'ought not to appear, as it
refers to some circumstances of improper Conduct of
Burns to Mrs. Walter Riddell which she represented to
Mr. Riddell and which he thought (in his Brother's
absence) he ought to resent and therefore declined taking
any further notice of Burns'. Miss Kennedy thus does us a
good turn in confirming further Walter Riddell's absence
and so fixing Mrs. Robert as the Sabine victim and
recipient of the 'regions of Hell' letter; but she does us a
very bad turn in every other way. Away goes the whole
picturesque story of the Sabine Rape and in comes a new
story altogether with a new picture of the relations of
Burns and Maria—which is yet perfectly consistent with
the quarrel and reconciliation between them which we
have just followed. And it will not do, of course, to say
that Burns's 'improper conduct' *was* the Sabine Rape,
because Robert Riddell must have been present at that
and seen it with his own eyes and had no need of any
'representation' from Maria or anyone else. To make
things a little more difficult, Miss Kennedy is to some
extent confirmed by Charles Kirkpatrick Sharpe, whose
acid description of poor Maria we have already recorded.
'There was a lady' wrote Sharpe (on the back of an old
receipted bill), 'whose intimacy with Burns did him
essential injury—their connection was notorious—and
she made him quarrel for some time with a connection of
her own, a worthy man to whom her deluded lover lay

under many obligations'. Sharpe's 'lady' is certainly Maria, and his 'worthy man' cannot be other than Robert, so this certainly sounds like the same story as Miss Kennedy's. It is dementing.

In a clash of evidence such as this one can do no more than attempt judgment on probabilities. Looking at it from this angle, Maria may have got hold of the 'regions of Hell' letter by a dozen different routes; it may have been made over to her at Burns's death with other *reliques* for use in Currie's edition, or she may have begged it still earlier from Mrs. Robert Riddell, who would have no particular interest in keeping it. Miss Kennedy may have known less than she thought or may have simply been prevaricating with a view to putting Currie off the scent and preventing publication; or—as is most probable of all—she may have confused the occurrence referred to in the letter (which Currie apparently did not show her) with the other occurrence which was in her own mind. The Sabine affair took place publicly before a 'fair circle' —which Miss Kennedy's 'improper Conduct' could hardly have done. There is no reason at all why there may not have been *two* incidents—a more private quarrel between Robert Riddell and Burns inspired by some tale-bearing of Maria's, *and* the Sabine Rape affair as well; indeed, Kirkpatrick Sharpe says that the quarrel between Burns and Riddell was only 'for a time', which suggests that *a* quarrel was made up. There was, as we know, no making-up after the Sabine Rape. And if there *had* been a previous row in which Burns had misbehaved and had been, after a time, forgiven, this would go far to explain the adamantine attitude of Friar's Carse towards the Sabine Rape, which would then be in the nature of a last straw. As to the Rape itself, by far the best evidence is the quite disinterested and independent correspondence between Maria and Smellie, and the 'regions of Hell' letter. If we can find a version which squares with both of these—as we seemed to have done a little ago—we need not be too seriously shaken by Maria's letter to Currie or by Miss Kennedy *plus* Kirkpatrick Sharpe.

Enough perhaps meantime on this particular riddle. I do not pretend that it is equal in importance to those on either side of it; but it is a worthwhile example of the mysteries, the contradictions, the confusions and insolubles that, even in minor matters, develop round the name of Burns.

III. Highland Mary's Grave

It will again be advisable to start here with a little recapitulation so that the story may be taken up where it left off. There was once, then, a young woman called Mary Campbell, one of the family of an obscure couple living on the Firth of Clyde, who wandered as far afield as Ayrshire and there took service, in one or more households, between the years 1784 and 1786. During the latter part at any rate of this period she was on very intimate terms with Robert Burns; he may possibly have seduced her; he may possibly have given her some sort of promise of marriage; he may possibly have intended to carry this promise into effect. However that may be, Mary Campbell left Ayrshire, rather abruptly and unexpectedly, in mid-May of 1786, and returned to her parents, who were at this time apparently in Campbelltown. In October of that year she 'crossed the sea' to Greenock, where her mother had relatives; so Burns himself put it, in those notes already cited, giving the date as 'the close of the autumn'. Again according to Burns, she undertook this journey 'to meet me'; but according to descendants or collaterals of the Campbell family[6] she was on the way to a new situation with a Colonel McIvor in Glasgow which she was to enter at Martinmas, and she was accompanied by her father and her younger brother Robert, who was to be apprenticed at the same time in Greenock. She *may* also have had yet another reason, not uncommon among her sex, for retiring temporarily to a shelter where she was little known. However all this may have been, in Greenock she presently died. A fever—apparently the seasonal typhus or 'putrid fever'—was raging in Greenock at the time, and this was the accepted cause of her death. Her burial was arranged by her host, Peter Macpherson, whose wife is said to have been a cousin of her mother's, and to whom, according to one story, young Robert Campbell was to be apprenticed. Macpherson interred her in the 'lairs' which he had just purchased, or inherited, in the old West Churchyard of Greenock; and as he heard the sods thudding down on the coffin he no doubt thought that there went the last of 'Highland Mary'.

He was, of course, very far wrong. Mary Campbell had left a tradition in Ayrshire, vague but melancholy; the ideas associated with her memory were those of remoteness, loss and might-have-been; as if some sweet but uncomprehended Gaelic air wailed over the prosaic cornfields of Kyle. Tradition in Ayrshire knew that there had been an exotic passing stranger, a figure almost from another world, who had meant a great deal to Robert Burns; and when he, in due course, issued nostalgic poems about a certain 'Mary', the countryside had no hesitation in identifying their heroine with the dim shape of Mary Campbell. Greenock was equally well informed; so much so that, as early as 1803, the Greenock Burns Club, the pioneer of these now ubiquitous associations, asked Peter Macpherson's permission to erect a memorial tablet on the grave in the West Churchyard. Its erection seems to have been deferred till the flare-up of Burns enthusiasm in the eighteen-forties, when public subscriptions were canvassed for a more ambitious monument. The response was not very generous; subscriptions are said to have totalled a mere £100; but the most pretentious monument which the taste of the time could manage for the money was in due course erected. It was not beautiful, but it served and serves, though transplanted and rather naked-looking for lack of the wall against which it stood, to this day. The reasons for its journey—together with all the contents of the grave it guarded—from the old West Churchyard to the new Greenock Cemetery have already been given, and need not trouble us here.

The point with which we are now concerned is that on
the 8th November 1920, during the exhumation—which
was carried out with religious reverence and care—there
emerged from Highland Mary's grave that bottom board
of an infant's coffin, perfect and unmistakable in shape,
though sodden with water. This object was immediately
seized upon as unmistakable corroboration of the theory—
which some had long suspected on more general considerations—that Highland Mary, at or just before her death,
had been delivered of an illegitimate child whose father
could only have been Robert Burns; and that, while no
doubt it was the 'malignant fever' which brought about
her end, a premature childbirth was a contributory cause
thereto.

It is necessary now to examine more closely how far the
coffin-board will support this version. The first of Burns's
major biographers to whom the new Material Object was
available were Mrs. Carswell (1930 and 1933) and Snyder
(1932); both made a good deal of use of it. To the former
it was a 'curious, though not by itself conclusive fact'
which strengthened a conviction by which she was
already obsessed; to the latter it was 'a piece of evidence
on the basis of which a new hypothesis may be constructed'.
Mrs. Carswell's conviction and Snyder's hypothesis were,
of course, the illegitimate-child theory outlined just
above. But what was this 'fact' or 'piece of evidence' really
worth?

A full and intelligent account of the exhumation is not
lacking; it may be found in an article headed *The Beginning of an Old Song* in the *Greenock Telegraph* of 4th January
1921, which I believe to have been written by a leading
member of the Greenock Burns Club, Mr. Archibald
MacPhail. Snyder at least had seen this article, for he
refers to it; but it seems to me that he could not have read
it with his usual close attention to detail or assessed it with
his usual judicial acumen. Snyder's account—and also
Mrs. Carswell's, who throughout simply states the illegitimate child as an accepted fact without (as usual) citation
of authority—leaves the impression that there was a

single grave or 'lair' known to be the peculiar resting-place of Mary Campbell; and that out of this, at the exhumation, there came what a century and a half had left of Mary *plus* that section of the infant's coffin. The connection between Mary and the coffin-board was thus inescapable. I can only say that this is a conclusion which must be considerably modified by a close reading of the *Greenock Telegraph* article.

This article, after preliminaries, states that on the fore-noon of Monday the 8th November 1920 the grave was opened 'not to be filled in again' and 'that which had formed its contents' was transferred to the Greenock Cemetery. It does not appear that the people of Greenock as a whole were greatly excited over the exhumation—in any case they would not have been admitted to it; but the work was carried out under the surveillance of com-petent authority, Mr. Sheridan, the Superintendent of Cemetery and Parks, and his staff. There were present other responsible persons—ex-Bailie Carmichael, the Convener of the Cemetery and Parks Committee (of whom we shall hear again); the Chief Constable of Greenock; Mr. Ninian McWhannel for the Burns Federation; four officials of the Greenock Burns Club and another; fourteen persons in all. The first earth had been removed before the Burns Club contingent arrived, and 'already several small bones had been unearthed'. All saw, however, the main exhumation—for which the weather, on a squally morning, mercifully held up. The grave turned out to be only four feet deep, 'stopping at gravel and clay'. The excavation took two hours, four men relieving each other by turns; four large boxes had been provided to hold the earth and a smaller box for any bones or remains.

Now come the important passages, on which one could have wished for even greater detail. *Three* skulls were unearthed, as well as a thigh and smaller bones and part of a jawbone 'with four teeth in good state of preservation'. There were also 'some human remains' which were 'black and quite hard'. 'One got a better idea of the number of interments from the considerable quantity of wood unearthed.' 'At the foot of the grave [this was later described by Bailie Carmichael as 'at the bottom of the North lair, in the north-west corner'] 'the bottom of an infant's coffin was found. This while sodden was quite sound.' The scene, says the author of the article, was like *Hamlet*, 'as the grave-diggers came on now an arm, thigh, jaw or skull'. In fact, it was made abundantly clear that— far from being the sole repository of Highland Mary and her putative infant—Peter Macpherson's lairs were as densely peopled as a modern tenement. *Three* skulls and an odd jawbone; and other bits and pieces; a 'considerable quantity' of coffin-wood besides that infant's board. None of those present appears to have been particularly interes- ted in this last relic—not interested enough, at any rate, to run for a timber expert or even an intelligent working carpenter from the adjoining shipyards who could have pronounced something reliable as to its date; a simple expedient which might have thrown a revealing light upon the whole problem. Instead, the entire contents of the grave were placed in a 'casket'—a sizeable object which, judging from the Press photograph, it took several men to carry—were removed to the Cemetery House and kept under lock and key till the following Saturday, when they were re-interred in the cemetery, without—so far as is recorded—any further examination. By a curious coincidence, there was arriving almost simultaneously at Dover the subject of another exhumation—the Unknown Warrior. How many Unknown Warriors went to the Greenock Cemetery with Highland Mary Campbell?

One of the surprising things about this exhumation— on which such weighty inferences were to be based—is the nonchalance with which it was regarded in Highland Mary's own town. The *Greenock Telegraph* gave space to the article I have just been quoting, but its account of the re-interment in the cemetery—which, judging from the Press photograph, was not very largely attended—is relatively meagre; it gave no notice of the exhumation in advance and its official account of that ceremony was a small paragraph sandwiched in mid-page between a 'Whiskey Dealer's Penalty' for charging too much and a 'London Blaze' which had turned out a hundred firemen. This may be immaterial, but is interesting in view of the hubbub that was to arise elsewhere out of the exhumation discoveries; quite clearly they did not disturb Greenock. The Editor never thought the item worthy of an editorial paragraph, and though the paper ran a correspondence column, the *Beginning of an Old Song* article drew no letters except one from a gentleman who wished to correct an alleged misquotation in the 'Old Song' itself. So far as I can see, no allusion to the event was made by the speakers at the (numerous) local Burns dinners a couple of months later. True, the local poets were better to the fore, and one of them at least kept the banner of the 'Mariolaters' flying in its full pristine colours. But in general one would be tempted to conclude that in Greenock, in 1920-1921, Highland Mary was not news; at any rate, so far as it knew of it, Greenock took the coffin-board in its stride.

The immediate effect of the exhumation, however, in such sectarian periodicals as, for instance, the *Burns Chronicle*, was that Highland Mary vanished almost entirely from their pages, and the 'Mariolater', who had made sporadic appearances therein, was heard of no more. This may, of course, have been a coincidence—but there does seem to have been a sort of conspiracy of silence. Ten years after the event the Burns Federation are reported as visiting Greenock; Highland Mary is referred to, but there is no word of infants' coffins—though Mrs. Carswell's book had by this time appeared, and was presently roughly treated in the *Chronicle's* columns. Indeed, this official organ of the Burns Federation made, so far as I can discover, only one more reference to Highland Mary between 1921 and the present day; on that occasion, however, in 1933, it returned to the charge—to some purpose.

The protagonist on this occasion was Dr. Lauchlan Maclean Watt,[7] a lifelong student and admirer of Burns, to whose earlier book on Burns I have been, with many others, indebted; he was at the time at Glasgow Cathedral. In the course of the year 1932 Dr. Watt had written to the *Times Literary Supplement*, criticising the inferences which Snyder, in his then newly published *Life*, had drawn from the infant's coffin-board unearthed in Highland Mary's grave. His criticisms were based not on the considerations I have been setting forth here, but on his long and varied experience as a Minister of the Church of Scotland. In thirty-five years as a Parish Minister, declared Dr. Watt, both in rural and urban areas, he had found it a universal custom that, when a mother died in childbirth, the mother and the child were buried in *the same* coffin, the dead child being normally laid on the dead mother's breast. There was, in all his great experience, *never* a separate coffin: and 'our largest funeral undertaker' (presumably in the city of Glasgow) would bear this out. From such an authority, such a view must necessarily carry very great weight; but it cannot, after all, be stronger than is any inference from generality nor can it outweigh the proverbial fact that there are exceptions to every rule. Further, it presupposes that Mary Campbell did die in actual childbirth—a supposition for which there is practically no evidence at all. Who knows exactly when Mary Campbell moved to Greenock or at what stage of her pregnancy—if she *was* pregnant at all? If the Campbell family tradition already mentioned is correct, she evidently expected to be fit to enter Colonel McIvor's service at Martinmas, but as Martinmas falls in late November, by which time any Burns child almost *must* have been born, that does not tell us much: though one may ask, of course, why she took no work during the supposed period of her pregnancy and was ready to re-enter service just when that period would have expired. Leaving that aside, she may have moved to the shelter of the Greenock relatives for her confinement some time in advance of it; and the child may have been born and lived there for some weeks and died of the same fever as its mother. I am not saying that there is evidence for this:

only that, on general principles, the one thing is about as likely as the other. When Burns said farewell to Mary in May of 1786 she may have been a month gone with child or two months or four—or, of course, not 'gone' at all. There simply are no *facts*; and Dr. Watt's argument was no stronger than any other inference proceeding from general expectation. However that may be, his letter to the *Times Literary Supplement* bore unexpected fruit, and he was presently in a position to offer some quite substantial confirmation.

For his letter to the *Times Literary Supplement* drew forth from Greenock a Mr. Hendry with a remarkable statement. (It is not clear whether Mr. Hendry himself read the *Times Literary Supplement* or whether some one else read it and produced him to Dr. Watt; it is immaterial.) According to Mr. Hendry, an ancestor or connection of his, Captain Duncan Hendry, apparently brought his wife from Campbelltown (surely an odd coincidence!) to Greenock at the end of 1826 for her confinement. A girl child, baptised Agnes Hendry, was born on 4th January 1827; it died, still in Greenock, on 27th February. Peter Macpherson, the friend and neighbour of Captain Duncan Hendry, then gave permission for the child to be buried in his family burial-place, in Highland Mary's grave. At the time of Dr. Watt's investigation a related Miss J. Hendry testified that she had often heard her father speak of this incident, and it was a tradition in the Hendry family that they had an 'auntie' buried with Burns's Highland Mary; all were clear about this and it was recorded in a "family tree" in their possession. Dr. Watt's Mr. Hendry was so certain of the story that when Highland Mary's grave was opened he anticipated that a child's coffin would be found in it, and when one duly appeared he knew at once whose it was. All this Dr. Watt set forth in a second letter to the *Times Literary Supplement*. He then weakened his case with some rather irrelevant arguments, but again led from trumps with a corroborative letter from ex-Bailie Carmichael (whom we met at the exhumation); the letter has other points of interest and may be quoted rather fully. Mr. Carmichael recalled that he was Convener of the Cemetery and Parks Committee 'when, owing to the Harland and Wolff scheme, the three lairs in the Old West Church burying-ground in one of which "Highland Mary" was buried were opened . . . I was present when the lairs were opened and saw everything that was taken out of them. The lairs were only four feet deep when the old shore was exposed. On the bottom of the North lair, in the north-west corner, was found the bottom board of an infant's coffin. It was perfect in shape, but sodden with water. I told my friend Mr. Hendry of this, when he told me that in all probability the bottom board belonged to the coffin which had contained the body of Captain Duncan Hendry's child, buried in 1827.'

This letter may not have been so valuable a corrobora-tion as Dr. Watt seemed to think; it only repeats Mr. Hendry, apart from whose bare statement Mr. Car-michael knew nothing about it; but incidentally, besides establishing more definitely the part of the grave from which the coffin-board came, it does tell us that there were *three* lairs, in *one* of which Highland Mary was buried. So here the procession of unanswerable questions begins. In *which* lair was Highland Mary? Was it the 'North lair', where the coffin-board turned up? Who else was buried in these 'lairs' and when? Is there any record of Captain Hendry's child? Whose were these three skulls? Nobody in Greenock now seems to know the answers; the Burial Registers of the Old West Churchyard and other relevant records are not forthcoming and cannot be traced. And once more one is left lamenting that no expert looked at the coffin-board from the point of view of date; there are forty years between 1786 and 1827; surely any man ordinarily used to handling wood could have said which of these dates was the more probable for it. But it was not done and cannot be done now.

If this version of Mr. Hendry's could be accepted as the solution, it would—as Dr. Watt claimed for it—'illustrate the whole case clearly' and, so far as the coffin-board is concerned, would go far towards showing that an 'unkind and ungenerous libel' had been perpetrated on Mary Campbell. But, without in the very least impugning the sincerity and veracity of Mr. Hendry, it must be pointed out that his story has obvious defects. The argument that it appeared extraordinarily pat to Dr. Watt's *Times Literary Supplement* letter may be ruled out—Dr. Watt would never have put his name to it if he had not been certain of its antecedents, and the suggestion would be a wholly unwarrantable slur on Mr. Hendry himself. One may be forgiven for saying, however, that in view of the publicity given to the exhumation and the subsequent tumult and shouting aroused in Burns circles by the publication of Mrs. Carswell's book as far back as 1930, it is surely a little surprising that neither Mr. Hendry nor Mr. Carmichael came forward earlier with this crucial piece of information. But apart from these considerations, the whole thing is hearsay, unsupported by one grain of solid evidence; and while family traditions and family trees have their value, they are not in the nature of scientific proof. And it is impossible to read the story without immediately catching curious echoes; again the expectant parent travels from Campbelltown to Greenock, again it is Peter Macpherson—who seems to have been remarkably free with his 'lairs'—who comes to the rescue and finds burying-space for the dead child. One may well suspect a certain confusion or overlapping of stories. All one can say is that if the coffin-board does not prove the Carswell-Snyder theory, the Hendry-Carmichael story does not disprove it; that the Highland Mary mystery is on the whole darkened by the exhumation results rather than clarified; and that the *Greenock Telegraph* article and Dr. Watt's Mr. Hendry have between them pretty well ruined the infant's coffin-board as a Material Object of any final significance.

How, then, does Mary Campbell stand? One can only reply, *sub judice*. What was she—a Beatrice or a lightskirts, spiritual or carnal, Angellier or Henley? It is

difficult to say. Did she and Robert Burns, after the
manner of dairymaid and farmer's boy, conjoin together
to produce an entity whose surviving particles, if any,
are now residing in the Greenock Cemetery? Again—'not
proven'. No jury on earth would convict on the existing
evidence; few juries would be left without a strong
suspicion of guilt. I do not think one can say more than
that—or less.

POSTSCRIPT

On this unsatisfactory note—a question-mark to which no answer can be given—this essay on Robert Burns must close. Yet if the note is unsatisfying, it is not perhaps inappropriate. Burns's whole life was a mystery—the original mystery of how genius can take birth in a market-gardener's cottage, how generations of good, ordinary, well-doing husbandmen can produce suddenly a blinding flash and flame; the mystery of how that flame, dampened and smothered by every possible circumstance, does not go out; the mystery of man's inhumanity to man—that ten thousand of Burns's fellows should watch him struggling through life and hardly one of them should hold him out a hand; and the mystery of how man's spirit, casting down all manner of barriers and blocks, can carry him through on the wings of courage, can master a sinking body and, in rough seas and cross-currents, keep it afloat till it will float no more. Small wonder that Burns's story has intrigued not only his own countrymen, but a great part of mankind; so that an American could say—with whatever hyperbole—that his name had been 'dearer to a greater number of hearts than any other save that of Christ'; and a Chinese could find him revealing 'our common humanity'; and a Canadian could write, 'He made the world his lover.' Whatever value may be attached to Burns's writings, verse or prose, whatever blame he may have earned by his faults and his failings, it is surely a poor heart that will not take fire at the warm blaze of his own and subscribe to the conclusion—'Here was a great *man*.'

FOOTNOTES TO PART FIVE

[1] *p. 215.* See D. McNaught's very useful article, 'Burns's Marriage', *Burns Chron.*, Vol XXVII. The view of irregular marriages and their effect in Scots Law which I have here adopted seems to rest on good authority.

[2] *p. 217.* Some writers, among them Mrs. Carswell, have denied this, being misled apparently by the unexplained fact that Burns entered the date of Jean's birth in the family Bible as 27th February 1767. The Mauchline Parish records, however, give 25th February 1765, and there is no reason to doubt them. (cf. Snyder, *Life of Robert Burns*, pp. 120 *et sqq.*)

[3] *p. 222.* For the text of this letter I rely on Prof. de Lancey Ferguson's 1931 edition of the *Letters*, as in the case of all my other quotations from these. It is the over-protestations of Burns in this letter, that Jean had *no* claim on him at all, that leads one to suspect that he feared she had a fairly good one.

[4] *p. 224.* Henley with his 'old Hawk', his impossibly Machiavellian Burns, seems to me quite off the track throughout these entire episodes.

[5] *p. 231.* For illuminating articles on this, see the late Sir Hugh Gladstone, *Maria Riddell, the Friend of Burns*; *Trans. Dumfries and Galloway Nat. Hist. and Antiquarian Society: 3rd Series, Vol.* 3; and J. C. Ewing and A. W. McCallum, 'The Falling Out at Woodley Park of Burns and Maria Riddell', *Burns Chron.* (1946)—to both of which I am indebted.

[6] *p. 377.* Peter Macpherson's daughter and J. C. Douglas, a clothier of Greenock. See Chambers: *Life and Works of Robert Burns*, Edited Wm. Wallace (1896), Vol. I, p. 428.

[7] *p. 247.* See Dr. L. M. Watt, 'Highland Mary', *Burns Chron.* (1933).

INDEX

Afton, River, 213 n. (9)
Aiken, Robert, patron of B., 19; and B.'s marriage, 156
Alloway, Wm. Burness at, 13
Angellier, on B., 83; on Mary Campbell, 142
Armour, Jean, antecedents, 154; B.'s letters on, 161, 221; in Commonplace Book, 19; 'desertion' of B., 20, 155, 156; at Dumfries, 160, 165; letters to Thomson, 165; and Jessy Lewars, 161; and Jean Lorimer, 112; marriage to B., 28, 139, 153, 156, 159, 215–30; and Mauchline Kirk Session, 155; and Anna Park, 108, 160, 164; portraits of, 160; first twins, 157; second twins, 138, 158, 219
Auld, Rev. Dr., B.'s 'single-man certificate', 217

Ballochmyle, Lass of, 82
Begbie, Alison, 113
Biographers of B., 10, 55 (see also Currie)
Blacklock, Rev. Dr., 21, 22, 115
Blair, Rev. Dr., 22, 84
Broun, Agnes (B.'s mother), 12, 15
Brown, Capt. Richard, 18, 138, 158, 221
Brow Well, 40
Burness, Robert (uncle), 88, 174
Burness, origin of name, 95
Burness, William (father), 12
Burns Begg, Isabella (niece), 48, 110
Burns Begg, Robert (grand-nephew), on Jean Armour, 164
Burns, Elizabeth (by Jean Armour), 121
Burns, Elizabeth (by Anna Park), 109

Burns, Elizabeth (by Elizabeth Paton), 166 n. (2)
Burns, Francis Wallace (son), 160
Burns, Gilbert (brother), on B.'s habits, 76; B.'s loan to, 29, 88; and Currie's edition, 56; and Taylor portrait, 47
Burns, Isabella (sister), on B. and Mary Campbell, 147; portrait of, 47
Burns, James Glencairn (son), 42, 160
Burns, Robert, aimlessness, 57; ancestry, 12, 95; apologia for marriage, 226; appearance, 45; and Jean Armour, 153–65, 215–30; bawdry, 80, 207; and Alison Begbie, 113; boyhood and adolescence, 17–20; 'canniness', 58; and Mary Campbell, 141–53; and Peggy Chalmers, 115–7; character, 44, 98; children, 17, 39, 41, 42, 109, 138, 153, 157; as dramatist, 31, 59; drinking, 69, 73; and Mrs. Dunlop, 117–22; education and reading, 16, 77–81, 185; at Ellisland, 29; exciseman, 28, 32–7; French Revolution and republicanism, 36, 39, 95, 97, 121; Horatian ideal, 31, 57, 66; illness and death, 37, 41, 68; imitators, 43, 211; 'independence', 85; Jacobitism, 36, 95, 96, 189; letter-writing, 173; and Jessy Lewars, 113; and Jean Lorimer, 111; loyalty to family and friends, 88; and Mrs. McLehose ('Clarinda'), 128–41; memorials and subscriptions to, 42; and Anna Park, 108; and Elizabeth Paton, 110; patriotism, 87; 'philosopher', 66, 190; 'Ploughman

257

Poet', 24, 62, 99 n. (2); on poetry, 188; political views, 91;
portraits of, 45–8; prize poem
on (1859), 44; relations with
women, 71, 103–8; religious
views, 91; and Maria Riddell,
123–8, 234–8; self-dramatisation
and posing, 59–66; 'single-man
certificate', 217; touchiness and
tactlessness, 82; venereal disease, 69
Burns, Robert (son), 52 n. (19),
157, 160
Burns, William (brother), 88, 138
Burns, William Nicol (son), 42,
160

Cameron, May, 72, 109
Campbell, Mary (of Dundonald),
143
Campbell, Mary ('Highland
Mary'), antecedents, 146, 242;
Bibles exchanged with B., 147;
death, 149, 153; exhumation,
150, 244; love affair with B.,
20, 141–53; tradition of, 243
Carmichael, Bailie (on Mary
Campbell's exhumation), 250
Carswell, Mrs., on B., 10, 71; on
Jean Armour, 165, 255 n. (2);
on Mary Campbell, 142, 151,
244
Chalmers, Peggy, 106, 107, 115–7
'Chloris'; see Lorimer, Jean
'Clarinda'; see McLehose, Mrs.
Agnes
Clarke, James (schoolmaster, Mof-
fat), 89
Clow, Jennie, 72, 109, 140
Commonplace Books, 18, 172
Crochallans, 26
Currie, Life of B., 32, 42, 55, 70,
75, 99 n. (1), 143

Drinking, B.'s, 69
Dumfries, B. in, 35, 36

Dundas, Robert, 22; B.'s verses on,
82, 203
Dunlop, Mrs., correspondence with
B., 117–22; defence of B., 90;
plans for B., 119; poem on B.,
101 n. (13); visit from B., 86

Edinburgh, B.'s stay in, 22–8
Edinburgh Edition, 21, 24, 28
Education, B.'s, 16, 77–81, 185
Ellisland, Farm of, 29, 159
Endocarditis, B.'s, 37, 68
Epigrams, etc., B.'s, 199
Excise appointment, 16, 28, 32–7,
133, 230

Fergusson, Robert, influence on
B., 80, 209, 213 n. (11); B. on,
63, 93, 99 n. (4)
Findlater (Excise) on B.; 75
Fintry, Graham of, patron of B.,
35, 36, 37, 58
Fisher, William ('Holy Willie'),
155
Freemasonry, 18
French language, B.'s knowledge
of, 63, 124, 212 n. (4)
Friar's Carse, quarrel at, 125, 231

Glencairn, Earl of, patron of B.,
23, 32, 203
Graham, Robert; see Fintry, Gra-
ham of
Gray (of Dumfries Academy), on
B., 76
Greenock, Burial of Mary Camp-
bell at, 243
Greenock, Burns Club at, 243
Greenock Telegraph, on Mary Camp-
bell's exhumation, 245

Hamilton, Charlotte, 115, 117
Hamilton, Gavin, and Mary Campbell, 146; and Peggy Chalmers,
115, 117; and Mauchline Kirk
Session, 146; patron of B., 19